The Life and Art of
HENRY FUSELI

Fuseli. Self-portrait. c.1780

The Life and Art of

HENRY FUSELI

with 267 plates, 13 in colour

PETER TOMORY

Thames and Hudson · London

Text filmset in Great Britain by Filmtype Services, Ltd, Scarborough
Printed in Austria by Brüder Rosenbaum, Vienna

ISBN 0 500 09086 6

Contents

NOTE

Letters of Fuseli quoted are from MacAndrew, Muschg, Federmann and J. T. Smith, *Nollekens and his Times*, 2 vols. London 1828. Poems of Fuseli quoted are from Mason and Federmann; other writings of Fuseli quoted are from Knowles and Mason. For details see Bibliography, p. 238.

All other quotations are as cited in the text, including the Northcote Letters Mss, the Ozias Humphry Letters Mss, and the bound volumes of Academy Miscellanea collected by Edward Basil Jupp and Edward Bell, respectively, in the Library, Royal Academy, London.

Preface

My reason for writing this book was that there was no recent study of the artist in English. Even in older studies, Fuseli is either treated as an international mannerist or as a gadfly in the otherwise smooth mixture of English painting of his period, depending on the nationality of the scholar concerned. From Federmann's pioneer monograph onwards, there has not been a comprehensive interpretation published, but rather studies of the artist, like Antal's posthumous work and Mason's treatment of Fuseli's writings and opinions.

I have laid particular emphasis on Fuseli as an artist in England, where he spent most of his adult life. Next I have illustrated and documented the sources which he and his contemporaries employed to form their respective styles, coupling this with an analysis of his work, his powers of invention and his influence. Most of all I have tried to set him in the context of English art.

I make no apology for the large number of prints amongst the illustrations, for the good reason that it would be through these rather than through the originals that any artist of this period would exert his influence. As supporting evidence there are these significant though unmemorable lines by Samuel Rogers, the banker-poet:

> What though no marble breathes, no canvass glows,
> From every point a ray of genius flows!
> Be mine to bless the more mechanic skill
> That stamps, renews and multiplies at will;
> And cheaply circulates, through distant climes,
> The fairest relics of the purest times
> And here the faithful graver dares to trace
> A Michel's grandeur, and a Raffaelle's grace!
> Thy Gallery, Florence, gilds my humble walls,
> And my low roof the Vatican recalls!
> *Epistle to a Friend*

Since the nature of his art and his working span make Fuseli one of the most interesting exemplars of the creative mind over the period 1770–1825, I hope that much of what I have written here may be applied outwards to the period at large. I have the intention of doing this myself, in due course.

7

My own specialized interest in Fuseli began nine years ago and during that time I have read most of what Dr Schiff has written, and worked with him for a brief spell in Zurich and corresponded with him on Fuseli. I would like, here, to record my sincere thanks to him for his always generous co-operation.

More formal acknowledgements are due to the respective authorities of the Department of Prints and Drawings, British Museum, The Warburg Institute, University of London, The Witt Library, Courtauld Institute, the Royal Academy, the London Library and the Department of Prints and Drawings, Victoria & Albert Museum, and the last three for allowing me to photograph material in their collections.

In New York I would like to thank for the same facilities, The Metropolitan Museum, and in person Mr Victor Wiener; the Library Services of Columbia University, in particular the Avery Library for permission to photograph works.

In Zurich I would like to thank Dr A. Schattler of the Kunsthaus for his speedy responses to my requests.

Since a great many of the findings in this book were explored initially in graduate lectures and seminars at Columbia University, I would like to thank the students who attended them for their enthusiasm and observations.

The quotation from Chaucer on p. 127 is from the modernized version by Nevill Coghill.

Last but not least there is my deep gratitude to my wife, for her endless patience, her photographic work and her assistance in checking the proofs and index.

Peter Tomory

I Life and Times

... the successful adventurer in the realms of Discovery, in spite of the shrugs, checks, and sneers of the timid, the malign, and the envious, leaps on an unknown shore, ennobles it with his name, and grasps immortality.

Lecture XI – on Michelangelo

Johann Heinrich Füssli was born in Zurich on 6 February 1741, a '. . . cursed cold month, as you may guess from my diminutive stature and crabbed disposition', as he observed later in life. Although physically he was never to grow much taller than five feet, his artistic and intellectual growth might have been predicted at birth. His godfather, Salomon Gessner, was a landscapist and theorist, and his father was a portrait painter, a writer and historian, a friend of the poets Kleist, Klopstock and Wieland, and a correspondent of Mengs and Winckelmann in Italy and the artists Rigaud and Wille in France. Another important family interest was entomology. Heinrich was to pursue it as an amateur all his life, while his brother Caspar was to beome a professional in the field.

According to his account, given to Farington* in Paris in 1802, Fuseli (as we may conveniently call him, though he did not adopt this spelling until much later) started to draw at the age of eight, making copies from the numerous engravings that he found at home, despite the disapproval of his father, who intended him for a more elevated career in the church. This aim was abetted, no doubt, by the prebendary Nuscheler, a friend of the family, who taught the young artist Greek and Latin. Nuscheler was also friendly with Pestalozzi, the educationalist and reformer.

Fuseli thus experienced, at an early impressionable age, an intellectual atmosphere continually energized by progressive and radical ideas. There is more direct evidence of this in some satirical portraits that he made, copying those which were being engraved by his older brother for their father's book on Swiss artists, *Geschichte und Abbildung der besten Maler in der Schweiz* (1755–57). The young Fuseli's drawings show the artists at work in their studios, suitably caricatured to fit their individual

1741 TO 1761

*Farington, Joseph, RA. 1747–1821. *The Farington Diaries*, ed. Gregg, London 1922–8.

9

genres. The sharpness of observation and the wit of these make it clear that he was used to a brisk, questioning environment.

The same tendency led him to the *Narrenbuch* (1640) by the Swiss artists Conrad and Rudolf Meyer and to their illustrations of human foibles he added his own pastiches. In the same vein are the satirical stories in which Till Eulenspiegel (1519) *10* featured, some of which were also illustrated by him during this period.

His earlier schooling over, Fuseli then passed into the orbit of J. J. Bodmer (1698–1783) who taught at the Zurich Collegium. The influence of this Swiss republican intellectual on the younger generation can be explained by merely quoting the last two lines of Klopstock's *Ode to Bodmer* (1750): 'How I have rejoiced since first I came into Bodmer's arms'. The poet, then twenty-six, was to provide the emotional stimulus of the *Sturm und Drang* movement.

The name Socrates-Addison, bestowed on Bodmer in the same ode, reflects the great range of interests of this philosopher and writer – he translated Milton's *Paradise Lost* (1732), the Ugolino passage from Dante's *Inferno* (1741) and a section from the *Nibelungenlied* (1757) besides nourishing a permanent admiration for Homer and Shakespeare. Nearby at Winterthur his friend Waser was translating Jonathan Swift. Thus long before he came to England, Fuseli was an enthusiastic and knowledgeable student of all the major literary sources which were to inspire his art.

His own relationship with the energetic teachers at this time is shown in a particularly telling drawing (Kunsthaus, Zurich) of Bodmer, Sulzer and Waser, arranged in a triangle of forces with the artist standing off to the left, an observer rather than a participant. Sulzer, Professor of Philosophy at Berlin, represented the opposite of Bodmer's emphatic espousal of feeling in poetry, for he had proposed to lay down a definitive German language and usage, which if ever adopted would have been the death of German poetry.

Fuseli's closest and most permanent friendship was formed during these student days with Johann Kaspar Lavater, a fellow scholar also destined for the church. From the letters that survive, Lavater seems to have been one of the very few, perhaps the only, person to whom Fuseli unburdened himself. They bear witness not only to the intimacy of their friendship, but also to Lavater's own innate goodness and kindness. Apart from a theological bond (they both held a highly subjective view of religion) they were united by a passionate belief in justice. In 1762 they issued jointly a pamphlet attacking the local magistrate, Grebel, a year after both had been ordained in the Zwinglian church. It was the first and last time that Fuseli was to take an active political role; thereafter he adopted a position of detachment, commenting on contemporary affairs through his art. The hubbub created by their publication was so great that both young men were advised by their friends to leave Zurich until the heat subsided. So in 1763, with another friend, Felix Hess, they set off for Berlin.

The short period in Germany was to be of immense importance to Fuseli. Not only was his transfer to England arranged there, but he came into close contact with the three main streams of European thought. The first was represented by Sulzer, already mentioned, the leader of German Enlightenment, whose lexicon *Allgemeine Theorie der schönen Künste* (4 vols. 1771) Fuseli was able to discuss with him, which meant discussing Winckelmann's and Mengs's theories on Ancient Art and Neo-classicism; the second by J. J. Spalding, whom he met at Barth in Pomerania, whose sermons and other texts were much influenced by Lord Shaftesbury and the Scot, Francis Hutcheson; and the third by Klopstock, at Quedlingburg, whose combination of strenuous country walks and pantheistic interpretation of nature made him a sort of founder father of romanticism – Lotte cried out his name to Werther in Goethe's first novel (1774). To borrow from part of one of Goethe's later works, this period was Fuseli's *Lehrjahre* – hardly an apprenticeship, but a testing period for all that he had learned from Bodmer. He had also to thank his old teacher for financial aid during this time.

He was, however, able to earn a little, as he reported to Bodmer in a letter from Berlin (23 November 1763) – seven gold louis for a translation of Lady Mary Wortley Montagu's *Letters*. This was an early example of simultaneous publishing in more than one language, with which we are familiar to-day, for the English edition had appeared in the same year. It is clear from the German title that this book included all the letters and not just those from Constantinople, so that the exotic nature of these was by no means the only reason for Fuseli's interest. There were Lady Mary's exchanges with Pope, for instance. Her name had been well known in Europe ever since Voltaire had publicized her introduction of smallpox inoculation to England in his *Lettres Philosophiques* (1734). He related there how it was practised by the Circassians, so that their women, so much in demand for the harems of Asia Minor, could have flawless skins, using this piece of esoteric knowledge in a famous episode of *Candide*. But it was certainly the letters from Constantinople that were the main attraction. They were to establish a myth for Northern Europe – the voluptuous houri, naked and unashamed, trained in the arts of love, but always subservient to her master – a dream of 'pneumatic bliss', the perfect antidote to the growing regiment of Blue Stockings and its dreams of emancipation!

This savouring of every literary dish was typical of the Enlightenment and is perhaps epitomized by Fuseli telling Felix Hess that Sulzer was reading Marguerite of Navarre's *Hepta-meron* in bed. He was, later, to use it as a source himself.

It was through Sulzer that he was to meet Sir Andrew Mitchell, the British Minister in Berlin, in whose company he was to travel to England. Shortly before his departure he was able to spend a few days with Klopstock and in one of his last letters to Bodmer from Germany, he tells him that he is translating the poet's *Messias* into English (three cantos – 1748;

the great religious epic was to be completed in 1773). In addition to this literary activity, Fuseli continued to draw. His major effort and perhaps his first cycle of works was eight illustrations for Bodmer's long poem *Die Noachide* (1765), but these were so mangled by the engraver, that they were never used. However, an engraving exists dated 1763, of a family gathering in Spalding's summer house at Barth. The scene is reminiscent of a centre panel of some Flemish triptych. Felix Hess, Lavater and the Spalding family are gathered in an open pavilion, like the stable of a Nativity scene, while Fuseli peers at them from around its right hand corner. In the same vein is another print entitled in German 'Love, Marriage, Death and Life' – an allegory of Spalding by the tomb of his wife, with his daughters. A butterfly flutters nearby, the Classical symbol of the departed soul. An inscription in Latin, 'Why this? You must seek much further', indicates the kind of religio-philosophic synthesis which will concern the artist in the future. In one of his later aphorisms (164) he remarked on the similarity of the principles of allegory and votive composition: 'they unite with equal right the most distant periods of time and the most opposite modes of society.'

This concern for the passing stages of life, symptomatic of his own age and his time, had already appeared in an ode (1760) which he addressed to Meta, Klopstock's young wife who had died at the birth of her first child. 'Fanny', to whom Klopstock had addressed some of his earlier poems, is also introduced. The poem takes the form of a monologue by Klopstock, who concludes by triumphantly claiming that through his poetry, Meta is immortalised on earth, and through his love rendered eternal in Heaven. Thus in two personal instances Fuseli recognizes the love of woman and union with her as a symbol of *virtù* and as a presiding genius of man's imagination. Meta had performed this role by encouraging the poet to continue work on the *Messias*. In that same year Fuseli published three other poems which had an intimate connection with Klopstock – *Hermann und Thusnelde, Thusnelde* and *Germanicus und Thusnelde*. These anticipate by eight years Klopstock's first patriotic drama *Hermanns Schlacht* (Hermann's Battle), and were probably inspired by an ode on the same subject by Cramer, a close friend of Klopstock. The third poem expresses eighteenth-century enthusiasm for Germanicus as a Stoic hero – a Trajanic statue, then believed to be Thusnelda, stood in the Loggia dei Lanzi in Florence. The poem is an early example of the fashion for investing Northern heroes and heroines with Roman virtues. Germanicus tells Thusnelde: 'Truly you have spirit, a Roman says that you are worthy of being a Roman too'. Admiration for Prussia, however, was a youthful enthusiasm on Fuseli's part; four years later at the end of his time in Berlin, he wrote to Bodmer that Prussia was in a lethargic state and nothing could be done but postpone its death. If Switzerland, a small and confined country, had to proclaim its principles so loudly, what must a kingdom of world status do? England attracted Fuseli above all because it promised liberty.

When he arrived in London in 1764, Fuseli could hardly be represented, even at the age of twenty-three, as an innocent abroad. Like most Swiss he had a gift for languages and already knew Greek, Latin, Hebrew, French, Italian and English, though he spoke the last all his life with a fairly heavy accent – at least according to some anecdotes, which may be exaggerated. Nor was there much in the literary and philosophic field, which he was not already familiar with. He arrived, therefore, with all the intellectual credentials expected by the international Enlightenment set – a working knowledge of Voltaire and Rousseau's *Julie or the New Heloise* (1761) and *Emile* (1762), of Addison, Steele and Lord Shaftesbury. To these he quickly added an admiration for Pope and Laurence Sterne and a reading of Hutcheson and Hume, the two reigning Scottish philosophers.

The Ossianic controversy was still much alive, since the previous year Macpherson had concluded the cycle with *Temora*. In July of that year Fuseli penned his long ode to Bodmer, in which he managed to refer to every kind of poetry and poet, including Ossian in a verse which captures the dirge-like rhythm of the original. Like the Rev. Hugh Blair in his *Critical Dissertation*, he may have noticed the extraordinary coincidences between Ossian and the Homeric epics, and perhaps shared Dr Johnson's opinion that the whole thing was Macpherson's own invention. At any rate he did no drawings connected with the Ossianic poems, a fact which differentiates him from the German *Stürmer und Dranger*; Goethe's young Werther, ten years later, was to exchange Homer for Ossian.

Fuseli's main purpose in coming to London was to act as a liaison between the German literati and their counterparts in England, though what exactly was required of him is not clear. It was possibly P. E. Reich or another bookseller who put the artist in touch with the firms of Millar & Cadell and Johnson* & Payne. Fuseli was a professional reader for both firms and usually engaged on the hack work of translation. Nevertheless, it enabled him to meet Johnson's circle of authors, and this was to be of lasting importance. As that circle grew, Fuseli found it his most sympathetic audience, and it is clear many of his drawings were made for the delectation of this particular group. He was to observe later, in his anonymous *Remarks on the Writings and Conduct of J. J. Rousseau* (1767) 'The poet writes to please all; hence he will be cautious of applying caustics to the darling vices of the public': but there was no reason why these 'caustics' should not be recognised by an 'in group'. Goya worked on a very similar principle.

Apart from Johnson himself, the most influential of this group was John Armstrong, medical practitioner, poet and essayist, whom Fuseli had met in Berlin and travelled back with to England. He was approximately Bodmer's age and became a similar sort of father figure to Fuseli, or rather uncle figure – a rumbustious uncle, strong in opinion and language, whose company Fuseli must have enjoyed. (They were later to set off to Italy together, although after a furious row they

*Johnson, Joseph, 1738–1809. Initially in business with Payne at Paternoster Row until the fire in 1770. Re-opened alone at St Paul's Churchyard. Johnson's home was in Old Church Street (now Upper Church Street), Chelsea. See P. G. Marin, 'Death of a London Bookseller', *Keats-Shelley Memorial Association Bulletin*, XV, 1964.

parted company at Florence.) Armstrong's claim to fame was his poem *The Art of Preserving the Health* (1744), which might be described as a socio-medical gloss on James Thomson's *The Seasons* (1726–30). It was divided, like Thomson's poem, into four parts – Air, Diet, Exercise, The Passions – in which the reader was abjured to keep an airy house, preferably on high ground, eat good wholesome food and never to excess, to take exercise sensibly and finally to maintain an equable temperament. Fuseli not only admired the poem but seemingly followed Armstrong's recommendations for Cunningham reported that he ate sparingly and never late. Fuseli himself boasted that he could walk from Old Church Street (Johnson's house), Chelsea, to Somerset House in under two hours. That he kept to such a sensible regimen possibly ensured his long life.

Not unconnected with the concern for health and fitness was his most important translation of this period, Winckelmann's *Reflections on the Paintings and Sculptures of the Greeks* (1765), which had been published in Dresden ten years before. Here, the health of the Greeks is extolled and the exercises of the Spartans praised. But of course its main purpose was to influence taste. It was one of the formative works of Neo-classicism, conjuring up a dream of a Golden Age and at the same time breeding a feeling of inferiority amongst Northern artists, whose climate, pock-marked skin and the after-effects of venereal disease, particularly amongst the English, were (according to the author) Herculean obstacles on the path to the beautiful in art. What might appear to be an observation of little consequence to us provoked, and continued to provoke, a strong reaction in England. That it provoked Fuseli may be guessed by his later comment that Winckelmann was not fit to eat the crumbs off Mengs's table.

Fuseli at this time seems, indeed, to have swung violently against Germany altogether: 'Since I have been in England, German literature is dead for me', he wrote in a letter to his friend Salomon Dalliker in 1765. He was impatient of the lethargic indifference of German writers to their political situation, and in the same letter Fuseli flared out against Klopstock for his empty rhetorical interpretation of religion: 'the gallimatia (nonsense) of a brain softened by apocalyptic weeping . . . his marble pyramid is inlaid with pasteboard, sugar paper and the motley colours of the clothes cupboard'.

Paradoxically, during the same year, Fuseli had to accept a situation so languidly endured by his German friends, that of a paid tutor to Viscount Chewton, the son of Lord Waldegrave. He gave this up as soon as he could. Through an introduction of Sir Andrew Mitchell, he was to gain a lifelong friend and supporter in the banker, Thomas Coutts. Fuseli had the capacity to keep his friends and they, however disparate their interests, continued to admire him.

Not least of his enthusiasms in London was the theatre;* it was Garrick and his company's new interpretations of Shakespeare that was the magnetic attraction. Garrick, almost anticipating the 'Method' system through gesture, expression,

*For most references in the text see: Allan S. Downer, 'Nature to Advantage Dressed', *Proceedings of the Modern Language Association* LVIII, December 1943; George C. D. Odell, *Shakespeare from Betterton to Irving*, 2 vols., New York, 1964; and Moelwyn Merchant, *Shakespeare and the Artist*, London, 1959.

14

timing and thorough analysis of 'character', had revitalized the tragic heroes. This experience for Fuseli was like 'an operation for cataract' (to borrow a phrase of David's describing his visit to Naples). One suspects that Garrick, to-day, might be put down as 'hamming' his way through a part; his own playing was certainly less restrained than that of Betterton, his predecessor. But it was Garrick's unique combination of the full range of the gestures of mime with a delivery in the broken rhythms of natural speech that must have appealed so much to his age. This blend of fiction and reality enabled the stage to become the most significant vehicle of metamorphosis of life into art. Fuseli was to observe later that his friend, the actress Mary Anne Yates, in the role of Hermione made 'no insignificant leap, as from Nature into a portrait'.

The most significant experience for Fuseli must have been to see Shakespeare *played*. It can be assumed that he knew the texts of many of the plays by heart, indeed he had translated *Macbeth* in Zurich. But to see so many familiar scenes enacted as dramatic situations would have revealed the possibilities of Shakespeare as a pictorial source. Garrick, who owned many engravings and paintings, must have based many of his scene positions on the compositions of the old masters. As early as 1719 Jonathan Richardson* referred to the theatre as 'a sort of moving pictures', implying a correspondence between painting and the stage. It would have required, therefore, no great leap of the imagination to 'picture' such scenes, but intuition was surely needed to recognize that these could replace the traditional moral scenes drawn from sacred and classical texts. In 1767, Fuseli referred to Shakespeare as 'the great instructor of mankind', who 'afflicts innocence and virtue'. Once again, it may be noticed that Fuseli is a realist, holding that moral principles are to be drawn from an analysis of life and not from ideal abstractions. Like Diderot in France, he admired Samuel Richardson's novels *Pamela* and *Clarissa* because they pictured life as it was.

*Richardson, Jonathan, 1665–1745, portrait painter and theorist. *Essay on the Theory of Painting*, 1715, with additions 1719, in French 1728, with additional chapters 1773.

There was one contemporary with whom Fuseli could identify himself quite closely – Laurence Sterne, whose *Tristram Shandy*, of which eight volumes had appeared by 1765, was then enjoying great popularity. On meeting the author Fuseli was shocked by his strong language, but he must have been impressed, for he in turn was to shock new friends by his own profanity. Indeed, Sterne's combination of Rabelaisian philosophic satire and wit, a sharp ear for vernacular speech and an acute perception of the commonplace situation runs remarkably close to Fuseli's observations in both literacy and pictorial form. In the letter to his friend Dalliker, for instance, he takes up the notion of metempsychosis, saying that there is no reason why the souls of an ass, scorpion, sheep, etc., should not be transferred to an alderman, a Zurich scholar or a Covent Garden singer . . .. And later when visiting Lyons he captured exactly Sterne's light touch in his *Sentimental Journey* of 1768. Writing to Lavater in February 1766, the artist related this episode: 'It is the custom here during Lent for ladies of the upper class to go on foot, through mud and rain, into every quarter of the town collecting alms for the poor house. One of these ladies visited Mylord (Viscount Chewton) and myself yesterday – this handmaid of mercy, what a Goddess was she! A cajoling eye of a serene, heavenly blue captured mine, a small lily-like hand enlivened mine! Her trembling finger against mine, I bowed over her and said (in French), "Madame, how happy the members of the church must be to have found such a hand to awaken the charity of heretics!" With delighted expressions of astonishment at the princely gift of a twenty florin piece, she curtsied, gave me a glance, laughed and flounced away.'

When he was first employed by Lord Waldegrave it was understood that he should accompany Viscount Chewton on a Grand Tour. In a letter Fuseli mentions a two-year journey and it would seem since their first main halt was at Lyons, that they would then proceed by the normal southern route to Italy. But this was not to be, and in fact they never went beyond France. Fuseli had no illusions about his young charge; writing to Dalliker and paraphrasing Pope's *Essay on Man*, he opines that since God had given the Viscount all the externals of life, but only two passions, the youth was somewhere in the middle between man and beast. He became more beastly as the tour proceeded.

They probably left England about 17 December 1765, since in a letter of the 7th, Fuseli tells Lavater that they will leave in ten days time, and spent January in Paris en route to Lyons. In a postscript to that letter the artist wrote, 'My name in Switzerland is Füssli, in England Füsseli, but nowhere Fyssli Magister artium', referring to a slip of his friend's pen, no doubt, but the last line has a plaintive ring. No one yet had recognized his true talent.

In Paris he was introduced to his idol, Rousseau, by David Hume, the philosopher, who was serving as Secretary at the British Embassy. Shortly after this Hume was to return to Britain taking Rousseau with him. Hume, who enjoyed much greater esteem in France at this time than in his own country, could have also introduced him to all the famous *literati* in Paris including Diderot, but we have no evidence about this.

Simultaneously, therefore, Fuseli met the two men who represented the two poles of European contemporary thought – the sceptical romantic and the romantic sceptic. In many ways Fuseli, like others of his particular generation, combined both, like a two-headed Janus – one face turned to the past of the Enlightenment, the other to the future Romanticism. As Hume wrote in *Concerning Human Understanding*, 'To form monsters and join incongruous shapes and appearances, costs the imagination no more trouble than to conceive the most natural and familiar objects. . . . all this creative power of the mind amounts to no more than the faculty of compounding, transposing, augmenting or diminishing the materials afforded us by the senses and experience.' This total rationalizing of the imagination, which would have made Blake spit with fury, was

I Fuseli. The Nightmare. 1781. This is the first version of Fuseli's most famous painting. Later versions are illustrated in plates 83, 137 and 222

II Fuseli. The Ezzelin Bracciaferro and the Dead Meduna. c.1784

16

I

II

tempered at the end of the century by Nathan Drake,* a not particularly distinguished belle-lettrist, but representing an average opinion. Defending 'Gothic superstition', he argued, 'it gives considerable latitude to the imagination, it seems to possess more rationality than almost any other species of fabling.' Fuseli, himself, was to explain the attraction of romantic fantasy by the fact that the Northern European had closer ties to it than to Greek mythology. But flights of the imagination had to be 'justified', as the compositor 'justifies' type in order to prevent it going, as Blake's went, beyond the 'verge of legitimate invention'.

*Nathan Drake, *Literary Hours*, London, 1798 & 1820.

It is unlikely that in Paris in 1766, or at any other time, Fuseli was aware of any 'paradox', 'dilemma' or 'conflict' in his position. These are all terms bestowed on his generation by the commentators of our time.

The meeting with Rousseau bore fruit later in the artist's anonymous pamphlet, *Remarks on the Writings and Conduct of J.-J. Rousseau* (1767), in which he supported the author in his controversy with Voltaire. This work never circulated widely since most copies were destroyed in a fire at Johnson's premises in Paternoster Row in 1770. The text, remarkable for the author's command of English, is in the customary polemical style, and it is the footnotes which more often reveal Fuseli's personal thoughts. Two quotations will suffice to show Fuseli leaning first towards Hume's cool reason and second towards Rousseau's warm sentiment. On tragedy, the artist notes that 'such a disparity (lies) between the spectator's and hero's circumstances, that it requires the most painful abstraction to snatch one useful lesson from all the flatulency of his passion.' In 1757, Hume† had expressed similar doubts, 'whatever dominion the senses and imagination may usurp over the reason, there still lurks at the bottom a certain idea of falsehood in the whole of what we see . . . We weep for the misfortune of a hero to whom we are attached. In the same instant we comfort ourselves, by reflecting, that it is nothing but a fiction.' It is also quite probable that Fuseli had read Lessing's *Laocoön* (1766), for Lavater had drawn his attention to it. Lessing, intent on demolishing Winckelmann's Stoic interpretation of the Hellenistic work, observed that, 'Stoicism is not dramatic . . . If we see him (the hero) bearing his misery with nobility of soul, he will, to be sure, excite our admiration; but admiration is only a cold sentiment whose barren wonderment excludes not only every warmer passion but every other clear conception as well.' The next quotation takes him nearer to Rousseau. In discussing how far the poet can go in 'applying caustics to the darling vices of the public', Fuseli drew the line at one subject – the slave trade. He cites the following lines from Thomas Southern's *Oroonoko* (1696):

†David Hume, *Treatise of Human Understanding*, 'On Tragedy', London, 1757.

III *Fuseli. Percival frees Belisane from the spell of Urma. 1783*

IV *Fuseli. Titania and Bottom. 1786–89. For other paintings on the same theme, see plates 76 and 99*

> I must not blush says Oroonoko
> A whitely shame
> To think I could design to make those free
> Who were by nature slaves: wretches design'd
> To be their master's dogs.

19

Fuseli upbraids the playwright for sacrificing 'the laws of nature, conscience and the truth' to the principle that 'Slave trade is legal, for we must have sugar.' Here he echoes the entry in the *Encyclopédie* on Negroes, 'this odious commerce and contradiction of natural law is justified by saying that these slaves usually achieve salvation of their souls through losing their liberty: the Christian instruction that they get is thus annexed to the indispensable need of them in the growing of sugar, tobacco and indigo, etc.' There is, in fact, an engraving by Fuseli, which, stylistically, dates from *c.*1766–74, and shows a dark-skinned man, a chain and a skin on his shoulder and a deckle-edged knife in his hand, striding away from some European clothes piled on the ground. Behind these are three white men dressed in the costume of the 16th, 17th and 18th century respectively. While this might refer to a freed slave returning to his homeland, there is a strong possibility that it represents Omai, the son of a Tahitian chief, who after being lionized by London society, returned with Cook to the Pacific in 1774. The subject was not to concern Fuseli again until 1806–07, when he painted *The Negro Revenged* for Cowper's *The Task,* in which an African and his wife watch a hurricane, as a symbol of apocalyptic vengeance, destroy a ship at sea. Two years earlier on a visit to Liverpool, he was to remark 'methinks I everywhere smell the blood of slaves.' While it is thus true that the artist was not a tardy supporter of Abolition, his attitude remained that of the Enlightenment generally towards slavery, which was not so much concern for the cause of the African, but a sense that such a bondage was a blot on the escutcheon of liberty.

Whatever the elevation of his thoughts in Paris, they were to be brought to earth in the next few months by the increasing friction between him and his pupil. It seems likely, from the change of address in a letter to Lavater from Lyons on 10th May, that Fuseli had resigned his position as 'bear leader'. There were also signs of friction appearing in the letters to his Swiss correspondents. In one to Lavater, Fuseli accuses him of impertinence, apparently, for castigating him over an affair. He continues, 'What right has that raw boy (Felix Nuscheler) to say I am going to the devil, treating me like one of his cate-chists in Turbenthal. Has Hess any right to take me to task . . . What does he mean by adventurer? Is it my fault that I could not earn a crust in my fatherland? We are not all made to press grapes in the church vineyard and smoke a pipe round the barrel. When he writes to me like a man and a friend, then I will answer him.'

Inevitably the gap was widening between the worldly 'adventurer' and his stay-at-home friends, but the gap that Lavater possibly had in mind was the one caused by his friend's slow shift to a position of non-allegiance to Christian doctrine *per se.* Goethe* was to describe this position rather well in a letter to Lavater in 1782: 'I am no anti-Christian, no un-Christian, but a decided non-Christian', or as Blake was to observe more coarsely:

*The best study in English on the Sturm and Drang is Roy Pascal, *The German Sturm und Drang,* 2nd ed., Manchester, 1968. Most references in the text are from this source.

The only Man that e'er I knew
Who did not make me almost spew
Was Fuseli: he was both Turk & Jew –
And so, dear Christian Friends, how do you do?

But this was written *c.* 1808–11, more than forty years later. In France, the artist had as yet made no declaration of independence of religion in particular, but his general tone of scepticism was, perhaps, sufficient to warn his friend.

The visit to France was completed by a short stay at Tours, then on to Paris. In all probability he returned to London in November 1766.

It was during the following year that Fuseli became really determined about taking up an artistic career. He had not forsworn literature, for he was busy writing his pamphlet on Rousseau, spurred on, according to Cunningham,* by Armstrong's enthusiasm. Also in a postscript to a letter to Bodmer from Tours, he mentioned that Winckelmann had been in touch with him about an English translation of the *History of Ancient Art* (1764). Nothing came of this. Without the income of his tutorship, Fuseli would have had to work doubly hard to earn a living.

His meeting with Sir Joshua Reynolds is generally ascribed to 1768, but for two reasons it seems more probable that he met him the previous year. First, his friend John Armstrong had sat for Reynolds in 1766 for his portrait (Adelaide, Art Gallery), and it is doubtful that the poet would have let slip this connection to introduce his young protégé. The second reason was the presence of Angelica Kauffmann in London. She had arrived in June the previous year and very quickly had made her mark through the attractions of both her appearance and her palette. She was also Swiss, which allowed Fuseli to see himself neatly sandwiched between her and another compatriot artist, Mary Moser, whom he had known since his first arrival in England. It would seem that he was as much smitten with Angelica as Mary was with him. There were, however, more serious links, namely her close friendship with Reynolds and Winckelmann, and her interest in German poetry, for she was certainly corresponding with Klopstock from 1769 onwards. It is not improbable that Fuseli arranged this. (The poet's patriotic drama *Hermanns Schlacht*, which had appeared in 1768, later inspired Angelica Kauffmann to paint her *Hermann and Thusnelda* in 1786.) Ever since his first arrival in England, Fuseli had been closely attached to the Mosers. The father, George Michael, was the first Keeper of the Royal Academy after its foundation in 1768, and therefore instrumental in introducing Fuseli to his own friends like Cipriani,† Romney and Mortimer.‡

However seriously he had taken his drawing before, it had ranked only as a secondary occupation, augmenting his other earnings. He certainly offered Lavater drawings as payment in kind, and had also illustrated Smollett's *Peregrine Pickle* and Dr Willoughby's *Practical Family Bible*. But this was sporadic *19*

*Cunningham, Allan C. 1784–1842: see Bibliography.

†Cipriani, Giovanni, RA 1727–85.

‡Mortimer, John Hamilton, ARA, 1740–79; see the Exhibition Catalogue, Paul Mellon Foundation for British Art, 1968.

compared to his literary work, which by this year would have included drafts on his projected history of German poetry.

Thus when an artist of Reynolds's calibre praised his drawings and urged him to become a full-time artist, he must have felt that this was indeed the finger of fate prodding him on to the right road. Reynolds seemed to have been more than merely encouraging, for according to the obituary of Fuseli* in 1825, he 'repeatedly begged from him (Fuseli) little unfinished sketches.' All this must have enabled the artist to overcome his natural diffidence – diffidence not of purpose, but of decision, of engagement. Northcote† was to describe him as 'timid'. Farington spoke of his reluctance to be drawn into any decisive expression of opinion. He might have described it himself as *Zeitlethargie* – a lethargy symptomatic of the period. The pains attendant on the birth of an idea, like that of a child, brought on such a lassitude that its complete fulfilment was endlessly delayed. Cunningham describes this state in Mortimer, 'when he desired to expand them (his designs) into full sized pictures, he found that the mechanical labour gradually crept, like the nightmare, over his performance, taming down the happy ecstasy of early thought.'

So when he announced the advice of Reynolds in a letter to Lavater, it appeared as a diffident and only half-serious interpolation: 'Something about myself? Well here is a bit of dry vanity: Reynolds has said for me to be one of the greatest artists of my time, there is nothing else to do but to go to Italy for two years.' Otherwise these letters to his friend between March 1768 and June of the following year are full of literary talk. From them one can compile an interesting list of authors and their books which Fuseli sent to his friends in Switzerland. Priestley's *Essay on government and on political and civil liberty*, Gray's *Odes*, Robertson's *History of Charles V*, Warburton's *Life of Pope*, Sterne's *Sentimental travels* and his *Sermons for asses*, Percy's *Reliques of Ancient Poetry* and Armstrong's‡ poem on *Health* and his *Sketches*.

One of these essays by Armstrong, published under his pen-name of 'Lancelot Temple', contained, *inter alia*, a sideswipe at Winckelmann and the first critical praise of Fuseli. Its title, *The Influence of Climate upon Genius*, shows the object of its attack very well. 'There are in this island some renegadoes absurd enough to tell you, that Britain lies at too great a distance from the sun to produce any genius', was the unequivocal opening. Armstrong continued:

I reckon that still, even in this age, our island may boast of several geniuses . . . in portrait . . . in landskip. But these geniuses are still alive; and some of them may be seen at a coffee-house, where they look much like other people. . . . As to history itself, besides some promising specimens of it at home, perhaps even this barren age has produced a genius, not indeed of British growth; unpatronized, and at present almost unknown; who may live to astonish, to terrify, and delight all Europe. But true genius is such an uncommon production of nature, and is so much superior to all quackish arts of recommending itself, that when it does appear, it is no wonder that a generation of people without taste do not know it.

It was indeed prophetic and although the subject himself might

* *The Gentleman's Magazine*, April 1825.

†Northcote, James, RA 1746–1831, also biographer of Reynolds and author of reminiscences.

‡John Armstrong, *Sketches or Essays on Various subjects by Lancelot Temple, Esq.*, in *Miscellanies*, 2 vols, London, 1770.

have only believed the half of it, his determination to turn painter must have been strengthened by this and other expressions of opinion by his English friends.

He makes this clear in a letter to Lavater of June 1769 as well as repeating his resolve to go to Italy for two or three years, 'when I have practised the rudiments of oil painting and daubed (gesuldet) a couple of paintings'. One of these, in all probability, was *Joseph interpreting the dreams of Pharaoh's butler and baker*, which was either purchased by or given to Joseph Johnson. Many years later, Fuseli was to lay 'the villainous clutch of restoration on it' and eventually it passed into the collection of the Countess of Guildford (1831). Apparently, it was this work which made Reynolds say that the artist could be a colourist too if he wished.

The letters to Lavater in the summer of 1769 are concerned with the raising of sufficient funds for the Italian journey and state his intention to visit Zurich on his return journey. Obviously he had no idea that his Italian sojourn was to last eight years. He records with gratitude the generosity of his English friends, particularly Thomas Coutts who was prepared to place a large sum at his disposal, provided he could raise a similar sum in Zurich.

The prospect of Italy no doubt fired him to write an Ode, *Über die Kunst* (On Art), which Mason dated between 1768 and 1770. Some of it is worth translating to show that his Muse often led him to exaggerated sentiment. On Correggio, for instance: 'Now let me in the caressing harmony/Of Correggio's soul lose myself, of which/ The magic kiss of light and shade/ Sacrifices neither truth, idea nor form./As full of ardour as the snorting/Horses of Apollo that disperse Dawn's robe,/Pure as the face of the Morning star/Or the dew that rises from the ocean.'

Certainly the gods had not done with him, for apparently on the eve of his departure from London, Johnson's house in Paternoster Row was burnt down. This cleared his past account with a vengeance, for the manuscript of his history of German poetry, the bulk of the copies of his Rousseau pamphlet and a large number of his drawings went up in smoke. But Fuseli apparently bore his misfortune with equanimity, for in a letter to Lavater from Rome, he remarked that bankruptcy was his lot, punning on *abgebrannt* (stony broke) and *Brand* (fire).

Before his departure there even seems to have been a celebration, that is if the date usually ascribed to Mortimer's *Caricature Painting* of 1765–66 can be moved forward to 1769, *3* for the man standing with a wineglass is certainly Fuseli as comparison with Bromley's engraved portrait shows. Mortimer is *2* seated, diminutive, on the left and the man looking up with pride at the artist is probably Dr John Armstrong, judging from Reynolds's portrait of him (Art Gallery, Adelaide). Both faces have the same wide bow-like mouth, the same lidded eyes. Only the nose presents a problem, but allowing for over-refinement in Reynolds's three-quarter view and exaggeration in Mortimer's full face, then both share a bulbous point. Others who

23

have been identified – Joseph Wilton,* John Ireland and a portrait of Joseph Wright of Derby on the back wall – suggest an artistic gathering but not one that can be identified, perhaps, with the Howdalian Society.†

Fuseli, with his friend Dr Armstrong, set off from Gravesend in April and twenty-eight days later arrived in Genoa. He went on by *felucca* to Leghorn, where apparently it ran aground, then continued by coach to Florence. On 14 May he was able to tell Lavater of his safe arrival. A month later he wrote again from Rome, but there was no mention of Armstrong; the two men had quarrelled and parted company. They were not to be reconciled until Fuseli's return to London in 1779.

It was perhaps the artist's determination to go quickly on to Rome that sparked the argument, since Florence was a much more attractive place to many Englishmen. This preference was largely due to the hospitality of the Hadfields, whose hotel was the headquarters of most English travellers. Hadfield,‡ who had formerly kept a house at Leghorn, also had two daughters and it was the elder, Maria, who attracted all who passed through. She was at this period very young, but she had a sweet voice, could draw well, play the harpsichord divinely and compose 'musick very finely', as Northcote observed to his brother (1778) and he went on, 'she will be another Angelica she is very handsome'. Fuseli was not exempt from her spell, nor were Tresham,** Ozias Humphry, Prince Hoare, a Mr Parsons, whose letter of serious intention to Maria's father somehow found its way into the Humphry Mss, and finally Richard Cosway, the miniaturist, whom she married. Why she did so was because he was, in her own words, '*Toujours riant, toujours gai*'. And that could not be said, possibly, about the others and certainly not of Fuseli.

It was not long before he was suffering from indetermination once more. In a tardy reply to a bubbling letter from Mary Moser in 1771, he excused himself, 'but I am often so very unhappy within, that I hold it matter of remorse to distress such a friend as Miss Moser with my own whimsical miseries; – they may be fancied evils, but to him who has fancy, real evils are unnecessary, though I have them too. All I can say is, that I am approaching the period which commonly decides a man's life with regard to fame or infamy.' Seven years before he had declared to his friend Dalliker that 'Fluctuation was the essence of life', but as he had found then as he now found in Rome, there was no such thing as perpetual motion.

How did he spend those eight years in Rome? Two to four years was the general average for working artists without secondary employment, for most were aware that it was professional suicide to absent themselves too long from the home market. Financially, Fuseli seems to have had little to complain about. It is reported that he earned at one time up to £1,300 in commissions from visitors, but it is also true that the subject of money came up regularly in the letters to and from

*Joseph Wilton, RA, 1722–1803, sculptor. John Ireland, close friend of Mortimer and author of *Hogarth Illustrated*, London, 1791 & 1798.

†A club of artists with Mortimer as President, which met at Munday's coffee house and was named after a Capt. Howdall, 'an enthusiast for the arts'. See *Memoirs of Thomas Jones*, Walpole Society, XXXII, 1946–48.

1770 TO 1778

‡Charles Hadfield was the proprietor of the popular hotel on the outskirts of Florence at which most English visitors stayed. According to Ozias Humphry he also had radical political opinions. His English origins are obscure; he is variously described as being Irish, or from Shrewsbury or from Manchester.

**Tresham, Henry, RA, 1751–1814, was also an art dealer. Hoare, Prince, 1755–1834, artist, dramatist and writer on the Fine Arts. Humphry, Ozias, RA, 1742–1810, miniature painter.

Lavater, for both he and Fuseli's brother in Zurich seem to have nagged the artist about his future.

There were in fact certain beguiling features of Rome besides those of its monuments, which would have enabled Fuseli to have put off, year after year, the decision to move on. First there was the coming and going of numerous artists so that every regretful farewell was countered by a joyful welcome. There was therefore always a reason to stay on another six months. If Mengs is taken as an example, and Fuseli seems to have been attached to him, we find him returning to Rome in 1772 from Madrid, away to Spain in 1774, back to Rome finally in 1777. English artists produce a similar pattern – John Brown arrives in 1771, Alexander Runciman leaves in 1772, Thomas Banks arrives the same year, Romney and Humphry in 1773 and independently, Joseph Wright. Then Tresham in 1775 and Northcote in 1777. Apart from English, others like Abildgaard and Sergel, David, Vien, Ménageot, Vincent, Sané, Peyron and Regnault were there as constant or inconstant companions. And besides the artists there was the steady though uneven flow of dilettanti to provide a variety of company and patronage.

Like almost every other resident of Rome, Fuseli contracted fever and was lucky to escape with his life, a trembling in his right hand and whitened hair. Northcote recorded in one of his letters going to a night funeral of the wife of an English artist, at which Thomas Banks read the service, and later the sculptor himself was to fall a victim. Life expectancy, for the unseasoned Northerner, could be grievously shortened in the Eternal City. To recuperate in 1772, Fuseli paid a visit to Venice and there acquainted himself with all the Venetian masters. It was still too early for him to have met Canova and they were to miss each other when the latter arrived in Rome in 1779. Fuseli's only other major excursion was the statutory one to Naples and the excavations at Herculaneum and Pompeii. All the works of art discovered at these sites were at that time removed to the old palace at Portici. Without the aid of an archaeologist, as David had in his friend Quatremère de Quincy, the remains of the old Roman cities might have proved baffling or worse. Northcote wrote: 'As to the other things which I saw at Naples they are not worth mention such as the ruins of Herculaneum and Pompeii which is only a few pillars and chambers of Rubish.' Fuseli, however, would have had access to specialists, since he knew both Charles Towneley, whose great collection of antiques was to enrich the British Museum, and Sir William Young, author of *A Journal of a Summer's Excursion by the Road of Montecasino to Naples* (1774) and whose joint draughtsman was John Brown. Another useful contact was Dr John Moore, the companion, or bear leader perhaps, of the Duke of Hamilton, whose European tour extended from 1772 to 1778. Moore was the father of Fuseli's later close friend Dr Carrick Moore and owner of the artist's Roman Sketchbook now in the British Museum. (Moore's other son, shown in the splendid portrait by Gavin Hamilton,

25

with his father and the Duke, was afterwards Sir John Moore who died at Corunna.) Fuseli's English connections in fact were excellent and entry into the household of Sir William Hamilton,* ambassador at Naples, was guaranteed. Hamilton at that stage was putting together his second collection of Greek and Etruscan vases. The first was to be shipped to the British Museum, the second unfortunately was to be lost at sea, but not before it was catalogued by J. W. H. Tischbein. Perhaps the most exciting excavation for an artist was nearing completion in 1778 at the so-called House of Cicero. There the well-known painting of the eight dancing girls and two mosaics of satyr play scenes by Dioscorides had been recovered. Many Greek vases had been removed from the tombs discovered further to the east at Ruvo, while excavations in Sicily were producing similar hauls. There could hardly have been a more stimulating period of discovery, certainly in the field of Classical Antiquity. To be thus presented with brand new Antiquities, unknown to the Renaissance, must have had a tonic effect. It was partly the domestic scale and character of so much of this new material which allowed the romantic imagination of the age to 'feel' the classical past instead of just admiring the ideal art of a distant age. Fuseli responded to these discoveries as much as anyone and it will be seen later how he accommodated them within his art.

*See Brian Fothergill, *Sir William Hamilton*, London, 1969.

Fuseli's interests and activities at this time covered an extremely wide range. He was studying art from the days of ancient Greece and Rome to the 17th century. He was compiling his own pictorial interpretation of Shakespeare (Lavater told Herder in 1774 that Fuseli had completed sixteen Shakespearean compositions in fourteen days). He was reading extensively in many literatures (Fuseli later told Farington that it was in Rome he applied himself to literature 'with inclination'), and he was wrestling, often in a spirit of frustration, with Lavater over the illustrations for the latter's *Physiognomische Fragmente* (Essays in Physiognomy) which appeared in German in 1775–78. In the end he was to do nothing for the German edition, as he explained to Lavater in a letter in 1773, 'I find myself neither suited nor disposed (and that is the truth) to draw physiognomic portraits, nine to a quarto sheet. To draw the *Iliad* on a nutshell or portray the chariot and the horses of Eleus on a gnat's wing, I leave to the "soulfulness" of Europe's illustrator (Chodowiecki). I need space, height, depth and breadth. He who wishes to can stir up a storm in a wine glass or weep over a rose, but I cannot. Nor do I know how to follow Le Brun's Passions,† for these passions do not match mine – nor would they match anyone else except a Parisian.' Lavater was in no doubt that his friend was unique for, with this letter at hand, he wrote to Herder, 'Füssli in Rome is one of the greatest of imaginative men. He is at all extremes – always original . . . His wit is boundless. He does little without pencil or brush – but when he does he needs a hundred yards of space, otherwise it is beneath his contempt. He has devoured all the Greek, Latin, Italian and English poets. His glance is lightening, his word a

†Le Brun, Charles, 1609–90, court painter to Louis XIV. His illustrated lecture, *Méthode pour apprendre à dessiner les Passions* (1669) was published in 1698.

storm – his wit, death and his vengeance, hell. At close quarters
he is not to be endured.' Again about a year later, in another note
to Herder, Lavater continues his catalogue of his friend's
powers – 'He is the most original genius . . . (he has) the
fierceness of a warrior – the feeling of the highest sublimity . . .
His spirit is the storm wind, his works flames of fire . . . (he is)
Jupiter's eagle.' While all this is the typical rodomontade of the
Stürmer und Dranger, it presents a true enough picture of Fuseli
as he must have appeared, a choleric, erudite, diminutive,
explosive Roman candle to his phlegmatic and more slow
burning acquaintances. Sergel, the Swedish sculptor, in a
caricature of his friend, shows the artist as a dynamic amalgam
of sharp angles ducking and dodging an onslaught of Olympian
rockets and thunder flashes. This view of him may well have
been inspired by Fuseli's real fright during one of the splendid
firework displays called La Girandola held during September at
the Castel di Sant'Angelo and which, according to Northcote,
was 'as much above all other fireworks to be seen anywhere.'
Fuseli's kind of aggressiveness is often found in men of small
stature and in the basically shy or timid. There is certainly
evidence of this in the artist's letters and the following may serve
as an example: 'I have only contempt for Klopstock's taste in
art, when he speaks of Preisler (an engraver in Copenhagen) or
the Germans; it is as arrogant as his judgement of the English.
His ignorance of their poetry is ludicrous. Citizen, Fatherland,
Freedom – if he was a Swiss he would know a little about these.
But where is the Fatherland of a German – a slave? Is it in
Swabia, Brandenburg, Austria or Saxony? Is it in the marshes
where the Roman legions under Varus were swallowed up?
Has Rome ever lost when she has fought *honestly* on her own
land and soil? A Frenchman – curse him – has more right to
call his land father than a Quedlingburger, Osnabrügger or
anyone else who pandered to that pen of arrogant toads from
Rügen to Ulm. A lackey, and what has he to be proud about –
his master's livery? And which one? The first, second or third?
Freedom! God! Freedom from that flatterer, Christian (King of
Denmark, Klopstock's patron).' Much is lost, it is true, in
translation but the mounting rate of his salvoes still comes
through in English.

The reason for this particular outburst was the copy of
Klopstock's Odes, which Lavater had sent him at the end of
1774, along with books by Herder and Goethe. The two works
of Herder, *Ältester Urkunde des Menschengeschlechts* (Vol. 1) and
Auch eine Philosophie der Geschichte, both published in 1774,
were of interest to Fuseli. The first, Oldest Document of the
Human Race, was an apologia for the book of Genesis, refuting
Voltaire's criticism of it as inconsistent and contradictory, but
at the same time, suggesting that as a primitive, revelatory
document of early man it could not and need not be dismissed
by modern, rationalist opinion. The second, Another Philosophy of History, was in a sense correlative to the first, since
it praises the early patriarchal and anarchic societies for the
independence granted then to the individual personality, in

contrast to his own age, in which personality was being emasculated. Contemporary man, therefore, must consciously strive through feeling to express his potential. By and large, Fuseli could share these views, although he might differ on particulars. They were consistent with his attitude to religious art. His devotion to the Michelangelo of the Sistine ceiling, for example, was not only artistic but dogmatic; here was a similar revelatory document – the ancient, oracular Sibyls, the old prophets as prefigurations of Christ, the primitive generative families of man and the successive creative, heroic and cataclysmic events of man's existence, fall and redemption.

During these years in Rome, the predominant influences on Fuseli's mind were not Italian, not even classical, but – however much he disclaimed the fact – German, and in particular Goethe. Among the books that Lavater sent to his friend were *Die Leiden des jungen Werthers* and *Götz von Berlichingen*. Rather like Herder's books, Goethe's novel and play are complementary. The young and contemporary Werther, with his yearning towards Nature, poetry and love, dies by his own hand, because he recognizes that the last can never be fulfilled in the existing state of things; Götz, at the opposite pole, stands as a purposeful and self-sufficient hero in a time of medieval anarchy. Together they represented the dual nature of the Sturm and Drang character, and perhaps originated that recurring Northern dilemma: how to reconcile poetry and life, spirit and flesh? To one of Fuseli's temperament, the best solution, if one would a hero be, was to take up a positive, confident and aggressive stance vis-à-vis the forces of the imagination, but towards those of reality adopt a much more accommodating posture. As Fuseli himself pointed out in a letter to Northcote, 'self-preservation is the first duty of the eighteenth century.' Many years later in one of his aphorisms, experience had taught him that 'Reality teems with disappointment for him whose sources of enjoyment spring in the elysium of fancy.' He did not, however, enlarge on either book although he does quote from *Götz* rather significantly on the subject of religion in relation once more to the unfortunate Klopstock, whom he accuses in the same letter quoted above of 'theological Hermaphroditism'. Then he goes on to quote from the play, 'For the majesty of religion I have the greatest respect, but as for you, Herr Hauptmann, or whatever they call you, you may lick my arse.' That in a nutshell describes Fuseli's view of all dogma – as it describes Goethe's.

Backwards and forwards across the Alps the correspondence flew. But in surviving letters there is very little information about the artist's own activities or about plans for his removal from Rome. One suspects there were several false starts, and it was not until the end of 1776 that there appears to have been a decision. Evidence of this is contained in a letter from Ozias Humphry to an unknown correspondent, possibly Sir William Young. Whoever it was had commissioned the Macbeth subject exhibited by Fuseli at the Royal Academy in 1777. As Humphry wrote, 'He (Fuseli) is very much connected with

Sir Joshua Reynolds and is therefore desirous that it should be sent to the Royal Academy and hopes you will have no objection to it . . . he proposes to be in England some time in March (1777) so as to be able to repair any little damage it may have sustained . . . Mr Fusielii (sic) says he shall esteem it a favour if it is not much seen before it is exhibited because he thinks it will be likely to produce a greater effect by coming unexpectedly upon the public.' First one may wonder why Humphry was acting as Fuseli's secretary, since presumably, if the correspondent was Sir William Young, the artist knew him well enough to write to him. On the other hand, it was not untypical of him to use an intermediary; he used Lavater in this way, perhaps because he was too diffident to make a direct approach himself. He did not go to London or anywhere else in 1777. If he had he might have prevented his name being mangled into 'Fusole' in the Academy catalogue.

However, in 1777 in May, Northcote arrived in Rome and the two artists struck up a friendship, which, on the available evidence, remained of a particularly venomous kind throughout their mutual lifetimes. If Fuseli was a butterfly (Northcote's epithet), he had a sting in his tail. Northcote was a wasp – that peculiarly English kind. He was, too, 'very much connected' with Sir Joshua Reynolds, from whom all blessings flowed as President of the still young Royal Academy. He was, therefore, in the very best position to give Fuseli the latest information on how the competition was shaping up in London. His gossip, nicely tinctured with nitric acid, must have helped in needling Fuseli into making plans for his return, via Zurich, to London.

So in October 1778, Fuseli set off northwards in the company of Sir Robert Smith and his wife. It was from Lugano, after having passed by way of Mantua and Bologna, that Fuseli wrote a warm, companionable letter to Northcote. Having made his comment about 'self-preservation', a term he had picked up in his reading of *A Philosophical Enquiry into . . . the Sublime and the Beautiful* (Pt. 1 Section VI), in which Burke* remarked that, 'The passions which concern self-preservation, turn mostly on *pain and danger*', appropriately Fuseli continued; 'At the sound of Rome, my heart swells, my eye kindles, and frenzy seizes me . . . I have lived at Bologna as agreeably and as happily as my lacerated heart and boiling brains would let me.' It would seem that he suffered from Winckelmann's disease, that the thought of returning to the North became more and more appalling. Winckelmann had got no further than Vienna when he decided to turn on his tracks and return to Italy, only to be murdered for a trifle at Trieste. Fuseli must have been feverish in Bologna, for like a Fragonard lover, he left a souvenir – *Fuseli amor mio* – under one of the nymphs tempting Saint Benedict in the fresco by Ludovico Carracci at S. Michele in Bosco outside the city. There, in 1792, W. Y. Ottley† saw it and added, *anche amor mio*.

Affairs of the heart were no doubt one reason for his reluctance to leave Italy; at the foot of his letter to Northcote he sent, in Italian, a love note to Nannina of the Palazzo Bolognetti.

*See *Philosophical Enquiry into the Origin of our Ideas of the Sublime and Beautiful*, 1757, ed. J. T. Boulton, London, 1958. This edition has a very useful Introduction.

145

†Ottley, William Y. 1771–1836, artist and art historian; Keeper of Prints, British Museum, 1833–36.

29

But as will be seen, the pleasure of Nannina* in Rome was to be succeeded by the pain of Nanna in Zurich.

*Her surname is unknown. See Stephen Gwynn, *Memorials of an Eighteenth Century Painter* (James Northcote), London, 1898.

This letter to Northcote, however, was not all complaint, for he enclosed a satirical drawing, of which the implicit meaning is not hard to discern. He warned his friend, 'Take heed of the mice', i.e. the competition each artist was up against in England. Benjamin West as the largest rodent was Fuseli's chief rival in history painting, Romney playing a smaller role. Northcote as a committed portraitist with history as his second string had both Romney and Humphry to fear. Fuseli, in fact, had already expressed his opinion of West to Lavater, when that innocent man had suggested using the American's painting of Orestes and Pylades in his book on Physiognomy: 'What you intend . . . God knows. For anyone must know, who has seen the Raphael cartoons and taken notice of the Antinous and Apollo, that he has tamed them with his drawing: his dismembering and joining of inexpressive and uncharacteristic marionettes to copied heads, which he himself has confessed at last, makes it good for nothing.'

As to the defecation on Switzerland, one wonders whether this act of relief and defiance had come from the artist's reading of Goethe's poetic riposte (1775) to Nicolai's travesty and parody *Joys of Young Werther*, for there he has Nicolai, having defecated on Werther's grave, admire the result and observe that if Werther could have done the same his suicide would have been unnecessary. Presumably, Fuseli meant that he would prefer to do this to his native land rather than go, unrelieved, through the pent-up agonies of returning to it. Since the artist has adopted the pose of one of Michelangelo's *ignudi*, next to Noah's Sacrifice in the Sistine Chapel, he might well be anticipating that great phrase, *Après moi le déluge*.

Almost every expatriate experiences a love-hate relationship with his native place. The sentiment that enjoins him to return to it is soon replaced by the ennui that drove him from it in the first place. Goethe had expressed this very succinctly in the case of Young Werther, who returned to his birthplace with 'all the veneration of a pilgrim', like Ulysses returned from the immeasurable sea: 'man can be happy on a few clods of earth', after all. Then the restlessness set in, 'I can stay here no longer' and 'time drags for me'. Then relief and departure, 'Yes, I am really a wanderer, a traveller of the world.' Fuseli, while perhaps ready to enjoy the fatted calf like the prodigal son had no intention of being fettered by the joys of reunion. He had in any case been too long away. But he did owe his father and Bodmer a visit before they died (as they did in 1781 and 1783). There was also Lavater. This good man as always had worked like a Trojan, arranging sufficient commissions to keep his friend busy and in pocket. Possibly he felt that, with plenty of work, and feeling the strength of the literary surge around him, Fuseli might be induced to stay. But like most stay-at-homes, Lavater did not realize that ambition knows no frontiers and

ZURICH 1778 TO 1779

1

success lies where the action is and not in the artistic backwater that was Zurich.

But it was there that Fuseli fell in love, possibly for the first and last time in his life. The girl, Anna Landolt, Lavater's niece, was already engaged. But there is nothing like playing with fire when it is well guarded; to be in love with love and to be safe, would suit Fuseli's shy and timorous nature. The declarations and exclamations of passion that he expressed in his letters, appear to grow stronger the further he was from Zurich. By the time he had reached Ostend, his confusion seems to have grown, for there he made a drawing referring to Nannina and her two sisters in the Palazzo Bolognetti, another of Magdalena Hess of Zurich to whom he was also attached and on the back of this a poem to Anna Landolt! For a month or two after he reached London, he was at his most feverish, and most secure one might add. There is good evidence to believe that he had a bad case of *Werther-fieber* (Werther fever), a term he had used himself in a letter to Lavater after reading the book. In a letter of June 1779, he repeats, admittedly with more erotic passion, the letter written by Werther in 'August', telling how, after troubled dreams he stretches out his arms to Lotte, seeks for her in his bed at night, groping for her half asleep, then awakes in a flood of tears. But all Werther desires is to sit with Lotte in a meadow and cover her hand with a thousand kisses. Not so, Fuseli: 'Last night, I had her (Anna Landolt) in my bed – my bed was rumpled – my hot, grasping hands wound around her – Her body and soul melted into mine – my spirit, breath and strength poured into her. Anyone who touches her now commits adultery and incest. She is mine and I am hers. And have her I will . . .' etc., etc. But the gale blew itself out, or rather the artist finally painted it out in *The Nightmare*. Yet *1* however self-induced this passion might have been, it prompted Fuseli to write his finest lyric, *Nannas Auge* (Nanna's Eyes). It had been preceded by one written at Baden, when he had been with Anna – *To Nanna's Pet Fawn*. Werther's Lotte had also a way with animals. It is no exaggeration to stress this connection since all Europe enjoyed a Werther cult. Young men affected Werther's yellow waistcoat and Lavater's own clerk shot himself, melancholy after reading the book.

By August, Fuseli had recovered enough to upbraid Lavater in his old tone: 'Urlsperger (a theologian) can go to the Devil with his Sacraments – Trinity! And you are surprised with sixteen exclamation marks, that because I offered up my lust to you, you can sacrifice me to every fool. Stop shoving my soul about and send me no more empty letters over the sea! . . . Answer me fully . . . (and) much about Nännen and Mäden (Nanna and Magdalena) and rescue me from Polly and Nancy and Peggy.' The last three names, of course, represent London's ladies of easy virtue, and for Fuseli, as one may see from some of his drawings, they came like the Fates, in threes. He was *182* never to revisit Switzerland.

*

On his return to London Fuseli naturally rejoined the circle around Joseph Johnson. With paintings to finish off for some of his Zurich patrons on his arrival, until his death forty-six years later, he kept up a ceaseless activity, missing only twelve Academy exhibitions, and these because he was busy. Although he continued his interest and activity in literary matters, these now became secondary to his work as an artist. He also seems to have been able to throw off his old enemy, lethargy, and whatever disappointments his career might have brought him, at least none were due to a lack of energy. But he was to confess to Farington that he had spent too long in Italy and had never had enough instruction in painting. He was, moreover, a late starter at thirty-eight and the competition was daunting.

Reynolds, West and Barry were now well established, and the last was in the middle of his large cycle for the Society of Arts. Mortimer died in 1779, but Romney was once more installed although he was always a doubtful starter in history painting. Northcote was to return in 1780 and Opie, 'The Cornish Wonder', arrived in London the following year. The artistic scene, however, to someone like Fuseli, must have appeared rather frivolous because of the great number of glamorous portraits and pretty classical subjects favoured by English high society. The following extract from his *Dunciad of Painting* (1780–89), gives a fair idea of his opinion:

> Where London pours her motley myriads, Trade
> With fell Luxuriance the Printshop spread:
> There as the wedded elm and tendril'd vine
> Angelica and Bartolozzi twine . . .
> Love without Fire; Smiles without Mirth; bright Tears
> To Grief unknown; and without Beauty, Airs;
> Celestial Harlots; Graces dressed by France;
> Rosy Despair and Passions taught to dance
> Irradiate the gay leaf – the charm struck crowd
> Devoutly gaze, then burst in raptures loud.

The artist was never to lower his sights for this kind of audience, even though he might, from time to time, do something that appealed to it. He was dependent on his own circle of patrons and admirers. But he could not escape the attention of the critics, of whom the most detested was probably Anthony Pasquin, the *nom de guerre* of John Williams. His treatment of Fuseli in the 1780 exhibition was true to form – 'This is the most miserable "Meduna" and deserves to be destroyed, & if a *II* Fuzee lay ready charged to destroy Ezelin it would be well for his detestable hard visage & baboon-like hands and fingers; he is just come in for a "chat" with his brother in iniquity opposite – Satan starting from the touch of Ituriel's Lance, which is the most ill looking devil I ever saw painted.' While it was not publicly expressed, Horace Walpole's famous comment on *The Mandrake* (1785), 'Shockingly mad, mad, mad, madder than ever', describes the general attitude of informed English opinion. It was Fuseli's and others' misfortune that they lived in a period when the fashionable taste of a single class of society precisely determined the mode and depth of expression in each category of painting – the wrong mode, too little or too much expression would damn the performance. Admittedly, longevity or a ranking position in the Academy would gain for the artist the respect of lip service, although not necessarily purchasers. Thus in 1788, Fuseli had his Ariadne called 'a sick idiot', but in 1790, when he became an R.A., he won a favourable review in the *Public Advertiser* only to have it made known that he depended on the eating of raw pork for his imagination. By the turn of the century, if he was the 'wild Swiss' and 'Painter in ordinary to the Devil', he was also the Professor of Painting, and reviews were milder and more congratulatory, from then on to his death.

A perusal of the Royal Academy lists tends to give a distorted view of painting activity in those days, since often it was not just artistic judgment that determined the choice of paintings to be exhibited. Thus the exhibition did not always represent the generality of an artist's work. If Fuseli's paintings in the Academy of 1781 are considered – *The Death of Dido, Queen Katherine's Vision, The Artist in Conversation with Bodmer* – one 7 may surmise that the first was meant to be compared with Reynolds' work of the same title on the theory that imitation is a form of flattery; the second was an earnest of the Shakespeare project; the third was to impress the President that the artist could turn his hand to serious portrait painting if he so wished. The previous year, three works had been chosen from pseudo-Italian history, Classical literature and Milton respectively, so that Fuseli had shown his paces as a history painter, and as one prepared to use English sources. The following year, 1782, the artist staked everything on one throw – *The Nightmare* – which had been painted the previous year, and it was by no means representative of his work as a whole.

Whatever the strategy may have been which lay behind his choice of pictures to exhibit, it succeeded. His name was made but not his fortune, for the money he got for a painting was a pittance compared to that gained by the printsellers. That problem was not solved until he took Moses Haughton, Jr in as his engraver, boarding him at 100 guineas a year in 1803. Until 1819, the two men published prints from the address of the Keeper's home, in Somerset House, a practice which today would raise a few eyebrows. By controlling both the manufacturing and retail ends of the business, Fuseli at last reaped a just reward for his labours.

While this is out of chronological order, it throws into relief the economics of artistic life of the period – if an artist would live at all, he had to have his work engraved to gain the kudos for continued sales, but without Fuseli's solution he had none of the income collected by the engravers. Thus in the case of *The Nightmare*, Fuseli must have painted *at least* six repetitions and variants for various printsellers for an outright and single payment.

Another problem, of course, and one which possibly led to his meeting with Blake, was that of finding a sympathetic engraver who would not butcher the original. That had been Fuseli's experience with the French edition of Lavater's

Essai sur Physiognomie (Vol. 1.2. 1781, Vol. 3. 1786), in which the French engravers had produced travesty after travesty of his original drawings. Blake had worked as an engraver for Joseph Johnson since 1779 and this may have brought the pair together – rather earlier than usually stated. Moreover, on returning to England Fuseli had taken rooms at 1, Broad Street, Carnaby Market (now Golden Square). (According to the Royal Academy catalogue this was the house of Mr Beyer – probably his friend, Peyer von Schaffhausen.) Blake also lived in Broad Street until August 1782, so the two were neighbours for three years. Apart from these connections, Blake had also been a pupil of Moser's at the Royal Academy Schools. Fuseli was sixteen years older than Blake and certainly at the time of their first meeting, must have appeared to the younger man a tower of erudition, not only intellectually but linguistically, for it should be emphasized that Fuseli could read Hebrew and Blake could not.

One may imagine, however, that Fuseli's first reactions were simply those of relief at finding not only a highly skilful engraver but one who was sensitive and imaginative enough to 'realize' the artist's intention, though this very capacity of Blake's was eventually to lead to their parting – as a copying engraver he would no longer do as he was told! In 1799, in a letter to George Cumberland,* Blake provides the clue: 'For as to Engraving, . . . I am laid away in a corner as if I did not Exist, & since my Young's Night Thoughts have been published, Even Johnson & Fuseli have discarded my graver.' It was in this aborted edition that Blake integrated the text as a vertical plane in the composition, using it to obscure most of the figurative image behind it and allowing only a head or a hand to appear around one or other side of this plane (e.g. Thunder, p.80). This kind of compositional 'eccentricity' may have led both Johnson and Fuseli to feel that Blake's usefulness was over, at least as a regular engraver.

In 1782, Fuseli moved to 100, St. Martin's Lane, his home for the next four years. In 1783 and 1784 he produced two more popular successes, the *Three Witches* and *Lady Macbeth Sleepwalking* (Louvre), showing that he could hit the right note of contemporary interest and also hold his own against the established artists like Reynolds and West, and *mirabile dictu*, the Hanging Committee of the Royal Academy. This committee, in the latter year, made Lady Macbeth contend with Reynolds's full length portrait of the Prince of Wales on one wall, and with Oedipus summoned to his death on another, dwarfed by West's three vast Prophet paintings for the Royal Chapel at Windsor. Politically, however, the 'hanging' was judicious.

In November 1786 occurred the auspicious dinner party, with Alderman Boydell† as host, at which the project for a Shakespeare Gallery was first broached. In none of the accounts is Fuseli mentioned as being present, which is strange, since the artists who were, West, Romney and Sandby, were hardly the leading lights in the eventual exhibition. Alderman Nicol, a

*George Cumberland, the elder, close friend of Blake for thirty years and author of *Thoughts on Outline . . .* , London 1796.

72

†Boydell, John, 1719–1804. Boydell was born at Dorrington, Shropshire. 1740, was apprenticed to the engraver Toms in London: 1745–46, published his first prints: 1782, became Alderman for the Ward of Cheap: 1790, Lord Mayor of London: 1796, complained that business was bad to a correspondent in Nuremberg. The capital he laid out on the Shakespeare Gallery was £150,000, not £350,000 as often stated. This was the sum that he and his 'brethren' had laid out in promoting the Fine Arts generally. He is buried in St Olave, Jewry, London.

V Fuseli. Thor, in the boat of Hymir, battering the Midgard Serpent

VI

VII

printer, is generally credited with the idea, although Fuseli's obituarist in the *Gentleman's Magazine* in 1825, wrote that it was in Rome that 'he suggested the original idea of the Shakespeare Gallery'. It seems more than likely that Fuseli, acting in his usual manner, used Romney as his proxy, who in turn found it politic to use Nicol as the mouthpiece. Romney, indeed, had made many drawings of Shakespeare subjects while he was in Italy and later, but there seems to be no evidence of him thinking of them as belonging to a cycle. If Lord Thurlow's remark is recalled, 'Romney, before you paint Shakespeare, do for God's sake read him', then one may doubt whether the artist was capable of such a conception, whereas Fuseli certainly was.

The Boydell scheme has to be seen in the context of others of its kind – particularly an earlier attempt, with Barry as protagonist, to provide a cycle of paintings for St Paul's Cathedral. When this fell through Barry, single-handed and on a miserable stipend, had completed his cycle 'Human Improvement' in the Society of Arts rooms between 1777 and 1783. West too, was fully engaged with a cycle of paintings for the Royal Chapel. Painters indeed were avid for such long-term commissions. They united artistic glory with a steady income.

Fuseli, the largest contributor to the first stage of the Boydell scheme, would obviously have preferred to be the *only* contributor, if he could have found a backer both confident and independent. But compromise there had to be, and with Boydell it had to be a sound business deal with all the options covered. To prevent any competition all the major artists would have to be contributors and if they were reluctant they would have to be bought. Every man has his price and Reynolds's was a five hundred pound note with the other half on promise. With the President in, the others followed – on the monetary scale in descending order – West at five hundred for his Lear, Barry three hundred for his, while Northcote and Fuseli were paired at the one hundred and fifty guinea level. While Boydell paid grandiloquent lip service to the Gallery, it was the sale of engravings from the paintings that had really attracted him to the scheme. Since the 1760s, he had been exporting prints to the Continent, but he also imported and thereby experienced a balance of trade problem, having to pay the difference in good English gold. The success of the Shakespeare scheme could put everything right, for his plays were being read and performed throughout Europe. In 1787 Boydell was in Paris, pleased to see English prints selling well and also doing some advance puffing of the Shakespeare project. With his eye also on the home market, he attempted, without success, to persuade David to visit England. The French artist was then enjoying a *succès d'estime et populaire*, and had Reynolds's unqualified praise for his *Death of Socrates*.

Boydell was beaten in the end, not by competition, but by the British naval blockade of the European ports. As he somewhat plaintively wrote, in his letter to Parliament to petition the holding of a lottery of all the Shakespeare effects, 'I certainly

VI Fuseli. Falstaff in the Buckbasket. 1792

VII Fuseli. The Shepherd's Dream. 1793

37

calculated on some defalcation (of revenue) by a French or Spanish war, or both; but with France and Spain (after 1792) I carried on but little commerce. Flanders, Holland and Germany, who no doubt supplied the rest of Europe were the great marts. But alas! they are no more' (1804). If Britannia ruled the waves, she also erased the profit margins.

There seems no doubt that the birth of Fuseli's Milton Gallery in 1790 was attended by a certain pain at losing artistic control over the Shakespeare programme, but also by pleasure at Boydell's morose hostility to the promise of competition.

Meanwhile in 1788 the artist had got himself married at last. His wife, Sophia Rawlins, of Batheaston, near Bath, is usually described as an artist's model, but one may guess not of the professional but of the amateur variety, and that Fuseli met her not in London but in Bath where his friend, Prince Hoare, whom he had known in Rome, had returned to practice as a portrait painter. In their choice of a mate Blake and Fuseli were a pair, for both married 'below their station', socially and intellectually, Blake having to teach his wife to read and write. Sophia must have had these accomplishments, since her husband would never have had the patience to teach her. Her attributes were good looks, good sense and good housekeeping. She also had the patience of Job. As Redgrave* suggested, it was perhaps his marriage that persuaded Fuseli, who was very much older than his wife, to make some provision for her, by applying for an Associateship of the Academy, so that a pension would ensue. But, at this time, it was good for any artist's business to acquire this cachet. It might well be a coincidence but the title of one of his paintings in that year's exhibition was *Theseus receiving the clue from Ariadne*, and perhaps it was Sophia's attention to her sewing basket which helped the artist to find the way out of his own labyrinth. In the following year, he exhibited *Beatrice*, who in *Much Ado about Nothing* had explained to her betrothed, Benedick,

> I yield upon great persuasion; and partly to save your life, for I was told you were in a consumption.

and Benedick later opines to Don Pedro,

> since I do purpose to marry . . . never flout at me for what I have said against it; for man is a giddy thing . . .

Whether this was his text or not, the sentiments expressed on both sides were probably true enough.

If marriage brought a certain contentment, it was his friendships that brought him sustenance. In 1789 an old one was reborn in the shape of Lavater's son, who after studying medicine at Leyden, came to England. Fuseli must have seen a great deal of him, for in *c.* 1790, he drafted on the back of one of his courtesan drawings, a poem, which, if he ever polished it, he sent to Lavater, extolling possibly with a streak of envy, the gift of such a son.

The poem is one of very few in English, so some of his sources can be pointed out. First the phrases 'the gorgeous east' and 'the wealth of either Ind' are derived from Shakespeare's '. . . man of Inde/ At the first opening of the gorgeous east' (*Love's*

*Redgrave, Samuel, 1802–1876, with his brother Richard wrote *A Century of British Painting*, London, 1866. Samuel also compiled *A Dictionary of Artists*, London 1876.

99

Labour's Lost IV 3) or Thomson's '. . . thro' gorgeous Ind' (*Summer: The Seasons* I. 825): while 'Gold of AurengZebe' and 'counterpoise' come from Dryden's play of that title (1676) and Armstrong out of Milton, respectively. The process of assembling together independent lines which pleased him is analogous to that adopted in his painting.

Another friendship, less sentimental and retrospective, but significant to both men, was with William Roscoe,* Liverpool banker and scholar. Once again, it was the ubiquitous Johnson who had brought them together. The publisher came from Liverpool and had taken the artist there first in 1767. It was in 1782, however, when Roscoe came to London on business that the connection began seriously. Roscoe was the younger by twelve years, becoming, it seems, an instant admirer of Fuseli's work, and from the surviving correspondence it is clear that Fuseli held his friend in great respect and affection. Roscoe was perhaps the only man, apart from Bodmer, whose scholarship and enlightened views matched his own. In both of Roscoe's Renaissance studies, *Lorenzo de' Medici* and *Leo X*, the artist carefully checked the sections on art, while the author repaid him by acquiring fourteen of his works, not counting prints and drawings, and acting as his agent in the Liverpool area. Thus, it was through Roscoe that Fuseli became something of a pioneer in tapping the resources of the provinces, sending paintings to the exhibitions which began to proliferate in the Midlands and the North. But Roscoe's greatest contribution was in financing the artist during the years he was working on the paintings for the Milton Gallery.

In 1790, Fuseli wrote to Roscoe: 'I am determined to lay, hatch and crack an egg for myself too – if I can. . . . a Series of Pictures for Exhibition such as Boydells.' To do this, he cajoled a very limited company of friends, Coutts,[†] Lock of Norbury, Seward, Steevens, Johnson and Roscoe to underwrite the years of preparation by regular subscription, to provide an annual income of £300. The upshot was that, by the time the exhibition was before the public, Roscoe contributed as much as all the others put together. This decade was perhaps the worst and best of the artist's life: worst, because of the nagging penury he had to endure and best, because he was engaged on a great monumental cycle which was all his own. Ironically it was to remain all his own until his death because of the complete failure of the exhibition. Possibly an earlier scheme, proposed by Johnson, to publish Cowper's edition of Milton with thirty engravings after Fuseli, would have proved more successful. But Cowper suffered one of his bouts of insanity and with Boydell growling, Johnson dropped the idea. That this scheme would have been more successful is attested by the plain fact that the only viable economic *and* artistic medium at this time was the engraving, as other artists, from Goya to Stothard, quite clearly recognized. Depending on the observer's point of view, the Milton Gallery was either a 'glorious failure' or a Pyrrhic victory, for it ensured the artist considerable artistic esteem in the two last decades of his life:

*Roscoe, William, 1753–1831, banker, historian and art collector of Liverpool.

†Coutts, Thomas, 1735–1822, banker and life-long patron of Fuseli. Lock, William, Sr, 1732–1810, of Norbury Park, art collector: see Duchess of Sermonetta, *The Locks of Norbury*. Seward, William, 1747–99, author of *Anecdotes of some distinguished Persons*. Steevens, George, 1736–1800, Shakespearian scholar and editor of the Rivington Shakespeare, 1805.

Whether his contemporaries were aware of it or not, the Milton Gallery was the last of the monumental cycles of European art.

During the 1790s, while the artist adventurer was leaping on to the strange shore of Milton's lost Paradise, he also had to face a reality on the domestic hearth in the 'termagant' Mary Wollstonecraft. The epithet was Fuseli's and confided to Lawrence in retrospect. Miss Wollstonecraft, who had been a teacher to 1788, had joined the Johnson circle shortly after as a reader, particularly of French texts, which she also translated. She had spent time as a lodger in the house of Thomas Taylor, the English Neo-Platonist and friend of Blake, who was to illustrate her *Original Stories from Real Life* (1796). The equilateral triangle, Blake, Fuseli and Miss Wollstonecraft, contained all the seeds of an Ibsenesque Battle of the Sexes. For Blake was so enamoured of Mary that he wished her to join him in a *ménage à trois*, while this was her own desire in regard to Fuseli. But Blake was to be disappointed and Fuseli immensely relieved when Mrs Fuseli forbade Miss Wollstonecraft the house. It has been suggested that the authoress's departure for France in 1792 was impelled by pique, but in fact there had been a tentative arrangement for Johnson, the Fuselis and the lady to make a visit there, and obviously the very unsettled political situation made them change their plans. There is little doubt that it was Mary Wollstonecraft who inspired Fuseli's *Aphorism* 226,

'In an age of luxury women have taste, decide and dictate; for in an age of luxury woman aspires to the functions of man, and man slides into the offices of woman. The epoch of eunuchs was ever the epoch of viragoes.'

In the same year that she left for France, her book, written in six weeks, *A Vindication of the Rights of Women*, appeared. For the moment, three passages from her introduction may serve as evidence –

'From every quarter have I heard exclamations against masculine women. If . . . this appellation . . . be against the imitation of manly virtues, . . . the exercise of which ennobles the human character, and which raises females in the scale of animal being, . . . I should . . . wish . . . that they may every day grow more and more masculine.' 'The only way women can rise in the world – [is] by marriage. And this desire making mere animals of them, when they marry they act as . . . children . . . – they dress, they paint. . . . Surely these weak beings are only fit for a seraglio.'

Finally there was this presumption, 'that rational men will excuse me for endeavouring to persuade them to become more masculine and respectable.'

Since the artist had met Miss Wollstonecraft the year after his own marriage, the concern of his wife was very real, even though the friendship was purely platonic, a condition seldom smiled upon by women in any case. Fuseli, at fifty, must have been considerably flattered by the attentions of this highly intelligent and good-looking woman of thirty one, who later was to warn him of 'the slime of vanity', but that daunting quality of the English bluestocking must have been too much for him in the end.

The early nineties were indeed devoted to 'vindication'. Thomas Paine's *Rights of Man* appeared in 1791–92, Blake's *Visions of the Daughters of Albion*, his own defence of women, in 1793, and to complete the cycle Thomas Taylor's* *Vindication of the Rights of Brutes* in the same year. The latter was a double slap for Paine and Miss Wollstonecraft, for Taylor's neo-platonism, ('love with me is only true in proportion as it is pure') and his great love of animals, lead him into a curious misanthropic position, as though he might be an implicit believer in the superior race of Swift's Houyhnhnms. For Fuseli this would be stretching the notion of metempsychosis beyond its satirical limit. His enlightened scepticism would for ever hold him back from *seriously* plunging into the heady abyss of that very English brand of irrational but imaginative speculation. To expand one of his own remarks, he was only interested in leaping from the peak of one pyramid to another and not in exploring the batty but thrilling ruins of some classicized Gothic cottage.

*See Kathleen Raine, *Blake and Tradition*, Princeton, 1968.

Accordingly, from 1785 onwards he had taken an active interest in Cowper's† translation of the *Iliad* and the *Odyssey*, which were finally published in 1791. In his letters Cowper not only acknowledges the erudition and poetic capacity of the artist but intimates that Fuseli accepted no payment for what must have been time-consuming work.

†Cowper, William, 1731–1800. *Homer's Iliad and Odyssey*, 2 vols. London 1791. *Correspondence of William Cowper*, 4 vols. London 1910.

In this same decade, Fuseli rose in the hierarchy of the Royal Academy, from Academician in 1790 to Professor of Painting in 1799. His election in both cases was accompanied by some unpleasantness, which in neither case was caused by himself. In 1790, Fuseli cleared his application with Reynolds only to find that the President was prepared to go to the wall on behalf of Bonomi the architect. The vote went against Reynolds, who was coming to the end of his presidency; Fuseli was elected, Reynolds – mortified – resigned; was mollified and resumed the Presidency for the last two years of his life. In the second case, it was the expulsion of Barry from the Academy over his *Letter to the Dilettanti Society* which created the vacancy. Fuseli may not have cared much for Barry who had voted against him earlier, but that Northcote and Opie should vote against him on the Professorship, must have hurt him, since he had helped both. However when they hurried round to him the next morning to explain, he welcomed them, calling Opie a 'bumbailiff' and Northcote a 'Jew broker'. He was not far wrong, since the Academy hardly distinguished itself in the matter of any election. Amongst many of the other members Fuseli conducted himself with probity – honest enough to vote alone against West as President, offering Mrs Lloyd (Mary Moser) since 'one old woman was as good as another'. It would appear that his behaviour gained him much respect. Fuseli was appointed Keeper in 1804, but only because the King vetoed the election of Robert Smirke, on West's advice, since the Academy was now split into those artists who had trained in Italy and those who had not. This was the reason Humphry advanced for his objection to Smirke. Under Reynolds, these factions had certainly existed, but his presence as founding father prevented outright war. His death, however, producing such phrases as 'we shall never see his like again', removed the only umpire both sides respected. West, as the King's man, became, inevitably, the next President, but he was no Reynolds. George III, shrewder and more thoughtful than most of the Academicians, was able through his power of veto to make sure that the Academy would uphold its dignity with a man of substance as Keeper. The exchange, which Farington records, between the King and West, is evidence that both considered Fuseli 'a man of genius', with West adding: 'He is distinguished as a Literary Character and known to all Europe.'

West had, no doubt, discovered this in Paris in 1802. During the brief armistice, there was a kind of Academic excursion to the French capital to see the works of art Napoleon had 'collected' from Italy. As an exhibition of masterpieces it has probably never been equalled, and for many of the English artists it made up for the deprivation of an Italian tour. Fuseli went with Farington and Dr James Carrick Moore. As Professor of Painting, he had already gained some renown with the publication of his first three lectures in 1801, and *pace* the usual acidity of the *Edinburgh Review,* one may gather from a later anonymous review in *The Examiner,* that the artist was at least seen walking in the shade of Reynolds. 'This Professor far surpasses the general class of lecturers . . . his discourses . . . boldly travel out of the beaten track; . . . Always animated, often glowing, he carries his hearers, with a pleasing avidity along his course' (1810).

In Paris, Farington did not see much of Fuseli, who was out and about on business of his own, looking up old acquaintances, amongst them the French artists he had known in Rome. He told Farington that he did not find France much changed since he had been there last. All in all, Fuseli's familiarity with so many people must have come as an eye-opener to many of his English colleagues, particularly since a stage was set for it in the shape of West's public breakfast on 27 September. Farington, whose jottings are always most animated in the presence of food, gives a very full description of the company, which seemed to comprise the whole international set in Paris. West, who took care not to seat Fuseli at the main table, nevertheless must have returned to England impressed by the Professor's performance.

The year of the publication (1802) of his lectures was Fuseli's sixtieth. This was the beginning of the Greek revival, and it has been said that Fuseli encouraged his students in the Academy Schools to adopt the Greek enthusiasm. The dandies and their girl friends affected all things Greek, including the highwaisted semi-transparent dress, worn with the minimum of underwear to resemble the Greek chiton as closely as possible. This craze for Greek dress extended across Europe. As early as 1785, Chodowiecki in the *Frauenzimmer Almanach* had shown his designs for a 'reformed' dress for German women based on Greek models. The 'English' fashion later called the 'naked'

42

passed to France and gained respectability by being called 'Directoire' or 'Empire'. In its extreme forms it was not popular, for when Mme Hamelin, wife of the Swiss banker, walked in the Tuileries gardens, apparently clad only in gauze, she was forced to retreat, while in England Mrs Jordan was cat-called off the stage when she appeared in a similar transparency. How far Fuseli really favoured it is not known, but a Swiss, Johann Caspar Schweizer, who had known Mary Wollstonecraft in Paris, described the artist as disgracing himself by 'wearing the clothes of a young dandy'. This might have been spite, for Schweizer was the husband of Magdalena Hess, upon whom Fuseli had cast an affectionate eye in Zurich. Fuseli always cherished the company of fair women. Perhaps after Mary Wollstonecraft's departure, he may have thought like Swift,* 'I have almost done with Harridans, and shall soon become old enough to fall in love with girls of fourteen', for he maintained through two generations a close and affectionate relationship with the daughters and granddaughters of Thomas Coutts.

*Swift, *Letters to Alexander Pope*, No. XI, 1757.

Amongst his other friends, there was William Lock, erstwhile pupil and patron, who married 'the beautiful Miss Jennings', and Opie's wife, who according to all was charm itself. There was also Lavinia de Irujo, a natural daughter of the Spanish Ambassador, who lived with her mother in Upper Church Street, Chelsea, where Johnson's house was also situated. Fuseli made drawings of her when she was in her late teens. However, it was with the Coutts family that Fuseli, childless himself, kept the closest company. Of the first generation there was Susan (b. 1771) who married Lord North in 1796 and later became the Countess of Guildford, the owner of the largest collection of Fuseli's works; her sister Sophia (b. 1775) who married Sir Francis Burdett in 1793. Of the second generation, there were the Countess's daughters, Susan and Georgina, born in 1797 and 1798 respectively, who provided the artist with several years of innocent delight. Samuel Rogers, the banker-poet, in his *Table Talk,* records that in the Countess' garden at Putney, there was a statue of Flora, at which the artist would leave scraps of poems and *billets doux* for the two girls. During this period of his life and for no other reason than convenience, Fuseli would spend nights away from home either at Putney or with Johnson at Chelsea. Mrs Fuseli seems to have accompanied him very rarely, for she was not in Paris, and she is never referred to as being with her husband at the several dinner parties that Farington describes.

The Fuseli home, however, was a shifting one in the early years of the century. From Queen Anne Street, where they had lived since their marriage, they moved to Berners Street in 1804 and the following year into the Keeper's house at the Royal Academy in its old quarters at Somerset House. While the last move brought the couple economic security, the changes would have been unsettling for a man in his sixties. What was more, his old friend, Lavater, had died in 1801. Not that the artist's activity was much affected by all this, since he was editing Pilkington's *Dictionary of Painters* (1805) and working on the illustrations for the Rivington Shakespeare (1805) during these years. A worse loss was to occur in 1809, when Johnson died; the annuity of fifty pounds that he left the artist was small consolation for his removal. More than anything it cut Fuseli off from direct communication with the literary world and at the age of sixty-nine he was unwilling to find another circle. Little is known about his reactions to the new poets. He appears to have admired Byron, but on meeting Coleridge at Johnson's was not much impressed by him – Fuseli was never very impressed by intellects which he reckoned were equal to his. His distaste was reciprocated. Coleridge, apropos the artist's *Macbeth and the Armed Head* (Folger Library Washington), remarked to Crabb Robinson on Fuseli's 'vigorous impotence', and Hazlitt wrote that Fuseli's 'distortions and vagaries are German, and not English: they lie like a nightmare on the breast of our native art.' Much of this may be explained simply by the impatience of a younger generation for an older, particularly when the former was more orientated towards landscape imagery and resentful of any attempts by artists to realize poetic images. Hence Charles Lamb's impatience with Boydell's Shakespeare Gallery – no artist was to foist on *him* what he could very well imagine himself: hence as Crabb Robinson* records, Lamb's praise for Robert Hunt's attack on Fuseli in the *Examiner* (1811). Lamb, too, wrote in high praise of Hogarth – English painting at its best – whose work now was resurrected and enjoyed a greater favour than in the artist's lifetime. Northcote, however, thought that Hogarth was overrated and Fuseli, while praising highly the artist's own engravings, did not think much of the paintings. There was still room and sympathy for narrative and landscape painting but little or none for Poetic painting. Fuseli knew this himself, and put it down quite correctly to 'that general change of habits, customs, pursuits and amusements, which for near a century has stamped the national character of Europe with apathy or discountenance of the genuine principles of Art' (Lecture XII, 1810). With hindsight one can recognize that when history is being made on a large canvas, as it was from the 1770s to 1815 on all fronts, military, political and industrial, the historical painter could attract little attention even with his own canvas of ten by fourteen feet, though it be suffused with 'the genuine principles of art'.

From 1809 onwards, then, Fuseli applied himself exclusively to teaching, painting and writing about art. At his age he would have had little enthusiasm for inserting himself into another literary set. Many old friends still survived and there was the theatre which he attended regularly. There was also another aspect which is never much stressed, and that is the growth of London. From an easily compassable city in the eighteenth century it had become a huge metropolis, the 'Great Wen' as Cobbett called it. Travelling about it was irksome, certainly to an elderly man and it would be easy enough not to see a friend for months. It is well known that Blake not only lost contact

*Crabb Robinson, Henry, 1775–1867: see *The Diary, Reminiscences and Correspondence of . . .* ed. Sadler, London, 1869.

44

with Fuseli after 1815, but with everyone else as well. His 'rediscovery' by Lamb and Crabb Robinson in the early 1820s, was almost like Stanley finding Livingstone in Africa.

Unlike Blake, Fuseli could not complain of lack of recognition in his own lifetime, for apart from his position in the Academy, an appraisal of his work, written by Johann Heinrich Meyer, had appeared in *Entwurf einer Kunstgeschichte des 18. Jahrhunderts* published together with Goethe's *Winckelmann und sein Jahrhundert* in 1805: in 1807 in his native Zurich, under the editorship of his old friend Nuscheler there was published *Heinrich Füessli's Sämtliche Werke nebst einem Versuche seiner Biographie.* Following Canova's visit to England in 1815, he was, in 1816, made an honorary Academician (first class) in the Academy of St Luke, Rome. Even his lectures were not overlooked, for the first three were translated by J. J. Eschenburg and published in Brunswick, 1803, while Fuseli himself had presented a bound copy of the English edition to the French Academy in Paris.

It says much for Blake's generosity of spirit towards Fuseli, that he could refer to their mutual neglect with such equal emphasis. But Blake lived alone, while Fuseli was entrenched at the Academy in daily contact with the members and with the students. It is astonishing to realize that Fuseli put through their first artistic paces almost every one of the painters that was to make a name for himself in the following decades – Haydon,[*] Wilkie, Landseer, Etty, Mulready, Linnell, Leslie – and most, particularly in Haydon's case, were appreciative of his teaching and his gifts as an artist. Leslie, from whom one might expect the least notice as the enthusiastic biographer of Constable, wrote in his *A Handbook for Young Painters* (1855) that Fuseli 'was a perfect master of chiaroscuro . . . he possessed such a competent knowledge of the anatomical structure of the human figure, as to be able to give ideal probability to attitudes, in which it was impossible he could be helped by living models. . . . in spite of his great faults, I cannot but look upon him as a genius of whom the age in which he lived was unworthy.' If one adds to this praise from a good technician like Leslie, the numerous anecdotes about Fuseli's kindness, his encouragement of Wilkie, his fondness for Landseer, and that he received the unprecedented gift of a silver vase from his pupils, then he must appear as an enthusiastic teacher and a disinterested judge of quality. It was, perhaps, his retention of an enthusiastic attitude that endeared him most to this generation of artists, and the high standards that he set himself and others. In his own word he 'enjoyed' life to such an extent that Samuel Rogers, twenty two years his junior and forever complaining of lack of notice, was refused his hand, since Fuseli 'was not prepared to make one [a handshake] in death's dance'. That was in 1819, when the artist was seventy-eight. He seems to have retained a remarkable vigour of action up to his last years, whether it was striding about amongst the Elgin marbles, crying 'The Greeks were Gods' or violently reacting to nature. This was described by Lawrence,[†] who had been

[*]Haydon, Benjamin Robert, 1786–1846; see *The Diary of Benjamin Robert Haydon*, ed. W. B. Pope, 5 vols. Harvard, 1960–63 and *The Autobiography and Journals of . . .* , ed. Malcolm Elwin, London, 1950. Wilkie, Sir David, RA, 1785–1841. Landseer, Sir Edwin, RA, 1802–73. Etty, William, RA, 1787–1849. Mulready, William, RA, 1786–1863. Linnell, John, RA, 1792–1882. Leslie, Charles Robert, RA, 1794–1859.

[†]Lawrence, Sir Thomas, PRA, 1769–1830; for the anecdote see Cunningham, Bibliography.

45

accused by the artist of plagiarizing his Satan figure. The portrait painter denied it, saying that it was based on Fuseli's own posture, standing on a high rock overlooking the Bristol Channel, crying out, 'Grand! Grand! Jesu Christ, how grand! how terrific!' Lawrence, put in mind of Satan looking into the abyss, made a sketch on the spot. By an extraordinary coincidence Fuseli's posture seems remarkably close to that deplored by Chodowiecki as an affected way of looking at Nature in his series, *Natürliche und affektierte Handlungen* (1779), the natural way being to stand still and bow the head slightly, in reverence.

His remaining years were well regulated. He worked on his *History of Art in Italy* and had completed Michelangelo before he died. He gave three more lectures by 1805 and a final three in 1810. He exhibited every year, except 1813, '15, '16, '19 and '22, at the Royal Academy. Not much more could be expected of an old man, who in his youth had declared that he would not live past the age of thirty.

He was out at Putney visiting his old friend the Countess of Guildford and expecting to dine that night with Lawrence, Samuel Rogers and W. Y. Ottley, when he fell ill. His life ebbed out over five days and his last words were 'Is Lawrence come?'

He was accorded full Academy funerary honours and was buried in the crypt of St Paul's along with others 'of the company'. For the sake of accuracy it should be stated that he is not next to Reynolds or Opie, but to George Dance the Younger and on the other side of Dance there is Benjamin West. With Dance between him and the late President, whom he disliked, Fuseli, if he had been able *post mortem,* might have declared that a Dance would prevent too close an attendance on West.

II The Artist as Autobiographer

It may be interesting to commence this chapter with Lavater's physiognomic analysis that accompanied Bromley's profile of the artist in the English edition of the Essays*:

> The curve which describes the profile in whole is obviously one of the most remarkable: it indicates an energetic character which spurns at the idea of trammels. The forehead, by its contours and position, is more suited to the poet than the thinker. I perceive in it more force than gentleness – the fire of the imagination than the cool of reason. The nose seems to be the seat of an intrepid genius. The mouth promises a spirit of application and precision, and yet it costs the original the greatest effort to give the finishing touch to the smallest piece. Anyone may see, without my telling it, that this character is not destitute of ambition, and that the sense of his own merit escapes him not. It may also be suspected that he is subject to impetuous emotions, but will anyone say he loves with tenderness – with warmth to excess? There is, however, nothing more true; though, on the other hand, his sensibility has occasion continually to be kept awake by the presence of the beloved object: absent, he forgets it, and troubles himself no more. The person to whom he is fondly attached, while near him, may lead him like a child; but, quit him, and the most perfect indifference will follow. He must be roused, be struck, in order to be carried along. Though capable of the greatest actions, to him the slightest complaisance is an effort. His imagination is forever aiming at the sublime and delighting itself with prodigies. Nature intended him for a great poet, a great painter, a great orator – but to borrow his own words, 'inexorable fate does not always proportion the will to our powers; it sometimes assigns a copious proportion of will to minds whose faculties are very contracted, and frequently associates with the greatest faculties a will feeble and impotent.'

No apology is offered for this long description, for Lavater gives here a more objective appraisal of Fuseli than anyone else of the time. Striking as it is as an example of physiognomic skill, one has also to remember that Lavater already knew a good deal about the man behind the profile. The analysis, however, is generally typical of Lavater's confidence in his science, although many contemporaries, including Lichtenberg,† were quick to point out how inexact it was. One example may demonstrate the elasticity of the physiognomic rules, namely that salient feature – the nose – which Lavater recognizes as the seat of 'intrepid genius' in Fuseli, but when he considers that of Socrates, which was pugshaped, in the same work, he falls back on the explanation that men of character and energy

2

*See Marcia Allentuck, 'Fuseli and Lavater: physiognomical theory and the Enlightenment', *Studies on Voltaire and the Eighteenth Century*, LV 1967.

†Lichtenberg, Georg Christoph, 1742–99, physicist and satirical writer: see *Lichtenberg's Commentaries on Hogarth's Engravings*, trans. I. & G. Herdan, London, 1966.

47

often look disagreeable and harsh. This emphasis on the nose goes back to Rabelais whose Friar John remarked *ad formam nasi cognoscitur* (by the shape of his nose shall he be known). Sterne followed this up in *Tristram Shandy* and Fuseli, not infrequently, refers to the nose in his letters, indeed in one written to Lavater from Namur in 1779, he suggests that the marrow of the nose is the nerve centre of friendship! Certainly in his drawings he gives often more than adequate treatment to this feature. Most prominent is the one he gives, very correctly, to Bardolph in the death of Falstaff. This interest *132* may serve as a reminder that men like the artist, however much they might be forward-looking, still retained to a large degree long-standing traditional beliefs which were not to be sloughed off until early in the next century.

In his youth Fuseli already saw himself as detached, for this is how he appears in the early drawings referred to previously, standing to one side watching the action he portrays – Bodmer in debate or Spalding in his summer house. Then the first years in London brought some confidence, particularly after he had arbitrated over the contest – Rousseau versus Voltaire – so that he might have thought of himself, with some justification, as 'the acute inspector, the elegant umpire . . . the subtle archer' of his life and times. These phrases from his first Lecture describe the Paris of Euphranor, also the subject of the drawing made in 1768–69. The moment chosen is that following Paris' ignominious battle with Menelaus (*Iliad* III), who, *5* his other weapons failing, dragged the reluctant hero through the dust by the plume of his helmet, until Aphrodite severed the chin strap that was near choking her protégé. First hiding him in a mist, she then carried him off to the safety of his room, where he was to be reconciled with Helen.

It seems reasonable to assume that to Fuseli this is an allegory about Beauty and Art. Such an allegory would not be unusual, for Reynolds had painted *Garrick between Tragedy and Comedy* in 1761 and West *The Choice of Hercules* in 1764, while Nathaniel Dance was probably already working on *The Interview between Helen and Paris*, which he exhibited at the Royal Academy in 1770. (Dance was devoted to Angelica Kauffmann, who would have readily introduced him to Fuseli.) There is moreover a remarkable similarity between Paris' features and *Frontispiece* his own, and we may read the allegory as meaning that Aphrodite-Beauty-Art is carrying the artist from the battle-field of literary hack work in London to Helen-Troy-Rome, for although the figures are Greek the stonework is the wall of Piranesi's Rome. Whether the artist, at this stage at least, identified himself further with Paris, as 'the deserter of Oenone, the seducer of Helen . . . that future murderer of Achilles', is very doubtful but in studying the pencilled self-portrait, it could be agreed that elements of character 'lurk(ed) under the insidious eyebrow and in the penetrating glance of beauty's chosen minion.' It is also worth noting that the artist, at this point, does not identify himself with one of the great heroes of the Trojan wars, but with a character, who while not a non-hero, was certainly a reluctant one, spurred on to the duel with Menelaus by the shaming tirade of his brother Hector, and nearly always, his survival is dependent on good fortune. In a later drawing (*c.* 1802–05) of *Fortune*, he shows her in a jester's cap with bells, as though the winning streak in life came only from being dealt the Joker in the pack. His remark, quoted by Lavater, that 'fate . . . frequently associates with the greatest faculties a will feeble and impotent', is illustrated in another drawing (British Museum) of the Roman period, in which two Michelangelesque men strain on the bars of a capstan, while a man of slight build, in a large shady hat, looks on. It could well be a study from life, but its implications are that the artist views the energetic activity of life as a spectator sport. More apposite is another of himself as the artist, crouching while a woman beats a large nail into his head – the indolent flesh (Sisera) being violently awoken by the spirit of Art (Jael). Fuseli was well aware, therefore, of 'his own merit', that he had 'a spirit of application', but that it would cost him 'the greatest effort to give the finishing touch to the smallest piece'. This is aptly underlined by his own remark to Knowles,* that lying on one's back absorbing the magnitude of Michelangelo's Sistine ceiling was ideally suited to one enervated by the pleasurable but exhausting activities of Roman night life.

*Knowles, John, Fuseli's biographer, see Bibliography.

Magnitude of a different order and the artist's reaction to it appears in a drawing of a valedictory nature, made between 1778 and 1780. First to be considered is the despair of the artist faced by the size of the left foot of the Colossus of Constantine. This emotion is consistent with the terms generally applied at this time to the more monumental antiques, which 'astonish' and 'overwhelm'. In the paintings of Pannini or the engravings of Piranesi, this is deliberately used in a way that foreshadows romanticism but it also stemmed from a feeling of inadequacy in the eighteenth-century artist, aware of what hindsight tells us, that he was in the trough of a great artistic wave. If he felt modest in comparison with artists of the previous century, in the company of ancient Roman art he felt like Gulliver in the Land of Brobdingnag. It is this which gives such intensity to the eighteenth century's attitude to fragments. When Fuseli had read Webb's *An Inquiry into the beauties of Painting* (1760), he had probably come across the passage where the author thought that, 'had the foot (of the Laocoön) only been discovered, the swelled veins, the strained sinews, and the irregular motion of the muscles, might have led us into a conception of those tortures, which are so divinely expressed in the face, so wonderfully marked throughout the whole body.' Webb and the artist would know that it was Constantine's foot in the foreground of Piranesi's *Frontispiece*, and Fuseli may have been just in time to see the marble antique foot, seventeen and a quarter inches long, which Nollekens the sculptor had obtained from Cardinal Albani by swapping a female torso. This foot, Nollekens took back to England when he left Rome in 1770. Later, when it was in his collection, Lawrence thought that it might have belonged to the *Belvedere Torso,* but discarded the

49

idea eventually since the foot stood flat on the ground. There was, in fact, a great deal of romantic infusion to be wrung out of such fragments.

A fragment of another order appears in the top left corner of the caricature Fuseli sent to Northcote in 1779, to which reference has been made. This Fuseli-phallus bird that wings its way back to Italy, is not only a fragmented member of the artist but refers directly to Hesiod's *Theogony*, in which Cronus dismembers his father Uranus, throwing the organs over his shoulder, to send them flying into the ocean, there to ejaculate in the waves and bring forth Aphrodite, the Goddess of Love. That the artist had been reading Hesiod is clear, since in his letter to Northcote he refers to that author's 'paradox' – that the half is fuller than the whole – from *The Work and Days*, but more of that in another context. The artist was by no means done with testing his friend's erudition, for he shows himself half-squatting like a frog, while the stools of this human toad drop on Switzerland and pass on through France into the waves of the Channel. One can be reasonably certain about this, because of the presence of the mice. 'Take heed of the mice' was Fuseli's admonition, referring obviously to the *Batrachomyomachia* (Battle of the Frogs and Mice) wrongly attributed to Homer, and in the eighteenth century included in editions of the *Iliad* and the *Odyssey*. Much later, Blake in his portrait of Homer (City Art Gallery, Manchester) flanked the poet's bust with a mouse and a frog. As Crabb Robinson observed to Coleridge in 1811, 'a perfect caricature should resemble the *individual* and yet having nothing *human* in it', true enough since Fuseli shows himself over life size. One may well reflect on all the implications that may be derived from this romantic inflation of the pygmy artist in one drawing to the giant man in another, like Gulliver translated from Brobdingnag to Lilliput by a few strokes of the pen.

Finally as a climactic moment of truth, there is the well-known double portrait with his old teacher Bodmer, whom he now saw for the last time. This painting, although it was commissioned in Zurich by Salomon Escher of Wollenhof, was painted in London on the artist's return there. Fuseli poses insouciantly like the adventurous traveller and not like a returned and respectful disciple. This and the fact that both figures are on the same level indicates that the conversation is between equals, the only dominating figure being the over life-size classical type bust. Dr Schiff believes this bust to be Noah, since Fuseli had made drawings for Bodmer's *Noachide* in Berlin, although only the frontispiece by him had appeared in the printed work. While this interpretation seems most reasonable, it does not fit the circumstances and conditions in which the work was painted, nor, on the analogy of the personal allegories discussed so far, does it agree with the artist's interpretative process. While stimulated by the particular he is ultimately only concerned with the general, or as he observed to Knowles, 'the moment of importance (is) the middle moment . . .: big with the past and pregnant with the future.' This last meeting

1 *Fuseli. Caricature of the Artist leaving Italy. 1778*

7

50

with Bodmer was indeed the 'middle moment', between the long apprenticeship in Italy and the professional career in London.

The generic source of this kind of 'conversation piece' was the painting by Rubens, called *The Four Philosophers* (Pitti Gallery, Florence). It shows Rubens and his brother conversing with Lipsius and another teacher; above them in a niche there is the bust of a Greek philosopher. In his fourth Lecture, the artist wrote, 'that portrait by which Rubens contrasted the physiognomy of philosophic and classic acuteness with that of genius', which seems to be what his own painting is about. In the Rubens, however, and to quote examples nearer in time, in the painting by Mortimer of himself and Joseph Wilton (1765) and in Angelica Kauffmann's portrait of Sir Joshua Reynolds (1767), the bust does not dominate the figures. But in the engraving by John Brown of Sir William Young, made *8* as the frontispiece to Young's *The Spirit of Athens* (published in English in 1777 and in German the following year) the bust (of Pallas Athene) is given special emphasis, as it is in Fuseli's picture. Earlier commentators suggested both Homer and Ossian and, as the bust here is also blind, Homer, at least, could be a tenable suggestion, particularly as Blake's Homer, mentioned above, is of the same type and not the more familiar long-faced, sunken-cheeked head. Hesiod is another possible suggestion, since there was a bust in the Blundell collection at Ince Hall, which Fuseli might have known. But neither Hesiod nor Homer quite meets the requirements of a controlling or directing presence, which might be expected on analogy with Brown's portrait.

In this instance, Noah, except that he was not blind, might be acceptable if it were not for Bodmer's pointing finger, which in itself does not suggest the spirit of collaboration which the presence of Noah would instill.

Surely this finger is the *monstrari digito*, referred to by Horace and Persius Flaccus and quoted from the latter by Fuseli in a letter to his friend Dalliker in 1765. It is the finger, as Horace explained, that points to Genius. There was one artist who had made particular use of this gesture, namely Salvator Rosa in his painting *La Menzogna* (Pitti Palace, Florence), in which a poet holds a mask in one hand and points at it with the other, while he looks toward a companion, the mask being the symbol of a satirist. In another Rosa, much the same message is conveyed although on another level. Here Phryne points at Xenocrates *9* as virtue personified, since he had been able to withstand her blandishments for a whole night. Some sources call her Lais. What may have led Fuseli to adopt this gesture, was the engraving of a pointing hand which appeared in the fifth volume of the German first edition of Lavater's Essays on Physiognomy (*Physiognomische Fragmente*) 1776. This hand, obviously Bodmer's, Lavater described as 'firm although tender, full of expression yet not sublime'. What can be recognized so far are the physiognomies of Genius and philosophic 'acuteness'; the bust must represent the physiognomy of 'classic' acuteness.

Recalling that as this is the 'middle moment' of Fuseli's career and he could hardly claim to being an established genius, then the classical bust could represent a prophetic figure and most probably Tiresias, the blind philosopher, whom Ulysses *41* consults about his future in Hades (Odyssey XI). The artist made a drawing of this subject in Rome and at the end of the seventies was engaged with other such visitations like the Witch of Endor. It was a common enough contemporary conceit to liken oneself and one's friends to characters in the classics. To go further and think of Bodmer representing Eumaeus, the faithful and loyal steward with whom Ulysses stays on his first arrival back in Ithaca, is perhaps to push the textual association too far.

With this 'conversation piece', which Fuseli exhibited at the Royal Academy in 1781 before he sent it to Escher, he ended his autobiographical cycle, knowing that whatever its reception in Zurich, the 'grand manner' of its conception would not be lost on the President, Sir Joshua Reynolds, and a note of alarm struck in West.

2 William Bromley. *Profile portrait of Fuseli*

3 John Hamilton Mortimer. *A Caricature Painting*. The occasion is some sort of gathering of artists. Fuseli is the man standing at the back holding a wineglass. Sitting, looking up at him, is probably Dr John Armstrong. The portrait on the wall is Wright of Derby. Mortimer, the artist, is the diminutive figure on the left

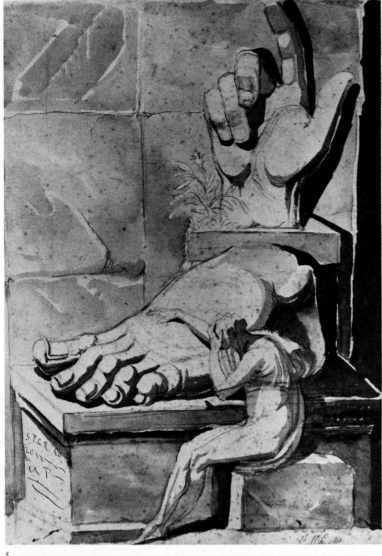

4

6

5

4 Fuseli. *The Artist in despair over the magnitude of Antique Fragments*, c. 1770–80

6 Piranesi. Detail of frontispiece to the *Antichità di Roma*, showing the same motif of the giant fragment of a foot

5 Fuseli. *Aphrodite carrying off Paris after his battle with Menelaus*, c. 1768–69

7 Fuseli. *The Artist in Conversation with J. J. Bodmer*, 1778–81. Fuseli is on the left, Bodmer on the right. The identity of the bust between them is a matter for conjecture

8 John Brown. *Portrait of Sir William Young Bt.* Again the motif of the classical bust dominating a portrait composition

9 Salvator Rosa. *Phryne and Xenocrates*. The pointing finger – '*monstrari digito*' – mentioned by classical writers is used by Rosa here and by Fuseli in the self-portrait with Bodmer

7

8

9

10

10 Fuseli. *Till Eulenspiegel and the Priest*, 1755–57

11 Hogarth. *Henry VIII and Anne Boleyn*

11

12 Fuseli. *Garrick as Duke of Gloucester* in *Richard III*, 1766. The scene is
Act 1, Scene 2, where Richard meets Anne with the body of Henry VI

12

13

14

13–15 The gesture of amazement, transferred from the stage to painting. Above: two works by Salvator Rosa – an astonished man (left) and *Job* (right). Below: Hogarth's painting of *Garrick as Richard III*, in the scene before Bosworth

15

16, 17 Both Ribera's *Joseph interpreting the Dreams of Pharaoh's Butler and Baker* (below) and Fuseli's *Measure for Measure*, 1805 (right) use the motif of the man peering down from an aperture

18 (bottom left) John Hamilton Mortimer. *Caius Marius musing on the Ruins of Carthage*

19 (bottom right) Fuseli. *Jonah's Indignation, c.* 1769–72

20, 21 Madness and plague: *The Madhouse Scene* from Hogarth's *Rake's Progress* (opposite top) and Poussin's *The Philistines struck by the Plague*. Both artists use the gesture of the man 'knuckling' his face to express anguish, as Fuseli does in his illustration of Jonah (below, pl. 19)

16

17

18

19

23

22 Fuseli. *Prince Arthur and Hubert, c.* 1775–76, from Shakespeare's *King John*

23 Domenichino. *Condemnation of St Cecilia.* Fuseli has taken Domenichino's composition and reversed it, keeping the seated judge with outstretched arm, the brazier of heated coals and the bending figures of the assistants

24 Fuseli. *Ajax raging, c.* 1770–72. Compare Ajax with the praying madman on the left of the Hogarth scene, on the previous page

25–27 Fuseli. *The Death of Cardinal Beaufort,* Henry VI Pt 2, 1772 (opposite, top) and two of the sources that went to its composition. From Raphael's *The Expulsion of Heliodorus from the Temple* come the line of men holding the king's robe and the two men turned towards each other on the left. From Giovanni da Bologna's *Hercules and Nessus* come the interlocking bodies and raised right arm

24

25

26

27

28 Fuseli. *Dante on the Ice of Cocytus*, 1774

29, 30 The antique *Gladiator* (above) was clearly one of the
models for Fuseli's *Lady Macbeth Sleepwalking, c.* 1775–76
(below). The attendant figures are masked, as in a Roman
theatre mosaic

28

29

30

31 Fuseli. *The Death of Brutus, c.* 1775, another adaptation of the pose of the *Gladiator*

32, 33 Fuseli. Two drawings for a Shakespeare Gallery: *King Lear and Twelfth Night, c.* 1775–76

32

33

34

35

36

34–37 Above: two more drawings for Fuscli's Shakespeare Gallery: *Macbeth* and *The Tempest*. Michelangelo's Sistine Ceiling provided the model for many episodes; compare the murder of Duncan with that of Holofernes (left). The whole scheme, however, would perhaps have been closer to that of Albani in the Palazzo Verospi (below)

37

38

38–40 Three etchings by Alexander Runciman, close in subject and spirit to Fuseli. Above: *Cromar attacking the Spirit of the Water*, from Ossian (compare Fuseli's *Tempest*, pl. 35, and *Brutus*, pl. 31). Below left: *Fingal finding Con-ban-Carglâ*. Below right: *Musidora*, from Thomson's *Seasons* (compare Fuseli's *Twelfth Night*, pl. 33)

39

40

41 Fuseli. *Odysseus before Tiresias in Hades, c.* 1776–77

42 Fuseli. *Witch of Endor,* 1777. Both pictures typify 'the moment of terror', the apparition of a supernatural being

43

43, 44 Fuseli. *The Escapee, c.* 1779, a real 'moment of terror' drawn, says
Fuseli's note, 'from memory after a mad scene in the Hospital of S. Spirito
at Rome'. Even so, memories of Raphael's *The Expulsion of Heliodorus
from the Temple* (detail below) have influenced the composition

44

45 Salvator Rosa. *The Apparition of Samuel before Saul*. A more conventional rendering than Fuseli's (pl. 42) but one which certainly influenced him. The ghostly horse's head was also to reappear in *The Nightmare* (pls 1, 83, 137, 222)

46, 47 Two engravings by Fuseli for Lavater's *Physiognomy*, c. 1779. Right: *Bust of Brutus*, representing 'a soul filled with agitation and uneasiness, yet still possessing itself sufficiently to think and act'. Below: *The Death of Abel* – 'suffering innocence is here presented in manly and energetic traits, under the form of a hero'

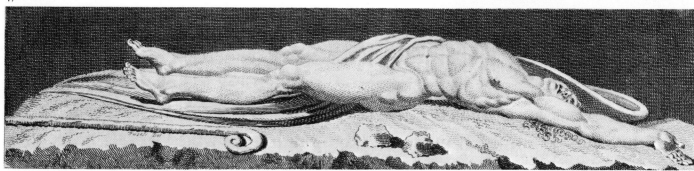

III Evolution and Sources

Every artist has, or ought to have, a character or system of his own; if, instead of referring that to the test of nature, you judge him by your own packed notions, or arraign him at the tribunal of schools which he does not recognize – you degrade the dignity of art, and add another fool to the herd of the Dilettanti.

Corollary to Aphorism 18

If Fuseli ever intended to be anything it was to be an original. Shakespeare was not to be 'arraigned at the bar of Drury Lane' by the critics, nor was he, Fuseli, to be similarly 'tried'. As a self-taught artist he had never experienced the subordination to a 'school' style. He could go to any pictorial sources which pleased him in their subject and their style, from Holbein's *Dance of Death* to the *Narrenbuch* of the Meyers. Whatever the sources, however, they would all be in black and white, in one or other of the graphic media – woodcut, engraving, etching – though not necessarily all cut by the hand of a master. Fuseli's early style reveals the nature of such sources, fluctuating in quality, according to how good or indifferent is the hand that he is copying. At no point does the question of colour enter his conception of form or space, which are determined solely by line and a minimal range of tone contrasts. The latter, in fact, he did not observe from nature, but derived them from the intaglio (reverse relief) or relief cutting of the block by the engraver. Evidence of this is given by his drawing of *Till Eulenspiegel and the Priest* (1755–57), where three tones only are 10 employed – black, grey, white – with such arbitrariness that there is no correlation of forms to space as would exist in nature. This can be called the woodcut style and can be compared to the engraving style of a drawing made ten years later, *Garrick as Duke of Gloucester in Richard III* (1766), which in turn can 12 be compared with Hogarth's *Henry VIII and Anne Boleyn*. Fuseli 11 thought that Hogarth's own engravings were 'exquisite' and this admiration seems to come out in the more 'pictorial' handling of the hatching stroke in the 'lights' to give variety of tone and fix the forms exactly in their spatial planes. The hatching also gives textural values, which are almost totally lacking in the earlier work.

69

Another of the early styles might be called the mezzotint manner exemplified in *Caius Marius and the Cimbrian Soldier* (1762–64), in which the overall dark grey tone resembles the 'ground' in this medium with the appropriate lights 'rubbed' in. This can be compared with the mezzotint of Reynolds' *Macbeth and the Witches* in terms of the medium's general effects. However the drawing of *c.* 1766, *Garrick and Mrs Pritchard as Macbeth and Lady Macbeth* reveals another influence, that of the wash drawing style of Etienne Aubry and J. G. Wille. Since the latter was a correspondent of his father, Fuseli may easily have seen original works. This latter connection indicates the quickening of the young artist's interest in pictorial effects, particularly after his arrival in England and possibly with the guidance of his compatriot Michael Moser. While there is evidence of drawing from life before he left the Continent, it is in London with all its enormous advantages, that Fuseli blossoms as an artist.

241

237

160

Since a great many of the drawings of this period were destroyed in the fire at Johnson's premises, it is difficult to trace his sources of influence and how he resolved them without considerable conjecture. However, there was one – the theatre – which can be examined. This is dominant in all three drawings referred to above. Even the Caius Marius scene, derived from Plutarch or Lucan, was included in Thomas Otway's play *The History and Fall of Caius Marius* (1679). Fuseli had read Otway before he came to England and the drawing might date from the Berlin period. There was also an opera (*c.* 1760) of the same story, since a design for the prison set by Galliari survives for a performance in Turin. Without pinpointing an actual performance, there is sufficient internal evidence to prove the artist's dependence on the stage. The stock two-windowed prison set is also to be found in Hogarth's painting of the prison scene in *The Beggar's Opera* (1729, Tate Gallery). The pose of Marius might have its origin in some Etruscan tomb figure, but it was a commonplace one in English seventeenth-century tomb sculpture. Since Marius in this scene is crying out 'Who dares kill Caius Marius', then the pose is a very apt one. With the pose of the Cimbrian one can go further for in Thomas Wilke's *General View of the Stage* (1759) there is this instruction to the actor on how to show astonishment, 'the whole body is actuated: it is thrown back, with one leg set before the other, both hands elevated, the eyes larger than usual, the brows drawn up, and the mouth not quite shut.' Hogarth shows *Garrick as Richard III* confronted by the ghosts, following this instruction and Fuseli shows him likewise as Macbeth. What is particularly interesting is to see these gestures used by Salvator Rosa,* in the soldier in *Job* and in the small etching of an astonished man. Betterton, who played Marius in the first production of Otway's drama, was the source of many of these instructions and as he had joined Davenant's company in 1661 was a contemporary of Rosa. Betterton, too, advised actors to study paintings by the Old Masters to gain insights into posture and gesture. This is not a matter of coincidence but clear

15

14, 13

*See Peter Tomory, *Salvator Rosa, His Etchings and Engravings after his Works*, Ringling Museum of Art, Sarasota, 1971.

evidence of a traditional declamatory acting style, with its origin in Quintilian's instructions to orators, which was common in Europe in the seventeenth century. Salvator Rosa himself, during his period in Florence, gained a reputation as an actor in performances at the Casino da San Marco, so it is not difficult to see why he should adopt for his painted dramatic encounters these gestures of the theatre. To cap this connection there is Horace Walpole's observation on the jailer in an oil sketch by Hogarth, 'It is the very figure Salvator Rosa would have drawn for Iago in the moment of detection.' Apart from the fact that there were several Rosas at Houghton Hall, the family seat, Walpole is voicing a commonplace association and not some personal idiosyncrasy. Uvedale Price* also links the names of Shakespeare and Rosa, both – as he thought – self-taught geniuses.

*Price, Sir Uvedale, author of *An Essay on the Picturesque as compared with the Sublime and the Beautiful*, London 1794. Lord Shaftesbury had already made the same connection in *Plastics* (1711).

There were two other lessons the theatre could teach Fuseli. The first, which can be noted in both the drawings from Shakespeare, is the minimal use of stage furniture and properties. In *Richard III* may be observed the use of a 'flat' behind 12 Garrick to carry an architectural reference, while behind the other figures there is a painted backdrop. In a painting by Mortimer from *King John*, a similar flat carries a Gothic arch, the backdrop a battle scene. In the Macbeth scene, an interior, a 160 folding screen is employed. Thus the main emphasis on the Georgian stage was placed on the actors, or as Fuseli observed to Knowles 'the actors are the luminous object to which the action points.' There is hardly a work by the artist that does not show this emphasis and consequently the minimum of 'props' to indicate period and setting. The second lesson was the angle of view obtained from a seat in the pit of the actors on stage. This groundling's view of the figures high against a low horizon was one of Fuseli's teaching dicta and appears almost *de rigueur*, from the late Roman period onwards. Certainly this lesson could be learned as well from studying paintings of the past, or present, but it was only on the stage that this could be seen combined with dramatic action.

Fuseli remained an inveterate theatre-goer all his life, which spanned a most brilliant period of the English stage. Like many of his contemporaries, he used the theatre as artists of the twentieth century have used the film. In a note (R.A. Mss), written with a shaking hand in 1823 or 5, he asked the unknown recipient, 'Did I not quote Dante à propos ? & is my Question about Garrick not worth an answer?' His knowledge and experience of the stage was an essential ingredient in his creative process. As remarked earlier, the stage was the vehicle of a metamorphosed reality in a society civilized by sense and sensibility. Reality was becoming too occasional with its aperçus and it was not given to everyone, like Stubbs, to see a lion attacking a horse.

Rosa's importance as an artist, and his influence on English art at this period, were of course not limited to his connections with the stage. It is as an 'independent' that he made his appeal to Reynolds, who, in his fifth Discourse, immediately after he had treated the grand manner of Raphael and Michelangelo, remarked, 'But there is another style ... the original or characteristical style, being less referred to any true archetype existing either in general or particular nature.' He observed that 'those who cultivated it were men of lively and vigorous imagination.' Rosa was one of the 'strongest-marked' of these, and what was to be most admired in his work was 'the perfect correspondence which he observed between the subjects which he chose, and his manner of treating them.' It is clear that Reynolds is referring to the whole of Rosa's oeuvre, and not just the landscapes.

Rosa, therefore, would appeal to artists of like mind, and one of these was the 'Salvator of Sussex', J. H. Mortimer,* with whom Fuseli was well acquainted; there were too many common interests, attitudes and friends to keep them apart. There is hardly room here to develop their whole relationship, but there are two instances which are remarkable. First is the engraving after Ribera, which was drawn by Mortimer and *16* engraved by Bannerman for Boydell's *A Collection of Prints* (1769). Not only is the title, *Joseph interpreting the dreams of Pharaoh's Butler and Baker*, identical with that of Fuseli's first painting, but the strong contrasts in the modelling and the coarse vigour of the faces can be found in Fuseli's Richard III *12* drawing. Furthermore the motif of the man looking down from the aperture, top right, is employed by Fuseli in his drawing of *Twelfth Night* and very much later in the scene from *Measure for* *33, 17* *Measure*. All of these scenes, including the Ribera, are prison scenes, Malvolio in *Twelfth Night*, being bound in a room, lunatic, exemplifying the 'correspondance between the subjects' and 'the manner of treating them'. Second, there is Mortimer's *Caius Marius musing on the Ruins of Carthage*, *18* etched by Blyth in 1782 from a drawing in Payne Knight's collection. Mortimer's work is difficult to date, but it seems reasonable to suggest that he was working on such subjects in 1770–72. Because of the strong similarities between this *Marius* and Fuseli's engraving of *Jonah* in Dr Willoughby's *19* Family Bible one might presume that although this was published in 1772, the artist had made his engravings for it before he left England. One of Rosa's predilections was his choice of subject from the lesser prophets of the Old Testament. To the *Job* one can add in this context his *Jonah preaching to the Ninevites* (Copenhagen) and engraved by Preisler, which was probably known to Mortimer since his *St Paul preaching to the* *14* *Britons* (Town Hall, High Wycombe) of 1764 is composition- ally close. Fuseli's choice of text is as unusual as Rosa's, for the prophet, seated outside Nineveh, is afflicted by the beating of the sun on his head. It is, then, curious, and probably not a coincidence to find in Otway's *Marius* (Act IV), the hero crying out, 'Oh my distemper'd Head!/ The Sun has beat his Beams so hard upon me./ ... Oh my tormented Skull!'

The Paris and Helen drawing, previously discussed, is also *5* evidence of a 'perfect correspondance' between subject and manner, for the marked contrast between the calligraphic

*See John Sunderland, 'John Hamilton Mortimer and Salvator Rosa', *The Burlington Magazine*, August 1970.

72

style of the figures and the heavy coarse style of the wall is not paradoxical, but a deliberate adoption and use of formal allegory. Fuseli borrowed the Greek 'characters' from a hydria by the Meidias painter (4th century BC, British Museum), *100* illustrated in d'Hancarville's edition of Sir William Hamilton's vases (Naples, 1766), but here the French edition (1787). The wall is from Piranesi and for convenience the detail *92* reproduced can be compared, although this is not necessarily the actual source. Fuseli had an infinite capacity in reducing or enlarging motifs from Piranesi; the arch and boat in the *Jonah's Indignation* is a reduction of the large *Ponte magnifico con* *19* *Logge ed Archi* . . . (Focillon 7). What the artist is clearly implying is that figures are fleeting and ephemeral while the wall is indestructible and permanent – *ars longa vita brevis*. It may also be observed in Rosa's *Phryne and Xenocrates*, that the two *9* figures are also posed against a blank wall, a feature of many of his moralities, suggesting that the eternal quality of the philosophic spirit is proof against the ephemeral temptations of the flesh.

What emerges from this synthesis of styles and sources is not only the artist's determination to find his own means of expression, that is to be an original, but also the speed at which he had moved to realize that often quoted aphorism of Simonides – Painting is silent poetry, and poetry is a speaking picture. Hazlitt,* in fact, was to put this in his own words, when he   *Table Talk*, 1821–22. described the artist's conversation. 'Mr Fuseli's conversation is . . . striking and extravagant . . . He deals in paradoxes and caricatures. He talks allegories and personifications, as he paints them.' Added to this is his almost Joycean capacity for association, an endless word and figural play, in which suggestions bound and rebound like the ball in *Gioco del Pallone*, an Italian game of which Fuseli made a drawing when he was in Rome.

As Joseph Addison* observed, 'There are in Rome two sets of   THE ROMAN PERIOD, 1770 TO 1778 Antiquities, the Christian and the Heathen. The former, tho' of   *Addison, Joseph, *Remarks on Several Parts of* a fresher Date, are so embroil'd with Fable and Legend, that   *Italy &c* (1705), Edition of 1753, from which all one receives but little Satisfaction from searching into them . . .   quotes are taken. There is however so much to be observed in so spacious a Field of Antiquities, that it is almost impossible to survey them without taking new hints, and raising different Reflexions, according as a Man's natural Turn of Thoughts, or the Course of his Studies direct him.' This was very much the case for any artist visiting Rome in the mid-eighteenth century, armed, as he probably was, with the Richardsons'† guide to Rome, in   †Richardson, Jonathan Sr & Jr, *An account of* English or French, the best there was, 'despite its many de-   *some of the Statues, Bas Reliefs, Drawings and* ficiencies and errors' as Winckelmann remarked. Fuseli would   *Pictures in Italy &c*, London, 1722, French also have had the advantage of the latter's *History of Ancient Art,*   edition 1728. the first coherent account of Greek and Roman art. There was yet another guide, available to readers of German only, in the introduction by the artist's namesake, H. H. Füssli, to the Zurich edition of Daniel Webb's *An Inquiry into the beauties of Painting* of 1766 and issued again in 1771, bound in with Raphael Mengs'

73

Gedanken Über die Schönheit und den Geschmack in der Mahlerey, the work from which Webb had 'lifted' most of his ideas. This latter printing, which with the earlier one was published by the artist's father, Caspar Füssli, was probably made when Winckelmann accused Webb of plagiarism. Fuseli, in a letter to Lavater from Lyons in 1766, remarked on the confusion of names and how he had been credited with the introduction, which he confessed he enjoyed more than the text of that 'bungler' Webb.

H. H. Füssli was himself a disciple of Winckelmann, whose introduction not only discusses ancient art but ranges over his own choice of masterworks by later Italian artists. His choice coincides to a considerable extent with the models to which artists were drawn at this time, a list so variegated that it gave rise to the charge of eclecticism. Raphael and Correggio, Michelangelo is a 'stormwind', Annibale Carracci, then with particular emphasis, Domenichino, Guercino and Guido Reni: Caravaggio he admires with the qualification that 'he shocks the soul in passing but brings about no lasting emotion'. His praise for Bernini is similarly qualified, his *Saint Bibiena* and the *Apollo and Daphne* are the best works but his *David* is a 'murderer'. Rosa's *Death of Regulus* is evidence of his 'wholly mad genius'. In many cases, H. H. Füssli counters the opinion of the Richardsons, but in general he does not break much new ground, except in one instance: to Reni's *Aurora* in the Palazzo Rospigliosi and Guercino's in the Villa Ludovisi, he adds Albani's *Apollo and the Seasons* in the Palazzo Verospi, now the *37* Credito Italiano bank. He particularly praises the figure of *Night* – she is both 'noble' and 'a quiet beauty'. Mengs thought that Albani had no equal in painting the female figure. Finally, H. H. Füssli puts himself very much on the side of Mengs and the angels, when he criticizes young artists who follow after Battoni, Caravaggio, Pietro da Cortona, Algardi and Bernini, instead of Raphael and Domenichino. The inclusion of Battoni reflects his rivalry with Mengs, which Northcote confirms in 1778; 'Mengs and Pompeo Battoni . . . both hold each other with the utmost possible degree of contempt.'

But Fuseli was not interested in any party alignment nor in following another artist's style, only in a 'character or system of his own'. He was by no means unique in this desire amongst the foreign artists in Rome. The best of them were intent on creating not only a 'modern' art, but an art which was relevant to the characteristics of their own countries, their own history and literature, and their own aspirations. The run-of-the-mill painters, of course, squabbled over their rival loyalties. In his second ode on Art, the artist said as much: 'Mixed up in that crowd which the North wind has blown into your palaces, Rome, there are mobs of Germans, Britons, French, mobs of Poles and Muscovites. One day, with trembling feet, I fled from that rabble of artists into your Temples (the Vatican), pent up with anger at London's and France's academics.' This prefaces his description of how he came into the Sistine Chapel to be overwhelmed in the evening light by the majesty and beauty of Michelangelo's frescos.

At this point it is best to admit that artists like Fuseli, a whole generation younger than Reynolds, did not think in terms of a 'grand manner' at all or even of components making up a unifying style. In fact, Reynolds' *Discourses* were more in the nature of an epilogue than a prologue; there is little evidence of any of the younger painters actually following his advice. What was becoming more and more prevalent, following such things as the organization of the French *Encyclopédie* or the taxonomic system of classification in the sciences, was a method of grouping according to subject-matter. For example, all paintings or engravings of the type 'Prison scene' would be placed under that head, regardless of the style or period. This is not to suggest that dossiers were actually kept in this way, but it was a new method of artistic thinking. It would come particularly easy to Fuseli since he was a practised entomologist, but hardly less so to anyone else of his generation, to whom the principles of Linnaeus were common knowledge.

As a matter of fact the word 'style' appears very seldom in writings of the period. It is supplanted by 'taste', 'intellectual relish or discernment' as the dictionaries of the time defined it. Mary Moser, in a letter to Fuseli at Rome, described Gavin Hamilton's picture *Briseis parting from Achilles*, as 'in taste, à la antique, elegant and simple'. When the artist came to discuss the same painter in his edition of Pilkington's *Dictionary of Painters*, he thought otherwise: 'Though he was familiar with the antique, the forms of Hamilton have neither its correctness nor characteristic purity, something of the modern eclectic principle prevails in his works, and his composition is not seldom, as much beholden to commonplace ornamental conceits and habits, as to propriety.' What Fuseli is criticizing is a failure in selection, not style, adopting almost a principle of modern criticism, of examining the success or failure of the artist's *intention*.

Fuseli was above all things, a man of 'principle', working always from a secure basis of conception of what his subject required. The major principle of his Roman period is that of *Terror*, derived largely from Burke, who had coupled it with the principle of *Obscurity,* remarking of Milton's description of Death, that 'all is dark, uncertain, confused, terrible, and sublime to the last degree'. One can see the point of Fuseli viewing Michelangelo's *Last Judgment* in the evening light. Another discussion of the principle which is closer to Fuseli is by his friend John Aiken: 'With respect to the well wrought scenes of artificial terror which are formed by a sublime and vigorous imagination . . . though we know before-hand what to expect, we enter into them with eagerness, in quest of a pleasure already experienced.' Aiken then goes on, 'A strange and unexpected event awakens the mind, and keeps it on the stretch: and where the agency of invisible beings is introduced [Hamlet, Macbeth, Richard III were cited earlier] of "forms unseen and mightier far than we", our imagination, darting forth explores with rapture the new world which is laid open to its view and rejoices in the expansion of its powers. Passion and fancy co-operating elevate the soul to its highest pitch, and the pain of terror is lost in amazement.' While much of this is a paraphrase of Burke, the examples of the supernatural from Shakespeare do not appear in Burke, nor do further exemplars cited by Aiken later in his essay – Aladdin and Sinbad from the Arabian Nights, Walpole's *Castle of Otranto* and Smollett's *Ferdinand Count Fathom* (1753). Aiken did, however, make one qualification – 'where they [scenes of horror] are too near common nature, though violently borne by curiosity through the adventure, we cannot repeat it or reflect on it, without an over-balance of pain' – which, of course, is a transcription from Aristotle's discussion on the cathartic effects of pity and fear in tragic drama. Similarly Fuseli later condemned the witchcraft scenes of Rosa, the martyrdoms of Ribera and other too realistic horrors of the seventeenth century.

This rather long preamble is necessary in order to define the artist's terms of reference in Rome. To demonstrate the taxonomic system, one may start with a single gesture – that of Jonah *19* 'knuckling' his face. Here is a man being plagued and maddened by the sun, so therefore one may look for the source in 'madness' or 'plague' subjects. Two of the best known at the time were Hogarth's Madhouse scene from the *Rake's Progress* and *20* Poussin's *Philistines struck by the Plague*, not the original re- *21* produced here, but the copy (National Gallery, London) which, in the 1770s, was in the Palazzo Colonna, Rome. Its popularity was due to being cited both by the Richardsons in their Guide and in the engraving by Picart (1670s). The mad Rake and the stricken Philistine on the right both 'knuckle' their faces.

Next one may proceed to a more complex example, the drawing of *Prince Arthur and Hubert* (*c.*1770–72) from *King John* *22* Act IV, Sc. 1, where Arthur cries, 'O, save me, Hubert, save me! my eyes are out/ Even with the fierce looks of these bloody men.' It is probably a preliminary sketch for the painting he sent to the Society of Artists in 1775 (86). While the style is still quite close to the Jonah, rather coarse with formal clichés in the drapery and anatomy, the mise-en-scène and the gestures are not exclusively those of the stage. For in order to stabilize the moral content of what is a passing dramatic episode, the artist uses major motifs from Domenichino's *Condemnation of* *23* *Saint Cecilia*, in S. Luigi dei Francesi, the seated judge and the two men on the left, and particularly the motif of the two arms. The sacrificial fire is paralleled by the basin of hot coals brought in by the executioners. Furthermore, Arthur is able to appeal to Hubert's better nature, while the blinding iron and the coals grow cold, and Cecilia, through her faith, persuades forty bystanders to turn Christian and her executioners are unable to accomplish her immediate death. However, Hubert's head turned across his shoulder and the first executioner's arm raised before his face are more likely to have been taken from Michelangelo's two Noah scenes (Ceiling, Sistine Chapel).

Apart from the content of the Sistine frescoes, their main appeal to Fuseli was the overall tonality and the dramatic

76

monumentality contrived by using few figures in an infinite
space, like the *Judith and Holofernes* spandrel, and conversely 36
the cramming of figures into a compressed space, like the
Brazen Serpent spandrel. In addition to these dramatic episodes, 167
the artist made many studies from the lunettes containing the
Ancestors of Christ.

Turning, then, to Fuseli's drawing of *Ajax raging*, the same 24
tonal and formal differentiations may be seen as they appear in
the Sistine *Judith and Holofernes* – the gloomy space containing 36
Ajax and the sharper delineation of Tecmessa with the infant
Eurysaces. But the latter are taken from Raphael's *Holy
Family* (1518, Louvre) and Ajax is a much nobler version of
Hogarth's praying maniac in the left hand cell of the Madhouse 20
scene. Not generally familiar is Hogarth's verse caption to
that plate:

> Madness, Thou Chaos of the Brain,
> What art? That Pleasure giv'st and Pain?
> Tyranny of Fancy's Reign!
> Mechanic Fancy; that can build
> Vast Labyrinths, & Mazes wild,
> With Rule disjointed, Shapeless Measure,
> Fill'd with Horror, fill'd with Pleasure!

It will be realized by now that the pool of sources for any
artist of this period is not only extensive but very deep, so that
he might fish for a motif from the surface of his own time or at
any fathom mark of the past. This applied as much to literary as
artistic sources, for Hogarth's verse had appeared at least
twelve years before Burke had commenced his interest in the
Sublime and the Beautiful.

A much more ambitious composition is *The Death of Cardinal
Beaufort* (1772), the artist's first exhibited work at the Royal 25
Academy. Most commentators have cited Poussin's *Death of
Germanicus* (Minneapolis), then in the Palazzo Barberini, as the
source, but apart from a very general resemblance, this work
can be discounted for the simple reason that Germanicus was a
Stoic hero and not a manic blasphemer. Except for the central
group, Fuseli drew on Raphael's two relevant works, *The
Death of Ananias*, a man who lied to God, and the *Expulsion of
Heliodorus*, a man who wished to appropriate the treasure of the 26, 44
Temple. By adding two more kneeling figures, Fuseli repeats
the diagonal group of the Ananias in his own. From the Heliodorus, the left middleground line of figures (the three women
and the two standing men) are reversed for Warwick and Salisbury and the three pages holding the king's robe. Studies from
this fresco are in the Roman sketchbook at Zurich. For the central group one has to turn elsewhere. 'I say', observed Burke, 'a
man in great pain has his teeth set, his eyebrows are violently
contracted, his forehead is wrinkled, his eyes are dragged in-
wards, and rolled with great vehemence . . . things that cause
terror generally affect the bodily organs . . . in producing a tension, contraction, or violent emotion of the nerves.' In a footnote
he explained that 'by tension, I mean no more than a violent
pulling of the fibres, which compose any muscle or membrane.'

Or as Shakespeare had Warwick say, 'See how the pangs of death do make him grin!'

In allegorical terms, the Shakespearean encounter is Virtue exhorting Vice and failing, so if the artist was looking for a suitable source, with the Burkean characteristics of terror and tension, he could hardly miss Giovanni da Bologna's famous 27 work in the Loggia dei Lanzi, Florence. In a masterly way Fuseli has turned the forms round so that the heads lie in the same diagonal plane as the upstretched arm, but has retained the motifs of one arm crooked over another and a hand placed below the shoulder. The expression of terror and pain in the Centaur is modified in the Cardinal, but the tension is as vigorously expressed. Lastly may be noticed the parallel motif of the knuckles of the hand on the pillow and the spread toes of Hercules on the rock.

In essence, Fuseli preserves Raphael's combination of spectators and dramatic action, except that all his are very properly riveted in their attention on three sides of the central group. Since the light also radiates outwards from the centre, there is the inevitable reminder of a painting like *An Academy by Lamplight* (1768–69) by Joseph Wright of Derby, which Fuseli would have seen at the Society of Artists, the year before he went to Rome. In that work some students are gathered around *The Nymph with a Shell* (Louvre), then in the Villa Borghese. Fuseli's choice of a sculptural source is not then so out of the way on that count, but it is more relevant on another. Since at least the beginning of the century there had been a poetic notion, which could be called the marble-izing of the passions, demonstrated by three couplets from well-known verse dramas:

> It drives my Soul back to her inmost Seats,
> And freezes ev'ry stiff'ning Limb to Marble.
> (Rowe, *Ulysses*)

> This is a Sight that like the Gorgon's Head,
> Runs thro' my Limbs, and stiffens me to Stone.
> (Dryden, *Cleomenes*)

> Who pants for Breath, and stiffens yet alive,
> In dreadful Looks, a Monument of Wrath!
> (Addison, *Cato*)*

*See Brewster Rogerson, 'The Art of Painting the Passions', *Journal of the History of Ideas*, January 1953.

In descriptions of actual stone statues, the same notion was used in reverse. Thus the Richardsons in their Guide were able to say of *The Gladiator*, 'he gains the Victory, through the supple 28 and firm movement that he makes: he throws himself forward with such speed, that all his muscles appear to tremble with ardour.' H. H. Füssli, in his guide, was to go much further, as any *Stürmer und Dranger* would, and reverses the decision of the Richardsons, 'His breast is swollen with thoughts of heroic deeds, in the outstretching of his mighty arm. He does not see this steady arm striking without anticipating the blow returned by the enemy; the terrible composure of his face announces death.'

There is more than a hint here of Fuseli's own eventual rejection of Le Brun's system of showing the passions in facial expression, as he explains it in his remarks to Lavater. Any

78

emotional tension must be seen to activate the whole body and as his knowledge of the various phenomena increased, he became more adept at rendering the correct tension.

Connected with this idea are the two drawings of *Lady Macbeth Sleepwalking* (*c*.1775–77) and the *Death of Brutus* of the *30, 31* same period, for both may be compared to the Gladiator. In *28* Lady Macbeth that forward lunge is devitalized by bending the back leg and lowering the forward arm, to arrive at a convincing image of automatism: whereas in Brutus welcoming death with open arms and an elastic spring, the legs and the front foot are splayed out. 'Elasticity' was a favoured word of the *Sturm und Drang*, applied by Herder and Bürger to the spirit, as though the mind itself was sinewed and muscled, so that it could spring and bound in unison with the body.

Compositionally, and in artistic influence, the drawings are different. The Lady Macbeth is cast as for a Greek drama, the two onlookers are clearly masked and probably derived from the well-known mosaic by Dioscorides seen by the artist on his visit to Naples in 1775; Lady Macbeth assumes the appearance of a somnambulant raving Maenad or avenging Medea, cast forever into a monument of tormented guilt. The space is determined by receding parallel planes as they might be on the Classical stage. The Brutus is based on the diagonal and compartmental space system of Michelangelo's spandrel frescos, and the figures are musculatured and heavily shaded to simulate those of the Master. But the motif of the head turned away in profile is from Poussin, for example in the Plague picture, and *21* the hand to the face in grief appears in three instances in the Germanicus. Then the head under the raised arm is identical to that of the angel in the crook of God's arm in Michelangelo's *Creation of Adam*. In the Zurich Roman sketchbook there are a number of such single heads taken from Raphael's frescos. All of this points towards Fuseli's increasing independence and dexterity in assembling his own compositions. Assembling was the key process for all the artists of this period, and each element of the assemblage had to be justified by association. This latter requirement led inevitably to 'suiting the action to the word', or in other words, adopting the mode of expression which would 'line up' with the artist's conception of his subject and the association he wished to make. This is plain in the Paris and Helen drawing, although there there is a pictorial dis- *5* juncture between the figures and the wall.

In the Dante drawing, however, total unity has been attained, not just because of the tonal and linear unity or the accuracy of *29* the textual association, but because of the association of a reality to which the spectator is linked. The last is established by the brilliant conception of merely showing the ankles and feet of the giant Antaeus and one of his companions on top of the wall, which simulates the same view that one would have looking up at one of the colossal, antique statues on a high plinth. The spectator is made to place himself on the same scale as Dante. Certain associations with the Sistine frescos are maintained – the bluish grey tone, the heads and the flat folds of the drapery. Since this is a repeat drawing from the original one in the Kunsthaus, Zurich, it is lighter in tone and line but not necessarily much later in date; a second drawing would always be a little more fluent in execution. While the planes are all frontal the space is deeply recessive, proper to the text description, the gesture of Dante is proper to the stage. Its seventeenth-century counterpart is to be found in Rosa's *Job*, *14* while an actor's handbook of Fuseli's time declares that the hands must never be raised above the head except for 'some very extraordinary occasion', since it was the highest on the scale of registering 'astonishment'. Thus the artist created a 'modern' conception for his time.

Next to be considered are the four drawings for a 'Shake- *32, 33, 34, 35* speare Gallery'. These are also repeat drawings similar in character to the Dante in that they are more fluently rendered and are lighter in tone than the originals (S. 471–4). The content will be discussed later and may be left aside, but the project itself is full of interest. It was novel for its time, and the surviving drawings raise the important question of what Fuseli intended for the ceiling itself – or was this to be glazed? It is to be presumed that he had no existing interior in mind, but it cannot be said that such a monument had sprung into his mind unaided, for without any doubt, he would have attended Garrick's Shakespeare Jubilee, which had had a run of ninety nights at Drury Lane in the autumn of 1769. The finale consisted of a grand procession, made up of scenes from many of the plays, the title of each being displayed on coloured streamers carried before it. In the middle of the procession was the Comic Muse in a car drawn by satyrs, with attendants representing characters of 'the ancient Comedy'. The rearguard was formed by Apollo with his lyre and the Tragic Muse in her car, supported by seven of the Nine Muses. For the final 'curtain', up front was Shakespeare 'from his monument in Westminster Abbey', garlanded with laurels, flanked by the Tragic and Comic Muses, and the major characters of his plays positioned on either side. The setting was 'a grand room, decorated with transparent pictures'. Mary Ann Yates herself took the part of the Tragic Muse.

The presence of the Comic Muse in a car drawn by satyrs puts one in mind of Annibale Carracci's ceiling fresco of *The Triumph of Bacchus and Ariadne* in the Palazzo Farnese, but Fuseli had a low opinion of that, calling it in his edition of Pilkington, 'a work whose uniform vigour of execution nothing can equal but its imbecility and incongruity of conception'. A more convincing source is again the Sistine ceiling – Macbeth taken from the Prophet Jonah, the dead Duncan from *34, 36* Holofernes, etc. But it is evident that Fuseli always made rational selections at all levels from conception to execution, and that he himself would consider the wholesale adoption of the Sistine ceiling for his selection of Shakespeare's plays, which includes both a romantic drama (*The Tempest*) and a comedy (*Twelfth Night*), besides the tragedies of *Lear* and *Macbeth*, as both 'imbecile' and 'incongruous'.

It is noticeable that Michelangelo does not use adult caryatids, but *putti*, whereas standing men and accompanying crouching figures appear in the Farnese ceiling and also in Lanfranco's ceiling at the Villa Borghese. But none of these uses a single figure on a pilaster below a spandrel – proof enough that Fuseli was intent on inventing his own scheme. At this point, Albani's *37* Palazzo Verospi ceiling, already mentioned, should be considered. It contained, above all, one of the most revered images of Night and her two children, Sleep and Death, based on the description in Cesare Ripa's *Iconologia*, the most important emblem book of the seventeenth century, and brought to attention in the mid-eighteenth by an edition by Orlandi (1764–66). In fact the whole of Albani's programme is an emblematic feast à la Ripa. Its significance is that it is a potpourri of earlier cycles, principally the Raphael studio *History of Amor and Psyche* in the Villa Farnesina, from which Fuseli took the Venus and Cupid for his Viola and Amor in *Twelfth Night*, *33* but also there are motifs and figures from Michelangelo and Annibale Carracci. Besides all this, Albani shows the passing of time from Night at one end to Aurora (Day) at the other. Close to them on the centre section are Evening and Dawn. In the middle panel there is Apollo flying through a hoop of the Zodiacal signs, with Flora (Spring) and Ceres (Summer) on one side and Bacchus (Autumn) and Vulcan (Winter) on the other. In the side spandrels are Ares or Mars, Hermes or Mercury, Jupiter and Juno. The smaller scenes depict the various episodes associated with Apollo. The inference of all this is the encyclopaedic nature of the cycle, embracing love and death, the seasons and time itself.

Was Fuseli planning a Shakespearean cycle analogous to Albani's? There is a reasonable amount of evidence available in the surviving drawings, since Fuseli planned a gallery of more than four plays, surely to support this connection. For the sake of brevity only *The Tempest* and *Macbeth* need be examined. *35, 34* Prospero and Macbeth are both overhung by winged figures, namely Ariel and the Witch, the former representing Day and the latter, Night, because *The Tempest* takes place during the day and *Macbeth* (mostly) during the night. Further analogies could be pursued, but it is perhaps sufficient to point out that Albani's ceiling is also astrological in meaning – Mars, Venus, Orion – so that as the planets control and direct the destinies of men Prospero and Macbeth do likewise in their respective spheres.

There will be further occasion to show Fuseli's attraction to Albani, but *en passant*, one doubts whether he missed the analogy of that master's *Rape of Europa* hung in the Palazzo Bolognetti, where Fuseli's Nannina lived.

There was also a living influence concerned with this concept of a Shakespeare gallery, absent in 1777 when the drawings were made, but who made a strong impression on Fuseli during his first two years in Rome. Alexander Runciman* was 'the best Painter of us in Rome', opined the artist in his already quoted letter to Mary Moser (1771). As 'Painter' and 'us' are

*Runciman, Alexander, 1736–1785, see J. Duncan Macmillan, 'Alexander Runciman in Rome', *The Burlington Magazine*, January 1970.

both underlined, a coterie would seem to be implied, of which John Runciman, Sergel the Swedish sculptor and perhaps David Allan were certainly members, while others, like John Brown and Abildgaard, would join in the following years.

Alexander Runciman was five years older than Fuseli and more professionally accomplished in those years; recognizing the bounding energy of his style, there is small wonder that Fuseli took to him. The range of his subject matter was also poetry and mythology, but directly relevant to the Shakespeare Gallery was the projected Ossian ceiling at Pennycuik House, near Edinburgh, which Runciman may have conceived, even while he was in Rome, for he was already enjoying the patronage of Sir James Clerk, the owner. As the *Perseus killing Medusa* is [62] dated 1774 and is more refined in style than the Ossian and [39] Thomson subjects, these may safely be assumed to be earlier. [40] When Fuseli's *Tempest* shipwreck scene is compared to *Cromar* [35, 38] *attacking the Spirit of the Water,* it shows how very familiar he was with Runciman's style, even to the use of the long hatching stroke over the figures. *Cromar* should be noted as a highly charged Highland version of *The Gladiator,* indicating the [28] same conception as Fuseli with his Brutus. In several figures of [31] the Shakespeare Gallery – particularly those imposing an- [35] drogynes, the large Miranda, Lady Macbeth by her candle and the three witches opposite – Runciman seems to have been Fuseli's model. Runciman's own source is, once again, Rosa, whose *Phryne* may serve as an example. However a particular [9] borrowing is to be found in the figure of Conban-carglâ [39] (corrupted by Cunningham to Corban-Cargloss), for apart from the position of the arms it is identical to the Goddess in Rosa's etching *Phytalus and Ceres.* Even Runciman's etching technique is derived from Rosa, who uses the same long hatch- ing stroke to tone down a figure and other parallels of technique can be traced from Rosa, through Runciman to Fuseli, for instance in Fuseli's figure of Caliban with his log. [35]

Runciman's ceiling, unhappily destroyed by fire, consisted of a large central oval of Ossian reciting before an audience of all ranks and periods, surrounded by twelve episodes from the poems, two of which are illustrated here, *Fingal finding* [39] *Conban-carglâ* and *Cromar attacking the Spirit of the Water.* [38] It might be possible to surmise, therefore, that Fuseli had twelve plays in mind with a similar centre panel of Shakespeare reading to an audience. Whatever his intention, it is interesting that five years after the departure of his friend, he should echo him so clearly. This could have been caused by the receipt of Runciman's etchings at that time.

While on the subject of Runciman it is instructive to compare the three artists whose close similarities have so often been noted – Runciman, Fuseli and John Brown* – for they were all originals, but Fuseli the only one not to die young like Runci- man or to dry up like Brown. Fuseli's Viola from *Twelfth* [33] *Night,* Runciman's *Musidora* and *Agrippina* and Brown's [40] *Virgin Mary,* for instance, provide a number of stylistic elements [85] which interlock. The colossal *Musidora,* a Courbet bather before

48 Alexander Runciman. *Agrippina weeping over the ashes of Germanicus*

*Brown, John, 1752–1787.

82

her time, has her left arm and hand extended and dropped like the *Viola*, while the latter, the *Agrippina* and the *Virgin Mary* share the distinctive long curve from the back of the head to the shoulder. This same treatment can be found in three works by Caravaggio, praised by Fuseli in his edition of Pilkington – the *Madonna di Loreto* (Sant'Agostino, Rome), *The Entombment* (Vatican, then S. Maria in Vallicella) and the *Madonna dei Palafrenieri* (Villa Borghese) – the principal attraction of such a motif being its air of languishment, as though the head was too heavy for the neck to support. As to their respective conceptions of woman, Runciman comes closest to a Michelangelesque androgyne – via Rosa, and possibly the man pulling on his stocking in Veneziano's engraving. Brown's Virgin is a 98, pre-Flaxman maiden of piety while Fuseli's *Viola*, despite all 33 its other associations, preserves the Rococo erotic form. But what is true of all three is that each was able to personify the role of each woman by the adoption of the relevant form.

For man, however, Fuseli had other ideas as may be seen in his *Back view of a Male nude* (1777). By 1772, at least, the artist had used an écorché type figure in his scene from Dante (*Inferno* Canto xxv) of the metamorphosis of the Thieves (S.424). One could assume, then, that Fuseli's interest in the flayed male figure commenced when he, like most of the other artists in Rome, first went to the French Academy (Villa Mancini) to practise his life drawing. There were Houdon's celebrated *Écorchés*, one of which is shown here, which he had made under the eye of the surgeon Ségnier, as 'mannequins' for his Baptist and St Bruno in the church of the Chartreux. Whether plaster casts of these had already arrived in London before Fuseli's departure is not known, but other similar models were available cast by the anatomist Cowper. Hogarth discusses and illustrates one of the leg in his *Analysis of Beauty* (1753): 'The winding figures of the muscles, with the variety of their situations, must always be allow'd elegant forms: however, they lose in the imagination some of the beauty, which they really have, by the idea of their being flayed; nevertheless . . . the human frame hath more of its parts composed of serpentine-lines than any other object in nature; which is a proof of its superior beauty to all others, and, at the same time, that its beauty proceeds from those lines.' Fuseli may not have followed Hogarth through the whole of his serpentine way, but at least acquired from him the germ of an idea, which he put into earnest after further study of the Houdon *Écorchés*. The figure, here, is not so much flayed as thin-skinned, semi-transparent, to show 'the model working' and, rather important, to arrive at a metamorphic and heroic image, in appearance and proportion, which would embody the artist's 'man of destiny'. By definition this image had to be timeless and physiognomically marked in no *ordinary* manner, so that in Elysium, Valhalla, Heaven or Hell, the men who bore this would be instantly recognized by the uniformity of their mould.

What is also true is that an heroic figure had to be as recognizable from the back as from the front. The 'back figure' was a

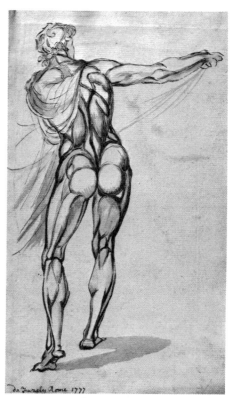

49 Fuseli. *Nude man from the back.* 1777

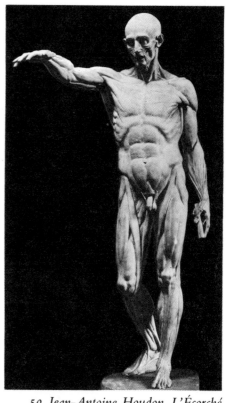

50 Jean-Antoine Houdon. *L'Écorché*

83

much favoured element in composition, principally as Fuseli explained later to C. R. Leslie, to lead the spectator into the picture. But from the mid-century, the back appears to have been adopted as the symbolic form of great strength. The *Belvedere Torso* was always to be admired from the back, as Hogarth showed it in Plate 1 of his *Analysis of Beauty*, in which he also shows the *Farnese Hercules* from the back. In a small notebook (Royal Academy) which West used in Rome (1760–63) there are back views of the same figure. There was, of course, nothing new in the employment of this painterly or sculptural device; Trajan's column is full of the back views of Roman soldiers and cohorts of them appear in the Renaissance and the seventeenth century. But for Fuseli, only those prototypes which showed the powerful play of muscular forces would do.

The drawing of the male nude is in fact a back view of one *49* of the Horsetamers of the Monte Cavallo. An almost identical *164* view was taken by Canova of the same figure including the horse (Museo Bassano B -13-40) in 1779–80. Of the Renaissance masters, the two most obvious sources would be Pollaiuolo and Signorelli. The latter's frescos (Orvieto) of the End of the World, the coming of Anti-Christ and the Last Judgment were very much to Fuseli's taste, not for style but for form. It may well be blasphemous to suggest this, but Signorelli was preeminently the 'backside' painter of the Renaissance, for what is typical of him, the hard contraction of the gluteal masses of the buttocks, is used by Fuseli in his drawing.

By merging these various studies, the artist formulated his own type of heroic image, tall in proportion, elastic in articulation, the centres most expressive of human energy clearly defined. There is more than a hint that Fuseli grasped here the same key as Delacroix offered to his friend Jean Gigoux as an aid to drawing, 'The artists of Antiquity took things by their centres, those of the Renaissance by the line.' While the point on which emphasis was put differed for each artist, Delacroix on 'masses', Fuseli on 'centres of energy', neither drew in continuous outline. This is best observed in the latter's drawing of Odysseus and Tiresias and in the satirical drawing. In these *41, 1* neither with wash nor line does Fuseli 'outline' the whole figure but builds it up through connected 'contours', analogous to those employed in mapmaking, delineating the shin, the calf, the thigh, the abdomen and so on. However, this method could be arrived at independently by the self-taught artist assembling his own formulae for the different parts of the body.

To return now to 'the moment of terror' 'where the agency of invisible beings is introduced'. *Odysseus before Tiresias in* *41* *Hades* (c.1775), *Samuel appearing to Saul, before the Witch of* *42* *Endor* (1777) and *The Escapee* (1777) represent a classical, a *43* biblical and actual example. The latter two are engravings by Thomas Holloway for the 1792 edition of Lavater's *Essays on Physiognomy*, supervised by Fuseli, but both had been prepared for the French edition of 1781–83. *The Escapee* is noted by the artist below the engraving as having been drawn 'from

VIII Fuseli. The Cave of Spleen. 1799

IX Fuseli. The Fire King appears to Count Albert. 1801–10

X

memory after a mad scene in the Hospital of S. Spirito at Rome'. which is significant on two counts; one being that whatever an artist's taste in expression might be in this period, there seemed to be a necessity for actual confirmatory experience, either imagined or real; the other, that visiting a mental asylum was a commonplace activity (in London a favourite Sunday excursion was a visit to Bedlam). Stimulated by the real scene, Fuseli has re-cast it – compositionally in terms of Raphael's *Heliodorus* fresco, and in feeling, as a more manic rendition *26, 44* of the *Death of Cardinal Beaufort*. Lavater reproduced only the *25* right-hand side in the French edition, and this might imply that he thought Fuseli was being intentionally critical of the Catholic Church, in showing the clergy on the left, waiting, like oppressive wardens, for the lunatic ministrant to be physically quietened and returned to them for spiritual absolution. If so, he was probably right. These aspects of organized religion were always repugnant to Fuseli, as they were to all adherents of the Enlightenment. Priests, as d'Holbach described them in the *Encyclopédie*, 'introduced ceremonies, initiations and mysteries, the dread of which, nourished in man that sombre melancholy, so favourable to the realm of fanaticism.' John Howard's *The State of the Prisons* (1777) would have been known in Italy, so that these one time *raree* shows, prisons and asylums, were now becoming objects of concern and their inmates worthy of intelligent sympathy.

While in this actual scene the demonic presence is truly invisible, in the other two drawings the invisible agent is embodied, at least to Odysseus and Saul. On the stage an apparition (e.g. Banquo's ghost) can be left invisible to the audience, but for the artist a 'presence' was essential both for meaning and composition. In fact, Fuseli progressively fleshes out these ectoplasmic forms until they are 'real' beings in every sense of the word, as Delacroix was to do in his etchings for Goethe's *Faust*. Nor did he make any differentiation between a ghost who 'wills' its own presence, and an apparition who is 'willed' to appear by sorcery, except through the addition of the medium.

Odysseus is both medium and supplicant, for he performs a *41* sacrifice to make Tiresias appear, but nevertheless is struck with amazement, in a proper stage style befitting the 'set' in which Fuseli places him; with the hero upstage, Tiresias is 'brought up' on a counter weighted trap, while behind him the 'shades' stream by on a painted backcloth. All this machinery was in use by the mid-century. Whereas Tiresias is dark, consonant with his environment, Samuel appears in lustrous white. The *42* Witch of Endor, her outstretched hands like electrodes, sparks up the apparition and fuses Saul into a stone-like trance. Her attitude, as Lavater explained, 'expresses energy and astonishment', and in the same section, on the artist he remarked that 'the form and bony system of his face characterize in him a taste for terrible scenes and the energy which they require.' Nowhere does Lavater admit to his own enduring weakness for the 'miraculous', whether it was effected by the animal

X *Fuseli. Satan's first address to Eve. 1802*

magnetism of Dr Friedrich Mesmer or divined by the dubious Cabbalist, Count Alessandro de Cagliostro, with whom Fuseli, like Goethe, would have had no patience whatsoever.

The renowned source for the Witch of Endor was Rosa's *The Apparition of Samuel before Saul*, in the Louvre when *45* described by the Richardsons, as 'the finest . . . seen of this Master: the Expression of Horror and Witchery is in Perfection'. In the 1770s, it was at Versailles, for Northcote saw it there. The spell of Rosa's witchcrafts, including the one above, produced a coven of echoes during that decade, two from Mortimer, one from West and the one above from Fuseli, who, however, departs notably from the Rosa recipe. First the witch is centralized, like Tiresias, making her a hieratic controlling power between the quick and the dead. Secondly Fuseli has departed significantly from the text, whereas Rosa follows it exactly, even to the *two* men. Saul was moreover dressed, not naked. How on earth Lavater was persuaded to accept such a travesty will never be known, for it is clear that Fuseli has interpolated a classical reading of some similar scene, based perhaps on Horace's *Epode V,* in which the Witch Canidia and her assistant strip a terrified youth naked, before burying him in a pit up to the neck. The group of the soldier 'inured to dreadful scenes' and the stiffened Saul is Hellenistic in origin; the intaglio gemstone, attributed to Dioscorides by Winckel- *109* mann in his *History of Ancient Art*, is one example, and known to the artist as it then was in the Farnese collection at Naples, besides being engraved in the book.

Another source has been cited, namely the neo-attic relief of a Dionysiac scene (Uffizi 314), which in the mid-seventies was in the Palazzo Riccardi. The group there is similar to the gemstone except that the male figure is standing. While there is no reason to believe that Fuseli did not use one of these sources, it is relevant to note that Giulio Romano had employed a similar group for his Achilles with the body of Patroclus in the Sala di Troia, Palazzo del Tè, Mantua and engraved by the Monogrammist L.D. (H.81); and that a similar group of God the Father supporting the dead Christ appears in a North- ern chiaroscuro wood engraving *Der Altar*, which was still attributed to Dürer in 1831. Thus, even if one knows that David copied the left half of the Uffizi relief, some caution is necessary in determining the primacy of one source over another.

Returning to the central figure of his composition, Fuseli's *42* intention was a kind of syncretic reference to the whole line of witches from Hecate onwards, like the goddess who changes Apuleius back into a human from an ass (Metamorphosis XI), claiming she is worshipped as Minerva, Venus, Diana, Proser- pine, Ceres, Juno, Bellona, Hecate, Rhamnusia and whose true name is Isis. A similar synthesis of text and form occurs in his engraving of the Death of Abel. For Abel is not derived as *47* might be supposed from Ghiberti's figure in the Baptistery door panel in Florence, but from the prostrate and dead son of Niobe (Uffizi, Florence) in the famous Antique group. As

Lavater explained, 'suffering innocence is here presented in manly and energetic traits, under the form of a hero.' It was, after all, the same source that Rubens had used for his prostrate foreground figures. Fuseli was interested only in the superior or heroic exemplar, 'a mediocrity of models' blasting, in his opinion, both virtue and genius.

Thus it was that Fuseli would choose *Brutus*, the patriotic murderer of Caesar the dictator, as a favourite subject. We have already looked at his drawing of Brutus falling on his sword; now he turned to him again at the instant of his victim's ghost appearing before him to announce that they shall meet again at Philippi – the same forewarning of death that Samuel gave to Saul. This is a rare occasion of Fuseli working without the 'prop' of an apparition, so that Lavater's gloss, 'The terror painted on this face announces a soul filled with agitation and uneasiness, yet still possessing itself sufficiently to think and reflect', is a necessary explanation.* It might, in fact, be applied, with a diminution of the term 'terror', to the artist's *Self-Portrait* (*c*.1779–80), in which the symmetrical arrangement of the knuckles provides an embrasure through which the artist peers uneasily but reflectively from the looking glass.

46

*Goethe wrote the original entry for Brutus in the German edition.

Frontispiece

At this point one has to look briefly at the political background to Fuseli's years in Rome, and the loyalties of those with whom he associated. That Fuseli was republican in sentiment hardly requires proof – he was Swiss, apart from all the evidence provided in his letters. His comments to Lavater, apropos Klopstock, that a Frenchman had more right to call his country fatherland – that there were Frenchmen who were patriots, whereas there was no one in the German states deserving of that name – show that for him as for the *Encyclopédistes*, patriotism was virtually synonymous with republicanism. Love of country, says De Jaucourt in the article *Patrie*, is 'the love of law and the goodwill of the state, a love particularly affected in democracies; it is a political virtue through which one renounces the self, preferring the public interest to one's own; it is a feeling and not a result of learning; the lowest man in the state can have this feeling as much as the head of the republic.' While Diderot and his associates thought only in terms of persuasion and not of direct action, they created a body of opinion which was to move from persuasion to action in the years to come.

In 1775 another painter came to Rome, also sympathetic to such ideals, also choleric in temperament, also devoted to antique sculpture as the 'living' image of the soul of Rome: Jacques-Louis David. Next year came an event which certainly impressed them both: the American Declaration of Independence, the distant smoke-signal heralding the events of 1789.

The last three years of Fuseli's residence in Rome would have been stimulated by David's presence, and the uncertainty caused by the ebb and flow of the war in America and its repercussions amongst the European States would have ensured that discussion of art and its relation to contemporary life would be anything but academic. The consequence was an interleaving of pages from classical history, philosophy and

89

contemporary aspirations. One example would be the chain of associations linking Winckelmann's praise of the Spartans, whose healthy regimen led to the body beautiful with the notion that the good republican should do likewise to keep himself disciplined and fit for service to the state, with the *Sturm und Drang* devotion to exhausting exercise to increase romantic empathy with Nature, and lastly with the English concern with health as the source of sound breeding, longevity and a clean mind. It would not have been difficult for the inmates of that Spartan institution, the French Academy in Rome, to bend on to all this the Platonic notion of the Beautiful as expounded in the *Symposium*, the theoretical bible of the David studio according to Delécluze.* The idea of scaling a ladder from physical life to the spiritual contemplation of the Beautiful had been revived by Lord Shaftesbury in 1711 and his observations translated by Diderot in 1745. Hence the upward pointing finger in David's *Death of Socrates* (1786), anticipated, more allegorically, by Fuseli in the drawing already discussed, *The Artist in despair over the magnitude of Antique fragments* (1778–80). 4 In this the ascending order of steps, with the artist on the lowest feeling, somewhat inadequately, for the form of that earthbound symbol, the foot, while the upward pointing finger soars above, combines the Platonic ideal with a thoroughly Piranesean romanticism, for it utilizes the same device of dissonance of scale as *Dante on the Ice of Cocytus*. In the later 29 drawing, the black shadows cast by a sun close to the horizon seem to accentuate the artist's despondency. His technical proficiency with wash tones is not in doubt however, for he is able here to distinguish, with considerable economy, the hardness of marble and the softer forms of the human body.

Closer still to David is the commission received by Fuseli from his native town, *The Oath on the Rütli* (1780). Whether the 57 artist had news of this before he left Rome is not known, but a drawing for the subject is inscribed and dated *Zurico 79* (Kunsthaus, Zurich). In most respects it sums up a great deal of what has been discussed above, depicting the legendary oath of concord of the three cantons, led by William Tell in 1307. Typically it incorporates Roman gestures and motifs of oath taking and concord with the upraised arms and faces of Christians calling on God as their witness. Left to his own devices it is probable that Fuseli, to express the feeling of patriotism, would not have chosen such a local event, since the general tendency was to fix such allegories in the earliest era of the Roman Republic. A work by Polidoro da Caravaggio, identified here as *Camillus and Brennus*, represents this 58 very well. Since it was engraved by Jakob Frey (1681–1752), a Swiss working in Rome, it was well known to all who worked there, including James Barry who used the whole group to represent Numa, Penn, Lord Baltimore, Marcus Aurelius, and King Alfred in his Society of Arts cycle (1777–83). Gavin Hamilton also owned a number of Polidoro's works, primarily because of his long standing reputation as an accurate portrayer of Roman modes and manners. It is interesting to note that of

*Delécluze, Etienne-Jean, 1781–1863, see Robert Baschet, *E.-J. Delécluze, Témoins de son Temps*, Paris, 1942.

the three Oath painters – Fuseli, Gavin Hamilton (*Oath of Brutus*, 1760–64, Drury Lane Theatre), and David (*Oath of the Horatii*, 1784) – all use the Roman custom of grasping the sword below the hilt but Fuseli is the only one to use the high figure and low horizon employed by Polidoro. The motif of the three clasped hands is a modification of the Roman *dextrarum iunctio*, two figures joining hands before a central person, for example on coins, inscribed *Concordia Aeterna*. It was Camillus who raised the first temple to the goddess Concordia, after he had defeated the Gallic chief in battle, challenging Brennus at the moment of his accepting the gold ransom for peace extorted from Rome – the event shown in the Polidoro engraving. In composition, Fuseli emphasises strength and equality with the equilateral triangle described by the figures and the square bounded by the sword and the arms in a centralized group. The absence of women, used by both Hamilton and David, points to that *Sturm und Drang* concept of masculine invincibility, a brotherhood of friendship, in which, obviously, there was neither place nor need for women.

59, 71

In colour and texture the *Oath on the Rütli* and *The Artist in Conversation with Bodmer* are flat and uninteresting, although both might be consistent with the artist's definition of 'negative' colour, the 'evanescence' of which Opie was to admire when he first came to London. Neither of these first essays in large oil painting is distinguished by that quality. What Fuseli was seeking was 'dead' colour to symbolize 'timelessness', bright tints and contrasting tones being too ephemeral, too 'fleeting' in effect.

57, 7

That he was not alone in this pursuit is attested by Reynolds in his notes to Mason's verse translation of du Fresnoy's *Art of Painting* (1782), 'There is [a] fault prevalent in the modern painters, – the predominance of a grey leaden colour over the whole picture: . . . particularly . . . remarked when their works hang . . . with pictures well and powerfully coloured.'

The two large oils just discussed were painted or completed in England along with a number of other commissions Fuseli had obtained in Zurich, about eight in all judging from the evidence of two letters to Lavater in 1781. Amongst these, he mentions two *Schwarzkunststudie* (Black Art works), a witchcraft and *das Schrättelin*, faun or satyr, but here a diminutive, shaggy creature of the woods, popular in Northern folklore. At the beginning of the century, Joseph Addison had noticed this *penchant* of the Swiss: 'I have often been tired with Accounts of this Nature from very sensible men that are most of them furnished with Matters of Fact, which have happened, as they pretend . . . The People are so universally infatuated with the Notion, that, if a Cow falls sick, it is Ten to One but an old Woman is clap'd up in Prison for it.' The reference to 'very sensible men' may suggest that, for all the rationalizing of the Enlightenment, Fuseli had his due share of this national predilection, without being 'infatuated' to excess.

1780 TO 1790

The *Nightmare* (1781) belongs in this context of *Schwarz-* I
kunststudie. While its content will be dealt with in a later section,
the style is full of interest, since it shows the overlaying of a
serious 'moment of terror' on an essentially Rococo composition, particularly that of Fragonard in his oriental Sultana
paintings, nor is the colour far distant from those either. For a
Rococo 'moment of terror' Fragonard's *Coresus sacrificing*
himself to save Callirhoe is also relevant since it received Diderot's 78
high praise and public acclaim when it was shown at the Salon
in 1766, a few months before Fuseli arrived in France. The two
artists may have met in Rome when the Frenchman made his
second visit to Italy in 1773, but in any case, the fainting or
sleeping erotic forms of women, *déshabillés*, were, one might
say, *de rigueur* in French book illustration of the period. Fuseli's
long limbed *houri*, however, is related more to Runciman's 62
Medusa and the Hellenistic figure of a dead Amazon in the
Naples Museum than to Fragonard's Rococo forms.

Two other motifs from Hellenistic sculpture are significant –
the extreme collapse of the head and neck and the knuckles of
the hand on the hanging arm touching the ground – for they
appear in the Runciman *Perseus and Medusa*, in the *Menelaus* 60, 62
and Patroclus and in *The Nightmare*. In comparison Barry's etch- I
ing of *Lear and Cordelia* (1774), while similar, is not based on this 61
extreme Antique source of death, but on the sleeping *Barberini*
Faun (Glyptothek, Munich). Notable also, is that Fuseli's
arrangement of the horse's head, the goblin and the afflicted
woman is identical to that of Rosa's *The Apparition of Samuel*
before Saul, in which the Witch of Endor appears to be almost 45
sitting on the back of Samuel on all fours. While *The Nightmare*
is an innovation, therefore, the artist employs, basically, many
traditional concomitants of the supernatural.

The Nightmare may profitably be seen in conjunction with I
The Ezzelin Bracciaferro musing over the dead Meduna (the II
original, exhibited in 1780, was sent to Salomon Escher in
Zurich). The version here was probably painted for the engraving of 1784, while the drawing (British Museum) is
inscribed and dated *Zurich feb 1779*. The story is well known of
how Byron, intrigued with the subject, asked Fuseli for the
source and was told it came out of the artist's head. What is of
immediate concern is that the scene shows a historical act of
retribution, while the same act in *The Nightmare* is imaginary –
the emotional state of each male protagonist, Ezzelin and Fuseli
however, being identical. Lavater's note to the engraving (1792)
runs as follows: 'Fettered by remorse of conscience, accused by
the presence of his [Ezzelin] victim, he deplores his madness, but
repents it not: he detests it, and yet still applauds himself for it.'
This is also quite an apt description of Fuseli's feelings for Anna
Landolt, whose portrait he painted on the back of *The Night-*
mare. The artist modelled his dreadful hero on the tyrant
Eccelino da Romano* (d. 1259), diminutive in stature, 'an
enemy to luxury' and 'proof against the seductions of women'.
The Northern motifs of the hourglass, crucifix and open bible,
familiar in Flemish and German paintings, help to round out

*See J. C. L. de Sismondi, *A History of the Italian*
Republics (Zurich 1807–1818). A much reduced
English edition, London, 1910.

this portrait of some northern Crusader – damned. As for Meduna, she had already appeared in his poem *Der Circassier* (1772), 'lying in the arms of death', the victim of the Corsair of Tunis, the robber of the 'glorious church of Istanbul' whose 'glowing eye rolled with dark jealousy'. The handling of the paint and colour is crisper than in *The Nightmare*, revealing the dual influence of Reynolds, in the hero, and Gainsborough, in the dead heroine.

There is little need to stress the continuity of Fuseli's interest in the 'moment of terror', but in the two paintings discussed above he had found it necessary, for one reason or another, to invent the situation, the result being that the spectator is prevented from comparing his own with that of the artist's interpretation of a known text. The emotional impact, if made, would be undiluted. But such independent inventions are not common in Fuseli's oeuvre, so that one must assume that he undertook them only when literature failed him or, as in the case of *The Nightmare*, there was a strong external stimulus. Unlike Blake, Fuseli always had to 'justify' his invention.

In the drawing *Fear* (c. 1780–2) he engages in another rare   *64* enterprise, that of depicting one of the passions without a visible and confronting 'presence'. There are two reasons why he might have done this; one, that with Chodowiecki's version of Le Brun's *Passions* from Lavater's French edition before him   *65* he wished to try out his own physiognomic interpretation; the other is the possibility of the drawing being connected with a proposal to erect a monument in Chichester Cathedral in memory of the poet William Collins (1721–1759). In 1787–88 Flaxman was to provide six designs, the cheapest of which was selected by the committee, one of whom was William Hayley. Collins, who died deranged, had written both an *Ode to the Passions* and an *Ode to Fear* (1746), from which the following lines might well have been the artist's text:

> Ah Fear! Ah frantic Fear!
> I see, I see Thee near
> I know thy hurried Step, thy
>   haggard Eye!

It is certainly the dilated eyes of the three girls which reflect their fear of the 'hurried step' of an approaching 'presence'. None of Le Brun's *Passions* is identical to Fuseli's, which is evidence not   *65* only of his rejection of Le Brun, expressed in his letter to Lavater, but also of his serious interest in physiognomic analysis, which, he thought, might lead to a more exact rendering of the emotions, particularly those which, like fear, tend to slacken the body and centre in the face, in contra-distinction to terror which runs through every nerve.

To emphasize this phenomenon, the artist adopts a style analogous to one employed in engraving, a combination of a tonal and line modelling, with the result that the eye returns again and again to the three faces.

Two other drawings of this period, the scene from *Timon of*   *66* *Athens* and the *Executioner*, reveal the artist's capacity in marry-   *232* ing style to interpretation. This is most marked in the *Timon of*

93

Athens, where Alcibiades and his companions are rendered frivolous and brittle by the spattering of highlights and decorative play of the drapery lines, and Timon solid and immovable by the way he is merged in with the rock forms of his cavern. The *Executioner*, while based on that of Andrea del Sarto's *Decapitation of St John the Baptist*, is made hard and aggressive, with pen and ink, in the manner of Bandinelli. The same subtlety is expressed in the low-centred, earthbound form of the shepherd and the airy flight of fairies above him in *The Shepherd's Dream* (1785), the most finished of all these drawings.

This mastery in the graphic media and the diversity of expression that Fuseli could achieve in them was not to be found so easily in painting. Oil was dense and obviously not so tractable as those other media. There is also evidence in many of his oils that he used the brush like a pencil, literally drawing in paint, thus ignoring a range of manipulations particular to the oil medium. While he certainly learned a great deal over the years, there is throughout his painting oeuvre a tendency to overwork certain passages, leading to unpleasant surfaces and muddy colour, and paradoxically a visible impatience with such a long drawn out process.

This said, Fuseli was by no means such a bad painter as some have suggested, for there is little to cavil at in his *Percival frees Belisane from the spell of Urma* (1783) in terms of the painted surface. Caravaggesque in lighting and colour and arranged in a shallow series of frontal planes, the composition is immediately arresting. The detail and spatial use of the chain is excellently handled, although one might jib somewhat at its conclusion on the right, secured to what seems a too abruptly amputated hand and wrist. Due allowance must be made here for the sinking of the 'darks', effected by time, which inevitably isolate the high-lighted areas. One wonders whether Fuseli's critics then or now would object to a seventeenth-century painting affected in the same way.

It is perhaps apposite to introduce here an influence which is rarely if ever mentioned – Florentine painting of the early Baroque. While recent exhibitions have brought an increased familiarity with the artists of that period, one tends to forget how many of their works would have been visible in Florence before the breaking up of the large collections at the end of the eighteenth century. Salvator Rosa was much affected by his sojourn there in the 1640s, and legend had it that Milton conceived his *Paradise Lost* in that city about the same time. Lady Morgan* in her book on Rosa (1824) hopefully ruminated on a collusion between the artist and the poet! When one compares Alcibiades and his entwining women in Fuseli's *Timon of Athens* drawing and *Hylas and the Nymphs* by Furini, with Hylas wearing a frown like Fuseli's *Brutus*, the connection seems clear. The general slumbrous tonality of many of these Florentine works is also close to that of Fuseli. Furini at least needed no introduction to English artists since Hogarth had patterned his *Sigismonda* on a work by that artist in Sir Luke Schaub's collection, a borrowing that gained great notoriety. It is also

67

77

III

*Lady (Sydney) Morgan, The Life and Times of Salvator Rosa, 2 vols., London, 1824.

232, 68

94

significant that the last man before our own century to praise, not to say mention, Giovanni di san Giovanni, Furini's contemporary in Florence, was Fuseli, in his edition of Pilkington's Dictionary. Giovanni, he says, 'may be ranked among the best fresco painters (e.g. S. S. Quattro Coronati; Palazzo Pallavicini, Rome) of Italy . . . his spirit soars above the concurrence of meaner artists.' Furini's *Hylas and the Nymphs* was in the Tassi-Galli collection, Florence, while Fuseli was in Italy and was engraved by Eredi (1780); later it was in English collections until its return to Florence this century.

Since it was related to his own interest in 'negative colour', the slumbrous tonality referred to above was one much admired by Fuseli in a number of artists, for example, Ludovico Carracci 'whose lights seem embrowned by a golden veil' and Rosso Fiorentino (*Transfiguration*, Città di Castello), 'that dying and nearly nocturnal light which tones the whole with sombre gravity'.

Not only was this tonality wholly relevant to witches and their spells but it suggests the 'timelessness' which the artist sought, to bring about a suspension of the consciousness of time, whatever the historical or mythical setting. To this end, he also eliminated as many vernacular details as possible, delimiting the spatial context so that each action took place in a kind of no man's land. Like Ezzelin Bracciaferro, Perceval never freed *II* Belisane in any known medieval text, although the artist *III* seemed to have been anxious to add an episode to Chrétien de Troyes' unfinished *Conte du Graal* (twelfth century), where the story of Perceval appears. This was not an unusual pursuit at the time. Chatterton had fathered his fine poems, on to Thomas Rowley, a mythical poet of the fifteenth Century, while nearer home, John Aiken had attached to his essay on Terror, already quoted, his own 'Gothic' fragment, entitled *Sir Bertrand*.

Two other works of the same year (1783) are not invented but drawn from Shakespeare – *Lady Constance, Arthur and Salisbury* (King John) and the *Three Witches* (Macbeth). Com- *69, 72* positionally these and the *Timon of Athens* drawing of the same *232* year vary a great deal but not because the artist was searching about for a satisfactory mode, but because each variation is adopted to suit its respective situation. Emerging from all his work in the 1780s is the idea of an emotional catalyst personified by a dominant being who radiates his or her mood to all around. The stage, once again, was a major inductor of this idea, for it was Garrick who had insisted that all 'on stage' must react or respond to the action or speech going on. Before his time, actors on stage not actually speaking would often engage in conversation with a friend in the audience or divert themselves in some other manner. Hence Fuseli had no need of studio models when the stage could provide him with all the *tableaux vivants*, and with the inauguration of the 'star' system by Garrick, all the dominating personalities he required.

However, Fuseli was not a theatrical painter, but an artist who wished to externalize and make permanent Shakespeare's moral force. To do this he had to establish a clear association between Shakespeare and the central allegorical tradition. Lady Constance is proof of one such attempt, for she is borrowed from Cesare Ripa's figure of Malincolia in *Iconologia* (1764–66), illustrating the line 'Here I with sorrow sit', with both Arthur and Salisbury affected likewise. In every way this centralized, grieving Sibyl dominates her dependants. Fuseli was not alone in borrowing from Ripa, for Goya made considerable use of these emblems, and even Gainsborough, whom one would not suspect at once, based his *Girl with Pigs* (1782, Castle Howard) on the emblem *Invernata* (Winter time), in which a woman sits melancholy, a hand to her head with a pig feeding before her. It is certain, with some evidence to be shown later, that this last edition of Ripa appeared at a crucial time, when artists were aware that they were at the crossroads of invention, that the traditional avenues were now revealing themselves as cul-de-sacs and new directions must be taken. To add maturity and fortify fresh subjects, what better than to incorporate one or more of Ripa's emblems?

The Three Witches are connected with another sort of emblem: the motif of overlapping profile heads found in Roman coinage and on bas-reliefs. Piranesi in his *Carceri d'Invenzione*, No. 2 (c. 1745–61) gave prominence to three overlapped relief heads and Chodowiecki employed the same device in the German edition of Lavater's Essays. In the Macbeth witches, Fuseli stresses the ancient and Sybilline nature of these androgynes, laying each a finger 'upon their choppy lips', while the repetition of their pointing hands makes their prophecy imperative. Never again, however, did the artist employ such a close-up view. What is significant is that this painting barely anticipates David's *Oath of the Horatii* (1783–84), whose protagonists use a similar imperative gesture. There is no case here of one artist seeing the other's work, but an underlining of the closeness of their association in Rome. Another instance is *The Death of Oedipus* (1784), where the two daughters collapse upon their father, stricken by his announcement, exactly as the women are by that of the old Horace in David's work. In each painting there is the centralized image of paternal authority, whose gestures intimate death, for either himself or kinsman.

This leads to what may be called the cumulative Ripa system, i.e. incorporating a number of those emblems in one composition. Albani had in a sense employed it in the Verospi ceiling, but here each emblem was framed separately, whereas both David and Fuseli thought in quite novel terms, of integrating them into fresh subject matter. The evidence of this system in David has never before been advanced, and since he uses Ripa directly his case must come first.

In the *Oath of the Horatii*, from left to right, one finds in the three Horatii the emblem of *Concordia Insuperabile* (Insuperable Concord), described as Geryon or three brothers who ruled together, having three faces, six arms, a lance and a naked sword; in the old Horace, an emblematic variation of *Amor della Patria* (Love of Country) represented as a Roman soldier standing on crossed arms and holding up two wreaths; in the two women,

69
70

72

59, 71

73

37

59, 71

in white and gold, *Fama Buona* and *Fama Chiara* (Good Fame), usually represented by a woman carrying a gold and a silver cornucopia; and lastly in the woman in black with two children *Fama Cattiva* (Bad Fame), also identified as Night and her two children, Death and Sleep. Not only does David make certain emblematic variations of his own, but fits these into the domestic pattern established by Corneille in his play, *Les Horaces*. The spatial voids often pointed out in this painting are occasioned by the necessity of keeping these *emblemata* reasonably separate, so that they could be read as such.

In one way David's was a very solid achievement, but his context did not require him to make inventive leaps to accommodate these abstractions, which *exactly* define Republicanism as it was defined by the *philosophes*, discussed earlier.

In contrast, Fuseli faced a very serious inventive problem when he attempted to 'realize' six lines from Milton's *L'Allegro*, 74 containing abstractions none of which are treated in the *Iconologia*. This drawing may be dated, fairly reasonably, to *c*. 1785, when he did another Miltonic subject, *The Shepherd's* 77 *Dream*. Furthermore the *L'Allegro* subject can be seen as an inventive 'breakthrough', for it was the breach in the wall, behind which lay the fairy land, his most poetic and distinctive contribution to European art.

The six lines from *L'Allegro* are as follows:

> Haste thee, Nymph and bring with thee
> Jest, and youthful jollity,
> Quips and Cranks and wanton wiles,
> Nods and Becks and wreathèd Smiles . . .
> . . . Sport that Wrinkled Care derides
> And Laughter holding both his sides.

In adopting the cumulative Ripa system, Fuseli would have had to search and invent, as Ripa had done, for close associative images to those he wished to illustrate, and surely these would have to be up-dated to weld together these abstractions and the associative capacity of a contemporary English audience. There were some clues to this problem in the *Iconologia,* for Orlandi the editor had seen fit to 'modernize' the dress in a number of the engravings, and even to add new emblems – for instance, *Conversazione Moderna* (Modern Conversation), a Rococo interior with a gentleman and his lady turned towards each other, which one may confess adds nothing to the storehouse of emblems!

How Fuseli proceeded is, of course, unknown, but the following may not appear too far fetched. Starting with the Nymph, Euphrosyne-Mirth, on the bed, Correggio's *Danae* 75 seems the obvious source and is also Love, since she was Jupiter's lover. A more recent association was Reynolds's *Snake in the Grass* (R.A. 1784, Tate Gallery) also known as *The Zone Unbound* on the basis of William Collins's couplet in his *Ode to the Passions*:

> Love framed with Mirth, a gay fantastic Round,
> Loose were Her Tresses seen, her zone unbound.

Fuseli's drawing is certainly a 'gay fantastic Round' as one passes, to be prosaic, in a clock-wise direction, from Sport and Care to Laughter 'holding both his sides'. Sport and Care are represented by a young girl and her nurse. In later paintings of Danae, she is generally accompanied by an old woman, for example Tiepolo's painting (1730–35, Stockholm), hence 'Wrinkled Care'; besides, there are the exchanges between Juliet and her nurse, the latter exclaiming at one point, 'I am the drudge and toil in your delight' (II. 3). Then there is Laughter, represented by Puck or Robin Goodfellow, who described himself in *A Midsummer Night's Dream* as 'that merry wanderer of the night'. After recounting some of his wiles he describes how 'the whole quire hold their hips and loffe' (II. 1).

The skill with which the artist personifies these abstractions and composes them in the order in which they appear in the poem is considerable. Also to be admired is the spontaneity of the action, in which the sudden rising of the Nymph sets off a chain reaction exploding at its end in Laughter.

Nothing better exemplifies the differences between David and Fuseli than this parallelism in their respective emblematic systems, for it displays the former's conservatism, in the true meaning of that term, and the latter's radicalism in relation to their definitions of a contemporary art.

After the *L'Allegro* drawing Fuseli must have felt as free as the air, Ariel himself, for in this twilight world of the fairy, time was suspended together with those rules of art canonized by a rational, human world, enabling him to create extreme divergencies in scale and operate them in a space which had its own rules.

The *L'Allegro* drawing, *The Shepherd's Dream (Paradise Lost,* I 781–88), *Titania and Bottom* and its pendant *The Awakening of Titania,* both from *A Midsummer Night's Dream* (IV 1) form a progressive sequence not only thematically but in the multiplying of the figures in each composition. There was, in fact, a precedent for the interlinking of Milton and Shakespeare, for Garrick, in 1755, had composed a kind of opera *The Fairies,* containing twenty-seven songs, with the lyrics drawn from Dryden, Milton (*L'Allegro*), and Waller, as well as from *The Tempest* and *Much Ado about Nothing,* and especially the fairy scenes of *A Midsummer Night's Dream.* The play, indeed, never obtained a fair hearing throughout the eighteenth century, since the adaptors cut it to suit their own preferences and not those of its author. But in this and other plays which lent themselves, a ballet was often introduced, of which the artist could also take advantage. Fuseli was much addicted to this form, as Farington tells of his enthusiasm in Paris (1802) for the ballet *Telemachos in Calypso,* which he thought was 'a luxuriant dream', the dancers' feet inspired to the extent of making Albani's sylphs look clumsy. This comment is instructive in the way in which Fuseli viewed one art in terms of another.

The world of fairies did not constitute light relief to the heavier themes of Milton and Shakespeare, for those 'incorporeal Spirits' could wreak havoc as well as pleasure, so that it is reasonable to suppose, that Fuseli thought of this essentially

74, 77

IV, 76

98

Northern world as parallel to that described by Hesiod in his *The-ogony*. After all, *A Midsummer Night's Dream* is set near Athens.

The Shepherd's Dream provides a clue to this analogy, for *77* seated behind the Sleeper is Pandora with her box open, having allowed out the evils that were to torment mankind. But also in the box was Hope. Hesiod in his *Work and Days* (90–105) described the primitive happiness of man before Pandora's advent and later (174–201) deplores, with an almost eighteenth-century misanthropy, the deterioration of his own age and gloomily predicts that worse is to come. The aptness of this Hesiodic reference is confirmed by the fact that Milton compares the Shepherd's dream to the first gathering of the fallen angels in Hell.

It is useful to compare Fragonard's painting of *Coresus and Callirhoe* with the *Shepherd's Dream* drawing, to see not only *78* how Fuseli utilizes certain Rococo characteristics but also how he distinguishes more exactly the elemental 'weight' of his figures, those which are air bound and those earth bound. Although one cannot be quite sure that the artist based his drawing on the Fragonard, there are so many coincidences, general and particular, that he must surely have had it in mind. It is apposite too to quote here a verse from Christopher Smart's poem *Night Piece*:

> Then came Sleep, serene and blind
> Bearing a death watch in his hand
> In fluid air around him swims
> A tribe grotesque of mimic dreams.

In addition to a beetle being ridden in on the left of the drawing, the notion of the 'mimic dreams' swimming in 'fluid air' seems identical to that which the artist conveys by the use of the arabesque patterns of the drapery, suggesting both movement and the density of the matter in which these beings 'swim'. At all times one can never forget that the artist was a devoted and very knowledgeable entomologist and that an interest in aerodynamics is not confined to the aircraft designer.

With the two scenes from *A Midsummer Night's Dream*, the *IV, 76* reference to Hesiod's *Theogony* is more evident, for here are Oberon and Titania, the fairy forces pitted against each other, embroiling man as a helpless pawn in their schemes. While the sleeper in *The Shepherd's Dream* can be identified with Epi- *77* metheus (Afterthought), Pandora's husband, his brother Prometheus (Forethought) may be identified with Bottom the Weaver, who like his progenitor, never loses command of a situation, despite being a prisoner of the cosmic powers. Since metamorphosis into an ass is the conception here, there is the further possible reference to Apuleius.

Turning to Fuseli's artistic sources, there is first Cunning- ham's interesting allusion, in relation to *Titania and Bottom*, to *IV* Hogarth's *Strolling Actresses dressing in a Barn*, for a play called *79* *The Devil to Pay* or *The Metamorphosed Wives* (1686) by Jevon, and also made into an opera by Coffey and Mottley. Like the Fragonard painting of Coresus, the Hogarth engraving offers *78* similar coincidences of figures and arrangement, besides the

99

general relationship of the Pantheon of gods and goddesses in the Hogarth and its fairy equivalent in the two Titania paintings. One of the best contemporary commentaries of this Hogarth plate was Lichtenberg's, which, published 1784-96 in the *Göttinger Taschenkalendar*, would not have been known to Fuseli until later. But the author certainly was, by repute at least, for he was a correspondent and sceptically amusing critic of Lavater's physiognomic diagnoses. The Lichtenberg commentary is extremely helpful in indicating the way in which Fuseli's imagination may have worked. For instance, Ganymede on the extreme left, in male clothes, is compared to *79* Mamselle d'Eon or the Chevalier d'Eon (1728-1810) who assumed female dress in his role as a French secret agent, while the girl holding the cat (background right) made Lichtenberg think of Titian's metamorphosis of the Laocoön group into three struggling apes.

It appears not at all impossible, therefore, that Fuseli had the famous *Farnese Bull* group in mind when he composed the *Titania and Bottom*. Considering the central triangular section *IV* of the painting there is a close resemblance in the placement of compositional diagonals, verticals and horizontals formed by the limbs and bodies of the figures. Even Titania's wand is angled in the same way as the rope in the Antique group. The artist's wit is shown in the way he replaces a son of Antiope holding the bull's horn by Peaseblossom scratching Bottom's head. Again, there is a relevance of association – Dirce tied to the bull, Pasiphae falling in love with a bull, Titania falling in love with an ass. To complete the analogy with Lichtenberg, one may pass to the gnome (bottom right) whose head is being twisted round with such force by the hooded hag, that he squints. For this figure Fuseli may have thought of an earlier acquaintance – Philipp Erasmus Reich – whom he described to Bodmer in a letter (March 1763), 'He is smaller than I am – he is like a comic-satyr story come true', and his eyes had distorted pupils which 'squinted a little'. There may be other such 'portraits' in Fuseli's paintings which could be identified, but this is perhaps sufficient at the moment to illustrate a little of his inventive process.

51 *The Farnese Bull. Hellenistic*

There is even a Miltonic echo in *Titania and Bottom*. Next to *81* the gnome is the Faëry Mab from *L'Allegro*, not only identified by her companion carrying a dish of junket, but by the diminutive friar who leads her:

> And by the Friars' lantern led,

wrote Milton, with a thrust at the orders of Friars, who deceived people as much as *Jack o' Lantern* or *Will-o'-the-Wisp*. A *81* reference not lost on Fuseli, either.

The fusion principle may be equally observed in *The Awakening of Titania*, for the image of the gnome on horseback *76* over Bottom's face is derived from Mercutio's description of Queen Mab in *Romeo and Juliet*, namely the three lines:

> Athwart men's noses as they lie asleep:
> And in this state she gallops night by night
> Through lovers' brains, and then they dream of love . . . 1 4)

The propinquity of this Awakening to the realm of the Nightmare is demonstrated by the suspended Ass's head above Titania and also by the demon rider, already discussed, for the latter is to be associated with Gottfried Bürger's poem *Lenore* (1773); here the girl's knightly lover returns from battle to carry her off to their wedding, but during their night ride a shaft of moonlight reveals to her that she is clasping a skeleton in armour. Chodowiecki's engraving (1778) illustrates the *80* couple leaving the girl's house, in a manner which incorporates a traditional witches' sabbath dance in the sky and a prosaic equestrian group. There could be no better comparison to demonstrate Fuseli's radical inventiveness in compounding the real and the imaginary to produce a 'third world' where the natural and supernatural could meet on common ground. It was not just common ground but commonplace as far as *A Midsummer Night's Dream* was concerned; Joseph Green writing to his friend Ozias Humphry (1 September 1773) of a newly married couple declared, 'They live quite in Fairy-Land and indeed seem the only Rivals of Puck and Peaseblossom'. As Gauguin remarked over a hundred years later, very little separates Art from the commonplace. In the last two decades of the eighteenth century, the presence of that latter ingredient, more often than not, signalled success for a painting.

The painting itself displays a number of artistic sources: from left to right, the fairy being kissed is similar to the couple on the left of Hogarth's engraving *Noon*, while next to them Puck is derived, very properly, in posture and expression from the artist's *Laughter* in the *L'Allegro* drawing; the sleeping *74* Bottom is closer to the *Drunken Faun* (1770–74, Stockholm) by Fuseli's friend Sergel than to the prototype, the *Barberini Faun*; then on the right, the fairy nursing an infant gnome is based on Luca Cambiaso's *Caritas* in the Palazzo Giustiniani, Genoa until 1815, which is a reminder of Pandora's box in the *Shepherd's Dream*. Finally, at the top with the Ass's head there *77* is the possibility that Fuseli was familiar with Claude Gillot's etchings of witchcrafts, for in one, *Rêve Magique* from *Scènes Humoristiques,* an ass's head floats in the air. This proliferation of sources and the subject leads to Sir Joshua Reynolds's dictum in his letter to *The Idler* (79. 20 October 1759) that the grand style was as separate from imitation of nature as Poetry is from History, and he continued, 'Poetical ornaments destroy that air of truth and plainness which ought to characterize History; but the very being of Poetry consists in departing from this plain narration, and adopting every ornament that will warm the imagination.' While Reynolds is referring to the literary modes, his words may have been the origin of a new classification, Poetic painting. Fuseli uses the term in his Lectures, but more often he uses 'History', perhaps because it was more widely understood. The important point, however, is that Poetic painting did not mean a slavish illustration of a literary text, but the adopting of 'every ornament that will warm the imagination', wherein lay the seeds of Romantic invention.

History, of course, was not a closed book to the artist, but mostly he preferred it to have been opened by some great intermediary, as in *Henry V surprising Cambridge, Scrope and Grey with their death sentence* (1786–89) one of the Boydell Gallery paintings. Fundamentally the work is a variation on the theme of David's *Oath of the Horatii*, Henry V taking the place of the old Horace as Patria, Exeter, Bedford and Westmorland as the three Horatii or Concordia and the three conspirators named in the title, are collapsing, like the three women, at the announcement of their fate. Further back in time the composition is a fusion of Raphael's cartoons *The Death of Ananias* and *The Blinding of Elymas,* with also the distinct possibility that such an arrangement was current stage practice. One cannot rule out either a contemporary allusion, since Henry V was about to set sail for France, and the artist is showing how one's country can be saved by closing the patriotic ranks and rooting out those that would destroy it.

This painting, because of its small dimensions, was obviously the one the artist made for the engraver. By comparing it with the engraving by R. Thew, one may see how well served the artist was by the print makers. Fuseli would see that he was, for engravers to him were craftsmen only, as may be gathered from his later opposition to them being admitted as members of the Academy.

This decade 1780–90 marks more than the threshold to his career as a painter; it was a whole ground plan of his future activities and the establishment of his reputation as a forceful inventor and pioneer of new frontiers.

This last decade of the century was mostly taken up by work for the Milton Gallery, but Fuseli had time enough for other themes. What is also clear is that he did not settle into a compositional rut, for both *Thor battering the Midgard Serpent* (1790) and the second version of *The Nightmare* (1790–91) show a renewed interest in Rubens; both the Titanias appear to be more svelte versions of the female nudes of the Flemish artist.

However, with these two paintings above, Fuseli adopts the full Baroque composition, almost for the first time, for in each he situates his figures in a series of advancing planes and fills out the forms with all the gusto of the Master. Perhaps a visit to the Banqueting Hall in Whitehall had stimulated him, for the Icelandic subject is close to Rubens's treatment of *Wisdom expelling War and Discord,* particularly since *Thor battering the Midgard Serpent* is allegorically equivalent. To the artist this was an important picture – his Diploma work for the Academy – so on analogy he may have felt he should do as well as Rubens had done for Charles I. The subject did not have to be researched, for he had reviewed for the *Analytical Review* (December 1788), Joseph Johnson's magazine, the *Edda Soemundar . . .* or the Elder Edda, which contains the story ('Hymiskvida' – Lay of Hymir) of Thor fishing for the serpent, Jormungard, the daughter spawned by Loki and the sister of Fenrir. This serpent, therefore, was not only a Northern Scylla but also the sister of the Miltonic

82

59, 71

82

1790 TO 1800

V

83

IV, 76

XI Fuseli. Garrick and Mrs Pritchard as Macbeth and Lady Macbeth. 1812

XII Fuseli. Chriemhild throws herself on the dead Siegfried

Sin. More directly than the scene from *Henry V*, it is a contem- 82
porary allegory of events in France, for Thor, crass, bestial but
courageous, was the hero of the Norse lower classes, as Odin
was of the aristocracy, so democratic Virtue overcomes the
strangling coils of hereditary Vice. Such a reading is indicated
by Carl Guttenburg's engraving of *William Tell* after Fuseli
and published in Paris in 1787. This later, but also mythical,
democratic Swiss hero was incorporated by David in his
drawing for *Triumph of the French People* (1793–94, Musée
Carnavalet, Paris).

Almost simultaneously with these political allegories, Fuseli
was wrestling with the problem of creating allegories of an even
more fundamental kind for Erasmus Darwin's *Botanic Garden*
(1791), a work which represents a radical change in the tradition
of poetic intention, as one may learn from Darwin's *Advertisement*: 'the general design . . . is to inlist (sic) Imagination under
the banner of Science; and to lead her votaries from the looser
analogies, which dress out the imagery of poetry, to the
stricter ones, which form the ratiocination of philosophy.'
There will be reason to examine three of these allegories in
another context, but the second version of *The Nightmare* is 83
markedly different from its predecessor not only in its com- I
position but in the extent to which it is influenced by
Rembrandt, for here the light emanates from the forms with
the intense illumination typical of that master. In terms of
sensation it is much more devastating than the earlier work.
The Baroque arrangement engages the spectator far more
effectively. Essentially it is a secularization of an Entombment
of Christ or an adaptation of Baroque ecstasy to Romantic
terror – a paralyzed rather than a swooning Saint Teresa.

There was running through Europe at this time a hysteria for
revelatory experience. In 1792 Joanna Southcott began to claim
prophetic gifts and supernatural powers. Lavater was a devotee
of Cagliostro and Mesmer, and late in life, searched for St John
whom he believed to be alive and well in Germany. The artist
Loutherbourg, also in his last years, became irrevocably
attracted to Mesmer's Animal Magnetism. Richard Cosway
was a dabbler in magic and the occult arts. Fuseli himself was
not immune. He was a contributor to the *Conjurer's Magazine*,
which commenced publication in 1791. How much he really
believed, it is impossible to say. One can hardly maintain,
confronted by his works, that he was totally uninvolved.

One of the few religious works that he painted, *The Appearance of Christ at Emmaus*, which hung formerly in the private 84
chapel of Lord North's house near Newmarket, demonstrates
that Fuseli, whether he formulated it or not, believed in some
sort of revelatory doctrine. Like Goethe, he may have thought
that one should believe, but not be concerned about what one
believed, other than in the existence of a Supreme Being. To
an orthodox Anglican like Farington, Fuseli appeared either
puzzling or shocking in his religious opinion.

*XIII Fuseli. Undine comes to the
Fisherman's Hut. 1821*

With its imagery of religious exhaustion, Fuseli's work is
close to John Brown's *Rest on the Flight* (c. 1775–80), particularly 85

in the figure of Joseph. Since this wash drawing was formerly in Lawrence's collection, it is possible that Fuseli may have owned it initially, as he may have had other drawings by Brown. Fuseli was certainly very sensitive on the subject, for Cunningham records Fuseli in a conversation bursting out with, 'Enough of Brown! Let us talk of Cipriani who is in hell!' Such an acerbic comment is a not untypical Fuseliesque ploy when discussion centred on those he considered his artistic peers.

In this painting, then, the artist chooses the revelatory 84 moment of the episode at Emmaus, with Christ disappearing and the two disciples left astonished or overcome. The handling of the disciples and their physique are reminiscent of Ludovico Carracci, as is also the placing of Christ. As for Christ himself, Fuseli made his views clear when asked by Lavater to provide him with a head of Christ for his physiognomical studies. The artist said that it was an impossible task and instead provided one based on a head by Verrocchio. Interest centres on the disciples and even with them one feels that the artist was averse to painting subjects from the Testament.

Purely as an exercise in compositional geometry the *Falstaff in the Buck basket*, exhibited the same year in the Academy, uses VI the same scissoring or jack-knifing of the acute triangle as *The Appearance of Christ at Emmaus*, this time to convey the most ignominious of all positions – a corpulent Hylas being drowned 68 by two nymphs in dirty washing! The idea for the composition may have come from Giulio Romano's fresco of Psyche and her Nurse tormenting Venus in the Sala del Psyche in the Palazzo del Tè, Mantua, which Fuseli had seen on his way to Switzerland, but otherwise it is quite original. By comparing it with Collyer's engraving after Mortimer of the same subject 86 (1781), one may see how Fuseli has translated that English comic rendering into a playfully sadistic and erotic event. Look, for instance, at the woman on the right and the use of the Rococo motif of the reflection in the mirror, shown in an orthodox version in Charles Ansell's work of the same period (*c.*1784–86), 87 like a vignette from *Naughty Nanette*, reflecting the impact on English society of French aristocratic themes. Coupled with this, however, is the possible reference to Ripa's illustration of *Lascivious Love*, for the feathers on the hat, arranged to look 88 like an alighting bird, may be a reference to one of the finches in the engraving.

It is rewarding in the work of this decade to examine the artist's interest in colour symbolism. In setting the painting of *The Shepherd's Dream* alongside this scene of Falstaff and *The* VII *Cave of Spleen* (1799), one may see how the general tonality VIII in each is adapted to suit the particular element concerned – a light, 'gaseous' tone for the fairy scene, naturalistic textured colours for the world of reality, and a clayey 'negative' tone for the underground world of the gnomes. Naturalistic local colours are also used in the studies of his wife which are numerous in this period, although one must distinguish between those in which she appears as Mrs Fuseli and those in which she acts as an emblem.

The emphasis on Woman during this decade was to a great extent generated by Mary Wollstonecraft, acting as the 'positive' pole to Mrs Fuseli's no less potent 'negative'. The artist was exploring the whole range of female experience and identity – as Eve, as Sin, as Knight-Errant (Britomart), as Titania or Queen, as Milton's Wife, as innocent, domineering, dominated, enslaved, bewitched and stark staring mad. In the titles of the Milton Gallery paintings Woman as Sin or Eve share the honours, so to speak, with Satan, but only in an earthly context. Satan falls or reigns in a cosmic territory.

It is in this territory that Fuseli makes a considerable contribution to pictorial invention. Views of the ether, described in the eighteenth century as 'commencing from the limits of our atmosphere and expanded through all the regions of space', were not unknown, but Fuseli gave them a new dimension. Until now the spectator at least was allowed to have his feet on the ground. In Fuseli's 'spacescapes', if one may christen them that, he too is suspended. Since so many of the Milton Gallery paintings are lost, recourse must be had to two compositions which post-date this decade, but repeat the nature of this invention: *The Fall of Satan* from Duroveray's edition   *90* of Milton (1802) and a late drawing, *Death and Sin bridging the 'Waste' of Chaos and met by Satan returning from Earth* (1819–21).   *91* Fuseli was not in fact wholly dependent on his imagination; on 29 June 1785, George Biggin and Mrs L. A. Sage had made a flight from St George's Fields to Harrow-on-the-Hill in Vincent Lunardi's balloon.* Mrs Sage in her published report the next day spoke of 'floating in the boundless regions of the air', and signed it, 'whether in heaven or earth, most affectionately yours'. Such eye-witness reports, multiplied in the following years, may have supplied the artist with the rationale for his invention. Even so, that he was so quick to utilize such an experience in a work of imagination is a mark of his progressive creative faculty. Thus the view of Satan falling away and down   *90* from St Michael conveys such a feeling of authenticity, that one is almost relieved to find oneself on the side of the angels.

In the drawing of *Death and Sin*, the spectator is once again suspended, but this time flying in echelon slightly below Satan, an effect no doubt much more convincing in the, untraced, original large painting, particularly if it was hung low on the wall. Furthermore, the light blue wash employed in this drawing characterizes that 'subtile, thin matter', ether. It seems certain that for *Sin and Death on the Bridge*, Fuseli devised a novel magnification of an artistic source, literally a 'blow-up' (in the photographic sense) of a detail from Piranesi's *Frontis-*   *92* *piece*.

The conviction that the Italian's minuscule figures on their enormous arch are the source is strengthened by the idea that it provides a sort of 'antithesis' to Fuseli's earlier 'thesis' of man being overwhelmed by antique monuments. Here in Chaos, Sin and Death, monstrous themselves, display their gargantuan power, by bridging that illimitable void. Thus, Man as spectator, dangled like a puppet on a string, is shown these demoniac,

*See Vincent Lunardi, *Account of the First Aerial Voyage in England*, London, 1785; also Rotha Mary Clay, *Ibbetson*, London 1948.

energetic forces of Destiny, exerting a will of a spiritual magnitude never dreamed of by any artist in Rome.

Only one other artist, Blake, conceived in this manner, but not even he thought to put the spectator into the same spatial ambience as these forces. One visual asset that Blake did not have, and probably never wished to have, was experience with the microscope. This Fuseli had and it is pertinent to quote what he had to say about it; 'After the discoveries of the microscope who can allow expression to a horse and refuse it to a beetle . . . man, formed for mediocrity, generally judges only from size: but size, whether immensely great or small, is a relative idea, and supposes somewhere an organ capable to judge of it.' As the microscope 'blew up' the insect world, the telescope 'blew up' the celestial. John Bonnycastle, mathematician and astronomer, was one of the closest of Fuseli's friends. In our century, science has quickly been recognized for its capacity to extend the 'verge' of 'legitimate invention'. This was no less true in the 1790s. Thus the painter's solution was to arrange for the spectator to view this or that 'world' from a seemingly relative position.

Very properly, not all the components of the Miltonic cycle were conceived cosmically. *Satan encountering Death, Sin intervening* (1793–96) proposes a frightening confrontation for *94* the spectator on a narrow spit running out into the black night of Chaos – a kind of violent paraphrase of Bernini's *Pluto and Proserpine* (Villa Borghese, Rome). Sin, as the lesser of two evils, strives to keep these colliding forces apart, like Proserpine straining from Hades to keep in touch with Earth. Apart from the scale, however, Fuseli follows the arrangement set by Hogarth's unfinished painting, *Satan, Sin and Death*,* as did also *96, 94* Barry whose painting of the same subject is approximately of the same date as the Fuseli. Neither of the two English artists come near to expressing the driving thrust of Fuseli's Sin, both preferring a somewhat old-fashioned static representation of the triad.

Since Fuseli's interpretation of Milton will be covered in more detail in a later chapter, the only other observation that need be made here is the difference between his and Barry's style. This may be centred on the two Satans, for they represent two different proportions and physiques. It might have been Mortimer, idealizing the Hogarthian English figure, who *18* started off a taste for this thick-set, stocky type, with its bulging thighs and calves. Certainly Barry gives it a more Michelangelesque treatment, but it remains recognizable as Tony Lumpkin – ennobled. In his published writings (1809), Barry, following an observation of Hogarth in *The Analysis of Beauty* (1753), remarked 'that the practice of boxing alone, in our countries, furnishes more frequent exhibitions of the naked and of the best kind, than any that are now to be met with in Italy'. The choice of English models, therefore, was deliberate, part of that aim to establish an English image, even for Satan!

Fuseli eschewed the pugilist, preferring the athlete – the lonely heroism of the long-distance runner to the matched

*See David Bindman, 'Hogarth's *Satan, Sin and Death* and its Influence', *The Burlington Magazine*, March 1970.

hearts of oak courage of the ring. His model for Satan is the *Apollo Belvedere*, and it is interesting to see that his heroic image has more in common with Francis Hayman's slim, damned Angel (1751) than with the sooty Fiend of Hogarth and Barry. Hayman and Fuseli are linked again in their respective *Satan, Adam and Eve* and *Satan's first address to Eve*.   96, X

Very characteristic of Fuseli's interpretation of the human body in action is the 'lift' he gives to the articulation even when the figure is nominally still, for instance in the drawing *Nude Figure of a Man* (1790–01) based on Veneziano's soldier dressing,   97, 98, 9 on the left of his engraving *Les Grimpeurs*. Barry's Satan is derived from the same model, but because the locomotor effects of the lifted heel are not carried up into the torso, the weight drops *down* instead of thrusting upwards. Fuseli grasps the nature of the elasticity of the man of action in repose, or at the arrested moment of an action, as he shows in *Britomart frees Amoret from Busirane* (1793).   102

The composition of this Spenserian subject is in marked contrast to that of *The Vision of the Lazar House* (1791–93)   101 and to that of the painting *Titania, Bottom and the Fairies* (1793–94)   99 for Woodmason's *Shakespeare*. Starting with the last, it is known that Fuseli was unhappy about the format adopted by Woodmason, and on comparing it with *The Awakening of*   76 *Titania* of the Boydell series, one can see why. In a way this unwanted discipline was to have an important effect on his later work. But at this stage, the narrow format required him to forgo the horizontal spread and to curtail the number of fairy attendants so that they had to be inserted around the principal subject like vignettes on the margins of a page. That they appear like this is due largely to the absence of the gradation of scale which he employed in the two earlier works and in *The*   IV, 76 *Shepherd's Dream* (1793). While in Rome he had commented   VII to Lavater, somewhat maliciously, on Chodowiecki's engravings, calling them *Vignetten-Statuetten* (statuesque vignettes), which in fact very aptly describes many of his own fairy figures. The insect man, below Titania, is a less horrific miniature of the   99 monster in Rosa's *Temptation of St Anthony* (Pitti, Florence) as though Fuseli had used a reducing glass: Theodore von Holst was also to blow up this figure in an etching.* The dancer to the   *Reproduced in Ruthven Todd (Bibliography). right, who might be a miniature of Mademoiselle Parisot, a celebrated dancer at the Opera that decade, owes her origin to the Greek vase painters. This demonstrates Fuseli's translation   100 of those red figures on black backgrounds on to canvas, projecting them with similar means.

The two drawings cited above show the artist deploying   101, 102 his action across the horizontal rectangle, as on a theatre stage. Fuseli required height, breadth and depth – room to move, as he had explained in an already quoted letter to Lavater. *The Vision of the Lazar House*, a drawing for a Milton Gallery painting, is dependent on the earlier work for Lavater, *The Escapee*, the right-hand group being pulled back to the centre,   43 the principal figure made recognizable as a manic Gladiator.   28 While it demonstrates the seriousness accorded, by this time, to mental disorders and attempts to distinguish them, the composition still echoes Hogarth's *Madhouse Scene* – the right-hand *20* triangular group of that work is repeated as is the placing of three figures around the maniac. Hogarth is also resorted to for the manic depressive seated on the right, but Fuseli's choice is not the obvious one, namely the staring man on the steps in the madhouse, but the depressed Highlander seated within the arch and knitting his fingers in the *Calais Gate* (Tate Gallery), which he had used before in *Twelfth Night* (1775–77). Since a *33* crazed woman flanks the drawing on the other side, one might be allowed to link these two, the most true-to-life, with Fuseli's much later remarks (2 April 1804) to Farington, that according to a medical friend the largest number of inmates at Bedlam were women in love and the second largest were hackney or stage coachmen, for the reason that the continual shaking they got affected the pineal gland (Descartes' theory)! It may well be that a number of Scots were employed in this trade, although one might prefer to think that Fuseli was pulling the leg of his humourless friend. But indeed, it was not such an odd notion in a period of odd ideas.

The composition of *Britomart frees Amoret from Busirane* (from *The Faerie Queene*, III, xii, 30–32) appears empty compared to *102* *The Escapee*, but the intention is of a different order. First it should be compared to the earlier painting (1783) *Percival frees Belisane from the Spell of Urma*, where Fuseli comes closest to cre- *III* ating the ambience of the Gothic novel. In the Spenserian version of this theme, however, the participants are separate and none is occluded by another. On the analogy with David's practice in *The Oath of the Horatii*, the drawing can be read as a contemporary allegory. In 1792 England had declared war against France, which proclaimed itself a Republic shortly after, and in January 1793, Louis XVI was executed. It is possible then that Britomart or the Britonesse, as Spenser also called her, is Britannia preparing to free Amoret or France from Busirane or the evil powers of the Revolutionary Tribunal. It is the first subject from Spenser Fuseli had done since 1769, so there is reason to believe that he turned to *The Faerie Queene* particularly to find a suitable allegory.

Admittedly the hypothesis that *Thor battering the Midgard* *V* *Serpent* (1790) and the Britomart drawing are contemporary allegories is largely a matter of inference. But their dates coincide conveniently with events, and the points made in them with the feelings of those of Fuseli's persuasion, particularly the Enlightenment generation. Edmund Burke, for instance, in his *Reflections on the Revolution in France* (1790) was all for the reform of the *ancien régime*, but not at all for its destruction. In addition the English had a regicide on their conscience, and would have preferred to see 1688 repeated rather than 1649. There is no doubt, moreover, of Fuseli's association with the radicals of Joseph Johnson's circle. Thomas Paine, warned by Blake in 1792, escaped to France; Thomas Holcroft followed during this decade; Mary Wollstonecraft also went to France in 1792; Thomas Banks, the sculptor, was arrested for sedition, but the case was dismissed; Horne Tooke was fined and imprisoned for sedition and even tried for high treason but acquitted. Last but not least, Johnson was fined and imprisoned for nine months for publishing a seditious pamphlet by Gilbert Wakefield, in 1797. One wonders who there was left to dine, but not at all that Fuseli kept his mouth shut. Apart from the fact that expatriates like to choose their own time for repatriation, the artist was genuinely of Burke's opinion, but was infinitely cautious, preferring to wrap even his conversation in allegory, as Hazlitt observed, than to be compromised by a brush with the magistrates. In the long run, however, the most effective restraint on his personal involvement was his own brand of misanthropic disdain for the age he lived in.

To return to the artistic source of the Britomart drawing: Andrea del Sarto's *Decapitation of St John* has already been mentioned and it is thus not improbable that Fuseli should also employ another of that artist's works, *The Naming of St John the Baptist* (Chiostro dello Scalzo, Florence). Furthermore, it was engraved by Domenico Cunego for Gavin Hamilton's *Schola Italica Picturae* (1773), an important source book for artists of that generation. The omission of the old woman on the left gives the compositional layout of the drawing, except that Fuseli has reduced the spatial distances and the recession on the left. Significant also is Andrea's simple but dramatic enactment of the event; the infant had just been called John by his mother Elizabeth, puzzling her relatives since there was no John in the family. She then turns to Zacharias, the father, struck dumb by the angel Gabriel, who writes in his book, 'His name is John'. The oracular nature of this revelation would have appealed strongly to the artist.

With Hamilton's book of engravings in mind, it is relevant to examine the figure of Busyrane, for he represents the archetypal character found in Oedipus and Lear, both powerful umpires of doom and destiny. The most primitive example of this archetype was Moses and it might be sufficient to relate Fuseli's figures to Michelangelo's sculpture. But that work lacks the electrifying spasm with which Fuseli endows this type, and it is more likely that Parmigianino's *Moses* (Madonna della Steccata, Parma) was the source of inspiration. The features of Busyrane, however, are virtually identical to those the artist gave to Autolycus in a drawing of 1765–69, in which that arch thief named his godson, Odysseus. On analogy Busyrane is also crafty and as an enchanter, a thief of man's mind. In the Parmigianino, one may notice that Moses' hair is blown in the manner approved for all such seers in English painting, although not quite in the windblown way that Rosa drew. Also significant are the treble darts of fire issuing from the head, for Fuseli has one of these arc-ing from the upflung hand of Death in *Sin intervening*. Lastly, there was academic sanction for this choice of source, for Reynolds in his fifteenth discourse observed,

'that our great Lyric Poet (Thomas Gray), when he conceived his sublime idea of the indignant Welsh Bard, acknowledged . . . he had warmed his imagination with the remembrance of this noble figure of Parmegiano.'

102
105
73, 240
104
94

Fuseli was similarly warmed when he came to do his own Bard from Gray.

The discussion of this decade's art may be concluded with *The Cave of Spleen* (1799) exhibited at the Royal Academy, *VIII* while another version appeared in Duroveray's edition of Pope's works (1798). As explained earlier, the last decade of the century had been very hard for Fuseli in a number of ways, but particularly in earning a living. It was not just his work on the Milton paintings but the reluctance of publishers to employ him that kept him poor. For he had to compete with a large band of illustrators most of whom would cater to the public taste, which he would never do. Stothard, Smirke, Singleton, Corbould, Westall and William Hamilton were some of these, and even Northcote and Opie did most of the work for Woodmason's *Shakespeare*. Apart from Johnson, therefore, it was only the singular publisher who would commission him. The letter that follows not only indicates the co-operation that existed between them but provides a useful introduction to *The Cave of Spleen*:

Queen Ann Street 20 July 1798
'Mr Fuseli presents his Comp. & thanks to Mr Du Roveray for the communication of the enclosed preface, written with equal propriety and ease, and to which in his opinion little can be added or excepted against unless perhaps in the quotation from Dr Johnson, the insertion of his shallow remark on the admission of allegorical actors; Spleen & her attendants bring nothing else.'

Indeed, with the evidence of the *L'Allegro* drawing, Spleen and *74* her companions are nothing else but 'allegorical actors'. That earlier drawing and this painting really form a pair, instructive of that inconstancy of mood and behaviour common to both the fairy and the human world. But in the painting the artist goes much further than he had in the drawing, inventive as that was, for surely in the painting, the yellowish brown tone reflects not only the grotto, but also Pope's couplet (*Essay on Criticism*):

All seems infected that th'infected spy,
As all looks yellow to the jaundiced eye.

The artist's own mood was little short of morbid at this time; in choosing the gloomiest part of *The Rape of the Lock* (IV. 16–88), he was expressing his own condition, but rather more importantly that of Europe too, as he saw it. To explain this, one must quote from his lecture on *Invention*, which he wrote only a year or so later. Dealing with Greek myths he draws parallels between 'Scylla and our Portress of Hell' and 'their naiads, nymphs and oreads and our sylphs, gnomes and fairies – ... differ less in essence than in local temporary social modifications', and towards the end of the passage, he remarks on Pindar's praise for Homer for the way 'he contrived to connect his imaginary creation with the realities of nature and human passions'. In essence, therefore, *The Cave of Spleen* is the Northern translation of Pandora's Box. Whether Pope intended the connection is not clear in the text. Spleen's 'Wondrous bag' is likened only to that in which Ulysses held the winds, but she is afflicted by Pain and Megrim and attended by Ill Nature,

Affection and Umbriel 'a dusky, melancholy sprite'. Hope or joy seems absent, until the two insects are noticed 'In lovely copulation, bliss on bliss' as Blake wrote in another context. In yet another one may note the two Loves together in Correggio's *Danaë*.

Over a hundred years later Worringer* was to observe that a hostile environment induces a tendency towards abstraction. In 1798 that tendency was to allegory by way of association.

75
*Worringer, Wilhelm, *Abstraktion und Einfühlung*, 1907.

In 1799 Fuseli had been appointed Professor of Painting, which afforded him a stipend and, as importantly, a rank of authority, so that this first decade of the new century brought new hope of security and recognition. This mood of optimism is reflected in the variety and volume of his production, after a second bitter pill of disappointment had been swallowed at the failure of his second Milton Gallery exhibition in 1800. But his achievement was recognized by artists and connoisseurs, not only for his invention but what must have been the magnitude and frightening atmosphere of this apocalyptic confrontation for those who could understand its implications. Such a confrontation was not 'well suited' to 'the debauched taste of the better Vulgar', to borrow from a Warburton note to *The Rape of the Lock*, and Charles Lamb,[†] thirty years later, writing of that arch-commonplacer of Fuseli, John Martin, aptly drew the right parallel between the latter's *Belshazzar's Feast* and a surprise display arranged by the Prince Regent at the Brighton Pavilion – a glittering transparency – BRIGHTON – EARTHQUAKE – SWALLOW-UP-ALIVE! – which threw the assembled guests into fits. In 1800 such popular surprises were more heroic but no less sensational – Fuseli wrote to Roscoe (18 June 1800) of the competition offered by Robert Ker Porter's *Storming and Capture of Seringapatam*.

Thus the modern allegorical content of *Satan's first address to Eve* was lost to all but the few. The painting, while it represents fairly exactly the original Milton Gallery work, was made for the engraver, W. Tomkins, for Sharpe's *The Works of the British Poets* (1805–08 and 1822). Since the painting was in Duroveray's collection, he had possibly commissioned it, but did not use it, for his edition of Milton (1802). This provenance and history indicate the heartbreak Fuseli must have experienced watching his original 7 × 10 feet painting being miniaturized eventually to a 3 × 2 inch engraving. The small painting does give some evidence of the artist's handling of oil paint at this period. He is best, for instance, in the Satan and the rose bush, which are both handled with an almost French feeling for the medium. Eve on the other hand, particularly her raised arm, demonstrates that drawing with the brush referred to earlier, and the artist's difficulty in determining flesh tones. It is the painting, not the drawing, that is deficient here, as a reference to *Ixion and Nephele* will confirm. The almost monochrome colour of the Satan derives from the artist's use of wash, and one may notice that, perhaps as a

1800 TO 1810

†See 'Barrenness of the Imaginative Faculty in the Productions of Modern Art', *Last Essays of Elia*, London, 1824–33.

X

105

solution to the painting of drapery, he adopts blacks and greys to a great extent.

The drawings selected to represent this decade exhibit two 'manners', the incisive pen technique and the fluid pencil and wash or watercolour combination; *Woman on a Sofa* and *Siegfried and Chriemhild* provide an example of each. The first demonstrates the *immediate* expression, the second the *resolved* expression, adequate evidence in itself that Fuseli, like Mortimer, 'found that the mechanical labour' of translating such a work into oil 'crept, like the nightmare, over his performance.' 188, 52

Since the visit to Paris occurred in 1802, the example of Baron Gros may be cited, for his drawings and oils evince the same states of expression, representing the transitional stage towards the Romantic adoption of the immediate as the final, resolved statement. Paris meant a great deal more for Fuseli than seeing Napoleon's cultural loot from Italy, for he was also able to meet the artists and examine the works which stood closer to his in the figurative tradition than any to be found in England. He may have noted, with some irony, that autocracy was a better champion of 'high principles' than democracy, but even if not, the artistic atmosphere would have been reassuring in the clear ascendancy and primacy of the history painters over that 'secondary' breed the topographers of land or face.

That he met David again is made clear by his remark to Knowles, 'that he could never divest his mind of the atrocities of the French Revolution, nor separate them from the part which he (David) had then acted, for they were stamped upon his countenance', (or words to that effect, for Knowles played a Bowdlerizing Boswell to Fuseli's Johnson, the unctuousness of the language being foreign to the artist). However, within this comment there is the implied criticism of David's betrayal of artistic integrity by his political activity. Nevertheless the latter's *The Sabine Women* (1799, Louvre), with Hersilia separating the protagonists, gave the same dominating role to woman that Fuseli was himself extending in a much greater variety of contexts. David's exclusive adherence to Roman history indicates, too, the effects of an autocracy which dictated the permissible limits of invention, although with the coming of Napoleon, these limits were being lifted. To Fuseli, the cult of Ossian, sanctified by Napoleon carrying a copy (in the Italian translation) in his campaign breast pocket, must have seemed quaintly old-fashioned, even though it offered the alternative of a Northern myth. Perhaps because of this paucity of themes most of the English artists returned rejoicing, their painterly inferiority complex eased by finding that the great Davidian productions were nothing but 'painted statues'.

An artist with whom Fuseli would have felt in tune was Girodet, who then was enjoying enormous esteem – *The Shades of French Heroes received by Ossian and his Warriors* was exhibited in the Salon of 1802. In 1799 Girodet painted the *New Danaë*, featuring Mademoiselle Lange as the goddess (Institute of Art, Minneapolis), in which her much cuckolded

52 Fuseli. Siegfried and Chriemhild. 1807

husband, M. Simons, appeared as a turkey cock, in revenge for her demand to withdraw from the Salon the portrait she had commissioned but had not paid for. In another vein, Girodet* composed a long poem in praise of Lavater, whose physiognomic studies he made much use of in his *Hippocrates refusing the gifts of Artaxerxes* (1792). There was, therefore, much in common between the two artists, so that it is surely more than coincidence that Fuseli's *Venus and Ulysses* (1803) is remarkably close to Girodet's *Birth of Venus* (1803, Private collection) and the latter's *Virgil holding the fainting Dante* (1805, Musée Fabre, Montpellier) is identical to the gemstone group which Fuseli employed again in his *Celadon and Amelia* (Thomson's *Seasons*) of 1801. Due notice, of course, must be taken of the fact that all the Roman-trained artists drew from the same reservoir of sources, but the proximity of these works in date indicates a closer liaison.

The visit to France and the great exhibition of works from Italy was not only generally refreshing to Fuseli's spirit, but essential to his literary occupation at that time – his edition of Pilkington's *Dictionary of Painters*. The classical sculptures, also, gave him food for thought vis-à-vis his conception of abstracted imagery and form, in the sense of a reduction of the parts and a simplification of the formal expression.

There is no need to enlarge on the general tendency in the 1790s to adopt simplified form. The outlines of Flaxman's engraved series are an instance, although it should be stressed that his drawings for them are not in single but often in treble outline and that his curves are constructed of straight lines. They are, in fact, 'relief' drawings as one might expect from a sculptor. And it was to sculpture that Fuseli turned for help in establishing a system of simplified formal planes. He shared the current enthusiasm for Egyptian art – there was obviously a great deal in Paris, and it is likely that he met Visconti there, the scholar responsible for the catalogue of the Museo-Clementina (Vatican Museum), a collection familiar to the artist for its Egyptian works. Another kind of 'sculptural' aid was German wood and copper engravings. These had long been familiar to Fuseli, but his interest was re-awakened at this period, partly by his own seeking and partly by the considerable English admiration for German literature and art in the 1790s. Coleridge and Wordsworth, for instance, met Klopstock on their visit to Germany in 1798–99. Blake provided the designs for a translation of Bürger's *Lenore* by J. T. Stanley (1796), one for the frontispiece being clearly influenced by Chodowiecki's engraving; in addition to translations of Schiller and Goethe, there also appeared in 1798 William Sotheby's translation of Wieland's *Oberon,* the second edition of which Fuseli was to illustrate in 1805. However on the pictorial side the fillip was given by W. Y. Ottley, an enthusiastic and erudite collector of prints, who published in 1816 *An Inquiry into the Origin and Early History of Engraving* (2 vols.), with a frontispiece of Dürer's seated *Man of Sorrows*. Blake's devotion to that master goes without saying.

*See George Levitine, 'The Influence of Lavater and Girodet's *Expression des Sentiments de L'Ame', The Art Bulletin,* 36, 1954.

106

107

108

80

There is no way of knowing how long Fuseli had harboured his own German engravings, nor whether he had encouraged Roscoe in that direction when he was putting together his own collection of prints, but it would seem that the origin of Fuseli's Horace engraving *Unde Unde extricat* (1795) goes back to a *109* small engraving by Altdorfer, *The Carpenter* (B.55), who sits cross-legged with a plank across his knees, via his own tailpiece *114* of a man in a similar pose reading a large book in Lavater's *Essays on Physiognomy*. The Horace engraving consists of such a minimum of planes that it looks as though it had been cut by chisel from a pyramid – the hieratic formal association sought by the artist for this eternal scribe. Horace's money lender, no less, and the inscription in full – 'It is difficult to procure, from wherever, interest or money' – was a reminder of the artist's everpresent financial straits!

In the first decade of the new century, this German interest is very much present – on the literary side in the illustrations to Wieland's *Oberon*, and in art, in the charming drawing of a *186, 111, 112* woman, once in Lawrence's collection, which is immediately reminiscent, in the style and the model, of Holbein's graphic work. In the drawing *Parental Care* (c. 1805) the source is an *216* engraving by Conrad Meyer, an influence in his youthful days: in *Hephaestus, Bia and Crato securing Prometheus* (c. 1810), the *113* splayed out hero is a typical German sixteenth-century motif, like *The Bewitched Groom* by Baldung Grün or – more relevantly *114* to the subject – an Altdorfer engraving *Jael and Sisera*, in which the victim lies flat on his back, foreshortened, and of which in his editions of Pilkington, Fuseli observed that it showed 'a sensibility of mind and a boldness of design'.

The effects of his study of German or Swiss graphic styles comes out in the Rivington *Shakespeare*, one of the best examples being the *Lear and Cordelia*, in which Lear's cloak *117* bends and breaks behind him in a woodcut manner, the grain not allowing any greater fluidity of line. Further the very deliberate gradations and economy of tone reminds one in general of Northern graphic art rather than Italian.

One major German cycle has not been mentioned as yet, *The Nibelungenlied*, in which, paradoxically, there is hardly *115, 116* a trace of German art. But Fuseli was never a *pasticheur*. For such heroic themes only classic sources would do.

These sources can be examined conveniently in some of the designs for the Rivington *Shakespeare*, for it was in these that the imposition of a narrow, vertical, rectangular format was combined with the artist's conception of an abstracted imagery. It was natural that he should try and do for Shakespeare within this compass what he had done for Milton in large. The problem was a different one, however, for he had to supply images for separate plays – there was no overall theme as in Milton. His solution was emblematic in nature, to try and fix for each play a simplified summation of its theme or the pivotal human attribute on which it rested. Opinion may differ as to the success of each emblem, but there can be no doubt of the felicity of the artist's invention.

The source of the *Lear and Cordelia* reveals itself as a combina- 117
tion of the so-called *Ludovisi Group*, in which a Gaul stabs
himself after killing his wife, and *Menelaus and Patroclus*, in 60
themselves a fusion of Northern and Greek tragic, heroic
figures. One may note also the ingenuity with which the curving
plumes of Menelaus's helmet have been extended into the angled
folds of Lear's cloak. This group, in terms of source, is related
to *Othello and Desdemona* and *Diomedes and Cressida* for the 118, 120
former is based on the *Satyr and Nymph* and the latter (Cressida) 119
on the *Dancing Maenad*. Fuseli had copied the Satyr group 122
(British Museum) when he was in Rome and a more exact
borrowing of the Maenad appears in *The Daughter of Herodias
with the Head of St John* (c.1791) which was engraved for the 121
English edition of Lavater.

Moving forward in time, *Pericles* is given the pose of Michel- 123
angelo's *Aminadab*, but with a conscious stressing of the 124
symmetry of the figure reminiscent of Egyptian royal sculpture.
The scene from *The Taming of the Shrew* is a paraphrase, a trifle 125
blasphemous perhaps, of Raphael's *The Freeing of St Peter*,
from which also the captain of the guard on the left is re-cast
as the Ghost in *Hamlet*. Then *Queen Katherine's Dream* is a mix- 130, 127
ture of figures from Andrea del Sarto's *Naming of St John* and 103
Ludovico Carracci's *St Benedict exorcising the demon from the* 128
kitchen, in which the demon's legs are shown, top left. Fuseli
owned engravings of these frescoes in S. Michele in Bosco,
Bologna. Perhaps he had recently acquired them for one of the
nymphs 'moulded by the hand, inspired by the breath of love',
as he described them in Pilkington's dictionary, appears as the
Girl on a sofa looking out of a window (1803). 195

To close this catalogue of sources, Houdon's *Écorché* reappears 50
as Caesar's Ghost in the scene from *Julius Caesar*. The old- 220
fashioned view that this is eclecticism run riot is unjustified
because of the aptness of Fuseli's sources. Nor was his use of
them a matter of calculation. There were other reasons such as
the preparation of his lectures, the work on the Pilkington
edition, and also an aborted project of writing a guide to the
Louvre; all would have brought this material floating to the
top of his imagination, which, in any case, was bent on establishing a monumental, canonical cycle to Shakespeare.

The free pencil sketch of *A man in bed* was probably a 133
rejected idea for the Rivington *Death of Falstaff*, rather than 132
for the *Death of Beaufort* in the same series; it supports contem- 131
porary comment on the ease and accuracy with which the
artist could sketch a figure, and demonstrates the economy with
which he could suggest the body under the bedclothes. It is
interesting to note in this respect that Constable, in his last
lecture in 1836, used an outline of the principal figure from
The Vision of the Lazar House, to demonstrate that 'the swellings 101
and depressions in the outline of a figure . . . never occur exactly
on the opposite sides'. For Fuseli the differentiation in the drawing of his figures is not so much that which lies between nature
and the ideal, since he often combined both, but that which lies
between ordinary man and exceptional hero. For the latter

there is *Roland at Roncesvalles* (*Fame*), a much more lithe and *134* graceful figure than Runciman's *Perseus*, or even their common *62* source, Guercino's *Fame* (Villa Ludovisi). That Roland is a 'stand-in' for Napoleon is very possible, since Fuseli, a hero worshipper, could hardly withhold admiration for that 'little corporal'. His opinion, given to Farington (1804) that 'Napoleon had courage but not comprehension – did not know how to estimate things', is so flat that it might be a smoke-screen, wise enough in the presence of Gossip itself.

A hero of another type is Count Albert in *The Fire King* *IX* (*c*.1801–04) from Walter Scott's poem of that title (Lewis, *Tales of Wonder*, 1801), for the author had explained in an introduction that his hero was based on a Knight-Templar, Saint-Alban who had deserted to the Saracens. In the poem Count Albert is spellbound by Zulema and renounces his true-love Rosalie, whom he later mistakenly kills, since she is dressed as a page. The Fire King is Paganism to whom Albert must submit to gain Zulema's hand. It is not hard to see why Fuseli should choose this theme, although he has added what must be the equivalent of *The Fatal Sisters* (Gray), a painting he exhibited in 1800. The mise-en-scène with the spiral steps echoes the atmosphere of Piranesi's *Carceri* series, and it could not have been many years after that Coleridge told de Quincey* about these engravings, describing them as Piranesi's *Dreams*, 'which record the scenery of his own visions during the delirium of fever'. While Fuseli probably knew that they were not, he seems to have borrowed from Plate III the stairs and from Plate X, the straining figures. The general greenish tone of this painting, which he adopted for a number of others in this decade, is symbolic, like the yellow brown of *The Cave of Spleen*, and Albert is dressed in yellow and red, the two colours admired by Goethe for their symbolic energy. However, this green tone was not admired by Leigh Hunt, who described it as 'livid', 'like brass diseased'. Fuseli, when asked about it, thought it was a 'pretty' colour, merely perhaps to confuse the questioner still further!

Another contemporary objection was to the skin-tight garment, a kind of attenuated leotard, which Count Albert and Achilles wear, a *cache-sexe* device employed by Fuseli in *248* his paintings only as a sop to convention. On the other side of the Channel, David was more adept, with sword or shield, in preventing embarrassment to the 'better Vulgar'.

Returning now to the question of influence, one finds in this decade the impact of the Venetian School as never before. Before citing specific examples it is useful to gather up some of Fuseli's remarks on artists of that school and its principal quality – colour. From Aphorism 176 comes *The Principle of Synaesthesia, Colour affects or delights like sound,* which confirms that the artist was familiar with the theories put forward by the Abbé DuBos in his *Réflexions* . . . (1719) and familiar through the work of Poussin. Fuseli was then able in his eighth lecture in 1810 to remark that Titian's eye was as musical as his ear, that his tints were 'deep toned' and the pinks, greys and light

*Thomas de Quincey, *Confessions of an English Opium Eater*, London 1823.

greens 'soothe, charm and melt like a sweet melody'. Finally, after his visit to the Louvre in 1802, the numerous paintings of Veronese seduced him to write 'the whole is a scale of music'.

Eros and Psyche (1808) shows a clear connection with Titian's *Venus and Cupid* (Uffizi, Florence), even though Fuseli has written in Greek on his drawing – 'This is indeed my Eros, not Titian's'. Of great ingenuity is the adaptation of Veronese's *St John the Baptist Preaching* (Villa Borghese, Rome) to *Hamlet, Horatio and the Gravedigger* (1804). The kneeling woman is replaced by the gravedigger, Hamlet's hand gesture is the same as St John's, and the distant cross on the left replaces Christ in the Veronese.

135

138
139

This induction of what could be called 'art historicism' into the conceiving of a composition was not only prompted by the artist's need for the sanction of the past, but also, as Haydon recorded in 1805, by his desire to 'interest, astonish or move'; and, let it be added, to break the scent for nosy plagiarists. Cunningham reports his reaction to the news that Lawrence was to exhibit a *Prospero and Miranda*, 'This comes of my blasted simplicity in showing my sketches'. About the same time there is an annotation opposite the catalogue entry of the Britomart and Amoret subject (R.A. 1793. [177]), 'We learn by private Anec[dote] on the party buz that presently in [a] corner of Somerset Place that the enchanting Amoret was exhibited to detec[t] [a] plagiarism'. Apart from some of the leading lights amongst his colleagues, Fuseli had buzzing about him a number of 'twangling' instrumentalists, like Shelley, the elder Haughton, E. F. Burney, etc., who played out their minor variations on his major scores. Fuseli, as *he* admitted about Blake, 'was . . . d---d good to steal from'.

The last time that Blake engraved for Fuseli was for the Rivington *Shakespeare* (*Queen Katherine's Dream* and a scene from *Romeo and Juliet*), and the last literary occasion of their connection was Fuseli's preface to Blake's edition of Blair's *The Grave* (1808), from which the following may be quoted: 'The technic part, and the execution of the artist, . . . claim approbation, sometimes excite our wonder, and not seldom our fears, when we see him play on the very verge of legitimate invention; but wildness so picturesque in itself, so often redeemed by taste, simplicity and elegance, what child of fancy, what artist would wish to discharge?' Fuseli was no exception, for in the following drawings there are indications, from slight to extensive, of his 'borrowings' from Blake, the inverted commas being necessary, for it is of conception rather than of form that the loan is taken. The three drawings are, *The great Father and Ancient Night* (c.1810), *The Nightmare* (c.1810) and *Hephaestus, Bia and Crato securing Prometheus* (c.1810), of which the first and the third reveal that kind of centralization peculiar to Blake – for instance (in the third drawing) the vertical lining up of the hammer, the stake and the genitalia along with the symmetrical balance of the two sets of legs. The same applies to the first, which also has some connection to Blake's *And he was given power over men* (1800–05, National Gallery, Washing-

127

156, 137
113

119

ton), while *The Nightmare* may be compared to Blake's *Death of the Strong Wicked Man* (Blair's *The Grave*), for both have a similar setting, a similar disposal of limbs and similar forces of evil leaving through the window. It seems that Fuseli 'steals' from Blake only in this way, apart from what he learnt in the use of watercolour and wash. This Blakean influence, of course, coincides with Fuseli's own interests in simplifying and abstracting, and it is a fact that *The Fertilization of Egypt* (1792), shows an interest in centralization which echoes Blake's without copying it.

To sum up the work of this decade, one may point first to the artist's astonishing variety, consistent with the earlier decades, and second, to the fact that the themes here offer an interpretation of the human condition on different levels, having their own logical relationship. In evolutionary rather than chronological order, the artist presents the creation of the world (*The great Father and Ancient Night*) and the Promethean myth; the social moralities implicit in the series from Cowper; the tragi-comedy and comical tragedy of Shakespeare's 'All the world's a stage and all the men and women merely players'; the delights and pangs of romantic love sheltered from the realities of life of Wieland's *Oberon*; the doomed hero and the *femme fatale* in the *Nibelungenlied*; finally, the Grave, Death and the Spirit in the scene from Hamlet and *Achilles grasping at the shade of Patroclus*.

136

140, 141

156, 113
142, 212

186
116
137, 248

In the last fifteen years of his life, Fuseli turned retrospective, working again at subjects which he had treated earlier, but at no stage losing sight of Life itself. Nothing illustrates this better than the quotation, obviously selected by him as Keeper, that appeared on the cover of the 1812 catalogue of the Academy exhibition:

1810 TO 1825

> Nature is made better by no mean,
> But Nature makes that mean: So o'er that Art,
> Which . . . adds to Nature, is an Art
> That Nature makes . . .
> the Art itself is Nature.
>
> (*A Winter's Tale* IV. 3)

What is surely apparent in all his work is the closeness of analogy between the subject matter he selects and the state of his own or society's condition. He would have agreed with Dugald Stewart* writing in 1814 on *The Pleasure Derived from Analogy*, that it is 'partly, from the mysterious wonder it excites, and partly from the convenient generalization of knowledge it affords . . . the faculty of imagination giving to these illusions a momentary ascendant over the sober conclusions of experience'. In no way, therefore, can these excursions into poetic and romantic literature be considered as escapes, for they are, in fact, the super-realities of an imagination nurtured by sober experience.

The Ladies of Hastings (after 1813?), for instance, is a significant painting, for it can be interpreted as a personal allegory. Part of an inscription on the frame reads *Vision at Margate . . .* , which

143

*Dugald Stewart, *Elements of the Philosophy of the Human Mind*, Pt II, Edinburgh, 1814.

will allow the reclining figure to be identified as the artist, since he is posed as he was in *The Artist in conversation with Bodmer,* except that here his head is turned away. He is to be identified not as some gardener with his spade beside him – difficult to see in the painting although clear in the drawing (Kunsthalle Basel) – but as a treasure seeker (*Schatzgraber*). A German tradition applied the name treasure seeker to the artist. Dürer's godfather, Anton Koberger, called his book of wood-cuts *Schatzbehälter* (Treasure chest). Inevitably Fuseli gave this a more extensive connotation, linking such a digger with the gnome, for instance, who offers gems to the goddess in *Flora attired by the Elements** (Darwin, *Botanic Garden* 1791) and by analogy to Proteus, who, Bacon said, 'resides in a cave under the vast concavity of the heavens' and denotes matter, since he was Neptune's herdsman tending the monsters of the sea. In addition he was also a seer, but difficult to approach, refusing to answer and disappearing in a variety of disguises unless he was shackled – a reasonable description of the creative artist. It is part of Fuseli's consistency that he gives the same elemental character to *The Lost Shepherd*[†] (1801) (Thomson, *Seasons, Winter* 277– 321), whose cloak is to become his winding sheet, for in life or death he is 'of the earth, earthy', the treasurer of his flock. Finally, there is *Timon of Athens*[‡] (1805), the most indifferent *Schatzgraber* of all, for he digs up gold only to throw it away. This misanthropic prodigality comes close to the picture Fuseli had of himself as a serious artist throwing away his art to a fashionable and fickle public. Thus the vision in *The Ladies of Hastings* is a Protean materialization, whose meaning becomes clearer by reference to Ludovico Carracci's *Nymphs tempting St Benedict in the Garden*; with the bank grown too high to climb, the nymphs become unattainable, and are soon out of sight, urged on by youth. The reality of this vision is attested by the rest of the inscription on the frame, *S.N.* (Susan North – sixteen or seventeen years old at the time) *opposite window on landing – end of study nr Billiard Room door.*

The same vision is embodied again in *Dante in Hell discovers Paolo and Francesca* (*c.*1818), the aquatint after his painting of that year. Here the lovers whirl past Virgil, while Dante, after hearing their story, 'falls, like a dead man, in a swoon'. It is not impossible that Fuseli saw this scene as an allegory of himself in old age contemplating the fading dreams of his distant youth.

Old age and youth are compared again in *Undine displeased leaves the Hut* (1822): the impotence of the old fisherman, clamped in by the table, contrasts with the virile elasticity of Huldbrand, who leaps up to follow Undine.

To understand the Dante aquatint we should glance back to the previous decade, when Fuseli exhibited *Count Ugolino and his Sons* (1806), a subject he had first treated in 1774–78 in a drawing. Here the group was set at a diagonal but the pose was the same. One presumes that it had been made in response to Reynolds' *Ugolino* (1773). In 1806 the immediate reaction was to compare the two works, and Fuseli's was lambasted in

53 Fuseli. *Dante in Hell discovers Paolo and Francesca. 1818*

**173, †144, ‡171*

145

53

146

147

148

Bell's Weekly Messenger (25 May), whereupon Blake wrote to the editor, saying that he was indignant over this criticism, and with the Reynolds work in mind explained that 'Count Ugolino is the father of sons of feeling and dignity, who would not sit looking in their father's face in the moment of his agony, but would rather retire and die in secret, while they suffer him to indulge his passionate and innocent grief, his innocent and venerable madness and insanity and fury.' Reynolds's Count Ugolino is obviously taken from Michelangelo's *Aminadab*, 124 but surely to support the expression of 'madness and insanity', Hogarth's manic depressive in *The Madhouse Scene* has to be 20 interpolated. Cunningham goes too far in describing Reynolds's Ugolino as 'a famished mendicant', but when Fuseli turned to Michelangelo's *Moses* for *his* Count, he was thinking of a noble man of action in forced repose. While it is probable that the *Pietà* in St Peter's served as a source for the dead son, there may be an influence from the *Pietà* by Ercole di Roberti (then attributed to Pollaiuolo), which Roscoe perhaps already owned when Fuseli visited Liverpool in 1804. There is a parallel also between the dead son's hand and the helmet and the Dosso Dossi *Portrait of a Man with a Helmet*, also in Roscoe's collection. Another interesting connection is with David's *Death of Socrates*, which Fuseli would certainly have known, either through the Martini engraving or by seeing the original in Paris in 1802, for the son on the left is posed similarly to the figure (Apollodorus not Plato in this writer's opinion) seated at the end of the bed, and both are based on the Phlegmatic in Chodowiecki's engraving of the four Temperaments for Lavater's work.

The merging of Michelangelo and Dante is carried further in the drawing *Virgil, Dante and Geryon* (1811); Geryon has 154 the *terribilità* visage of a beardless *Moses*, very correctly, 'His face was a just man's', said Dante of this 'image of Fraud'. The curving walls of the block-built cliff enclose the group in the same way that the walls of the Colosseum surround Michelangelo in the engraving made by Blake after a Fuseli drawing 155 for the first edition of the latter's *Lectures on Painting* (1801). Michelangelo bears the same intense look and appears almost to dominate the Colosseum, figuratively denying Fuseli's inscription, *Ancora imparo* (I am still learning). This is a new and romantic interpretation of the great artist standing in the Colosseum by moonlight, an experience no tourist to Rome could deny himself. Goethe, for instance, writes of April 1788: 'My farewell to Rome was heralded in a particularly solemn manner: for three consecutive nights a full moon stood in a cloudless sky . . . one evening I went out quite alone. . . . But when I approached the grand ruins of the Colosseum and looked through the gate into the interior, I must frankly confess that a shudder ran through me, and I quickly returned home.'* One wonders whether Fuseli, like Goethe, thought of Ovid's elegy to Rome, with its line:

* *The Italian Journey.* trans. W. H. Auden & Elizabeth Mayer, London, 1962.

> Lunaque nocturnos alta regebat equos.
> (And a full moon ruled the steeds of night)
> (*Tristia*, Bk. III)

for Geryon was such a steed, taking the two poets mounted on his back 'round and down' to a lower and more dismal level of the Inferno.

With Lavater dead in 1801 and Johnson in 1809, Fuseli had lost two of his closest and oldest friends at a particularly vulnerable time of life, and, he may have felt that he too was close to 'the mansions of the dead. . . .' It was by night that Blair had conjured these up, and it was night that preoccupied the artist, frequently, from 1810 onwards.

He turned to another long dead friend for his text in the drawing *The Great Father and Ancient Night* (c.1810). This was 156 John Armstrong's *The Art of Preserving the Health* (1744), but re-issued in *British Poets* in 1795 and again in 1805–08 and 1822, and since Fuseli had done work for the 1805–08 edition, this was probably the reason. However the lines which apply to this composition are:

> and ancient Night
> Again invoke the desolate abyss
> Till the great FATHER thro' the lifeless gloom
> Extend his arm to light another world,
> And bid new planets roll by other laws.
>
> (lines 545–549)

The Father here, of course, is not God but Oceanus from Hesiod's *Theogony*. To explain his gesture a gloss can be added from Erasmus Darwin's *The Temple of Nature* (posthumous 1803):

> Organic life beneath the shoreless waves
> Was born and nurs'd in Ocean's pearly caves
> (canto I 295–6)

So here Oceanus holds up two pearl-seeded oysters (sea eggs?) which will fertilize new life.

Night's children clinging to her are not Sleep and Death being cradled by Albani's *Night,* but Day and Night, according 37 to Pausanias's description (5 : 18,1). The idea of a close supernumerary, however, comes from Albani's *Aurora,* and in *The Dream of Prince Arthur* (1788) she appears as the Faerie Queen. 157 In the distance to the left in the Armstrong subject, Charon in his boat is represented not so much as a butterfly as a bat. Its position in the composition associates it with the bat in Guercino's *Night* lunette in the Villa Ludovisi, in which Night is posed as 158 Dürer's *Melencolia.* No great stretch of the imagination is required to see the connection between Guercino's *Night* and *The Witch and the Mandrake* (c.1812) (a soft ground etching 159 made by the artist after his painting of that year); the rocky background, the witch and the owl are only in reverse. The subject comes from Ben Jonson's *Masque of Queens* (Witches' Song), in which one of them lay at night 'to heare the Mandrake grone' and then plucked him up. The witch's breasts are exposed for she has been nourishing the mandrake with her milk. It was an earlier essay on this theme (1785) which had promoted Horace Walpole's diagnosis of madness in the artist. Then in 1793 Johnson had published Blake's *For Children, the Gates of Paradise,* of which Plate 1 shows a woman carrying a baby plucking a mandrake in the form of an infant from the foot of a tree. Blake's association is the mandrake as an aid to fertility, but Fuseli's treatment has a more ancient connotation, for this witch on a mountain can be equated with Cybele, the earth goddess with many breasts, nourishing all living creatures. In Italy she was known as Rhea and was associated with Faunus at the Albunea spring, the oracle which Aeneas consulted. Albunea was also the name of the Tiburtine Sibyl, the prefiguration of the prophetic witches in *Macbeth*. Faunus himself, or Pan was the source of the *incubus* or nighmare. As for the mandrake, it was used as an anaesthetic and also an aphrodisiac in the East. As an opiate, it was administered by Friar Lawrence to Juliet, who exclaimed:

And shrieks like mandrakes' torn out of the earth,
That living mortals, hearing them, run mad; –
(*Romeo and Juliet*, IV 3)

Johannes de Cuba showed in his *Hortus Sanitatis* (*c.*1498) that there was a male and female mandrake, the latter being the sex of Fuseli's homuncula; the plant in fact often grows in anthropoid form and was believed in Germany and elsewhere to be inhabited by familiar demons, hence its use as a talismanic instrument in witchcraft. To complete the circle, Cybele was connected with the Dionysiac rites, the shrieks and howls of the Corybantes, the priests of Cybele. References to this can be found in Euripides' *Bacchae* and *Hippolytus*.

If this appears to be too exhaustive, then one can turn to Fuseli's note to *The Daughter of Herodias with the Head of St John* 121 in the Lavater English edition, explaining why he had shown Salome as a Bacchante; it was her Greek mother (Herodias) who had prompted her to dance the 'orgic ballet' of Antonae, mentioned in the *Bacchae* of Euripides, the *Lenae* of Theocritus, the Sixth Satire of Juvenal and in all probability the First Satire of Persius.

It was, therefore, the hybrid God Cybele-Dionysus that Fuseli identified as the ancient source of the *femme fatale*, and it may be mentioned that the Levant, where Salome danced, is given as the locus of *atropa Mandragora* (the mandrake), a hardy perennial, in the *Hortus Cantabrigiensis* (6th ed. 1811).

In this Corybantic lineage, Lady Macbeth had a rightful place. In *Garrick and Mrs Pritchard as Macbeth and Lady Macbeth* XI (1812), the artist is mythologizing the much earlier contemporary action of his drawing (*c.*1766). While still an active 160 theatre-goer, the artist could look back to Garrick and his company as the dramatis personae of a Golden Age, the gods and goddesses of a Pantheon theatrum.

Thus these galvanic transparencies perform against a background of dark purple, the most imperial tone of tragedy and noble grief. While they are literally drawn in paint, in a way very close indeed to Tintoretto's practice, there is another element present in this painterly draughtsmanship. That element is electricity.

Since *The Poetical Works* of Erasmus Darwin had been re-issued by Johnson in three volumes in 1806, one may pause there, before going further back for more exact scientific corroboration. In a footnote the poet and natural philosopher suggested that if a paralytic limb could be made to move by electric shock, this might indicate 'some analogy between the electric fluid, and the nervous fluid, which is separated from the blood by the brain, and thence diffused along the nerves for the purposes of motion and sensation'. Some more analogies to explain this can be drawn from the writings of Dr Joseph Priestley (whose portrait by Fuseli hangs in Dr Williams Library, Gordon Square, London).

From *The History of the Idea of Positive and Negative Electricity* (1775), the following extracts are relevant, the first to Darwin's   XI suggestion, 'all the operations of electricity depend upon one fluid sui generis, extremely subtile and elastic, dispersed through the pores of all bodies': the next extracts may be applied analogously to the scene from *Macbeth*, bearing in mind Darwin's analogy of the electric to the nervous fluid. In reference to 'the doctrine of *plus* and *minus* electricity', Priestley observed:

When the equilibrium of this fluid in any body is not disturbed; . . . it does not discover itself to our senses by any effect. . . . This equilibrium being forcibly disturbed, the mutual repulsion of the particles of the fluid is necessarily exerted to restore it. If two bodies be both of them over-charged, the electrical atmospheres . . . repel each other, and both the bodies recede from one another, . . . if one of the bodies have an overplus of fluid, and the other a deficiency of it, the equilibrium is restored with great violence. . . . The Light which is visible . . . is generally supposed to be part . . . of the electric fluid, which appears when it is properly agitated . . . the light, and the phosphoreal smell . . . arise from particles of matter much grosser than the proper electric fluid, but which may be driven from bodies by its powerful action.

The 'moment of Terror' now becomes a violent electrical discharge, with its accompanying light and smell. Sequentially one may relate the painting *Chriemhild throwing herself on the dead Siegfried* (1817) to the same analogy, for Priestley observed   XII also that, 'If both the bodies be exhausted of their natural share of this fluid [electric], they are both attracted by the denser fluid, existing . . . in the atmosphere contiguous to them', but he concluded that this 'occasions them still to recede from one another', as much as the dead recede from life, once the spirit has been exhausted from the body.

Like Fuseli, the members of the *Sturm und Drang* moved from the notion of 'elasticity' to that of 'electricity' almost as soon as books on it appeared. Two years after the first edition of Priestley's history (1767), Goethe was writing that happiness and heroism 'are as communicable as electricity' Herder (*Vom Erkennen und Empfinden* 1778) drew analogies between elasticity, magnetism and electricity, as natural energies, and those of the human spirit. It is significant of Fuseli's whole approach to a new conception, however, that he should justify it by employing Tintoretto's stylistic technique, itself sanctioned by time and approval. Nor might it be impossible to relate the Rembrandtesque light of *The Nightmare* (1792 Darwin, *Botanic*   83 *Garden*) to that of sheet lightning, for Priestley in the same article observed that those killed by lightning were generally found to have their lungs full of air. Indeed, Darwin describes the victim's 'suffocative breath', as 'Her interrupted heart pulse swims in death'.

To return to a more orthodox system of analysis, the drawing of *Chriemhild throwing herself on the dead Siegfried* (1805) may be considered as 'preparatory' for the painting of 1817,† in the same way as Delacroix's drawing *The Barque of Dante* (National Gallery, Ottawa) is for the painting (Petit Palais, Paris) of 1821, that is, all extraneous detail inclusive of the precise definition of space is eliminated, leaving the central action 'floating' as a poetic super-reality. In his drawing Fuseli's hand remains strong and vigorous and it is not until about 1814, for instance, *A Woman gazing into a mirror*, that the penstrokes look a little shaky and about 1822, in *Undine displeased, leaves the Fisherman's hut*,** that the application of the washes becomes less fluent than it used to be. While the tone of these colour washes is often lighter in this late period, for example in *A Capriccio of the Horsetamers* and in *Undine and Huldbrand*,‡ it is occasioned more by the nature of the theme than a fading of the vision. From all accounts Fuseli remained vigorous to the end.

His choice of Friedrich de la Motte-Fouqué's novel *Undine* (1811) is entirely consistent with his central interests and also with his revived interest in German art and literature. Motte-Fouqué, moreover, not only set his story in a quasi-medieval context, but also in language, phrasing and vocabulary sought to establish a 'vernacular' for that period. This was compatible with Fuseli's adaptations from an engraver like Altdorfer. It is worth recording that Sir George Beaumont in 1823 wanted to bring Fuseli to see the early Flemish and German paintings in the collection of Charles Aders,* amongst which there were works attributed to Van Eyck, Van der Weyden, Memling and Dürer. Aders was an intimate of Coleridge, Lamb and Crabb Robinson, who met Blake in the Aders home.

Undine, a wayward watersprite, can only gain a soul by marrying a mortal: Huldbrand von Ringstetten is the 'bewitched groom', but Bertalda estranges his love. On their marriage day, however, Undine appears and bestows on Huldbrand 'the kiss of death'. Fuseli's interpretation is as felicitous as ever, from Undine's arrival in the hut, to her precipitous flight of displeasure and her balletic collapse in her lover's arms.

It may seem a shade invidious then to introduce, on the basis of analogy, the two engravings by Chodowiecki, *Der Tanz*, from *Natürliche und affektierte Handlungen* (Natural and affected behaviour) of 1779. There is no need to say which is which, but it is the one with the girl, her hat like Pelion piled on Ossa, and her partner, bent into a serpentine which Hogarth would deplore, that strikes a chord, dissonant perhaps, with *Undine comes to the Fisherman's Hut*. It would seem, with another example to be cited later, that Chodowiecki was the shadow, unlike that of Peter Schlemihl, which Fuseli would have liked to be rid of. It is difficult, in this period, to say who owed what to whom amongst contemporaries. Nevertheless, Chodo-

54 Fuseli. *A Woman gazing in a mirror. c.1814*

*Charles Aders and Sir George Beaumont: see M. K. Joseph, *Charles Aders, University of Auckland Bulletin* 43, English Series 6, 1953.

XIII

146, 165

55

XIII

†*116 and XII;* **146; ‡163 and 165.*

126

wiecki, better than almost anyone, demonstrates pictorially that shift in social behaviour in the 1780s and 1790s towards restraint and refinement of gesture that took place amongst the cultivated classes throughout Europe. In the first decades of the next century, it is no wonder that Fuseli amongst the English would appear as a wildly posturing throw-back and the energy of his art distasteful to an enervated society.

This would be true even when the subject was English like *The Devil and the Sompnour* (1821) from Chaucer's *The Canterbury Tales* (the Friar's Tale). While Blake's *Canterbury Pilgrims* of 1809 was a possible stimulant, there was another – the re-issue in 1816 by Palser of Mortimer's Chaucer illustrations, originally published in 1787. The engraving of the same subject* by James Hogg, after a Mortimer of the mid-1770s, shows the Englishness of that artist in contrast to Fuseli's almost Goethean interpretation of Satan as Mephistofeles. The vernacular exchanges in *Faust* and *The Canterbury Tales* are very similar, for instance Chaucer's devil says:

> 'What are you cross about,
> Dear brother? You and this pan are mine by right.
> You yet shall be in Hell with me to-night,
> Where you'll know more about our mystery
> Than any Doctor of Divinity.'

Then he swooped down to claim his own; Blake described the Sompnour, companion of the Pardoner, 'the Age's Knave', as 'a Devil of the first magnitude, grand, terrific, rich and honoured in the rank of which he holds the destiny'. Fuseli agreed, for his devil and man are twins. It would also appear that he considered Chaucer required reading for his students at the Academy, for in a handwritten list, dating probably after his re-appointment as Professor of Painting in 1810, of books ordered for the library there, along with Aeschylus, Euripides, Sophocles, the Classical poets, Lemprière's *Classical Dictionary*, Dossie's *Handmaid to the Arts,* Carter's *English Painting, Sculpture and Architecture,* Johnson's *Dictionary*, is a folio edition of Chaucer's works.

In these last years, not all was retrospection. The drawing, *Woman with a Stiletto*† (*c.*1816–17) (the inscription is not Fuseli's) can be connected to a real-life episode. Cunningham records a dinner party at Thomas Coutts, when the banker's second wife, Harriet née Mellon, whom he had married in 1815, came dancing in, dressed as Morgiana (Ali Baba's inamorata) pointing her dagger 'at every breast'. When she came to Nollekens, Fuseli cried out, 'Strike – strike – there's no fear; Nolly was never known to bleed.' Nollekens, than whom, according to J. T. Smith, a man no meaner came, was the special butt of Harriet Coutts's mimicry, as one learns from Haydon's *Autobiography* (December 1817). He records that he had known her in her actress days when she had been living with Maria Foote at Holly House, 'under the protection of Mr Coutts, but certainly not in vice', and how he had played blind-man's buff in the 'fun room' there. Fuseli must have made his drawing almost immediately since in the top right corner there is a

55 Daniel Chodowiecki. *Two engravings from 'Der Tanz'. 1779*

*161, 162
†56

127

reasonable resemblance to a pop-eyed Nollekens, while Harriet Coutts is shown 'turning that eye of hers' (Haydon) on another 'victim'.

To complete this section, it would be proper to consider the drawing, *A Capriccio of the Horsetamers* (*c.* 1810–15). Since his early days the group of the Monte Cavallo had epitomized for Fuseli heroic energy and immortal fame. This is the only time that he shows both Castor and Pollux, and for some reason, he places them in the sea. Significantly the five-year period allotted to this drawing on stylistic grounds is marked at the beginning by a flurry of artistic activity over a monument to Nelson (Flaxman, West, Blake and the ever ambitious Haydon had planned or executed their own characteristic monuments or apotheoses) at the end, and equally important was Canova's visit to England. That eminent sculptor had observed to Haydon (in French) that 'the divisions of the stomach in the statues of Monte Cavallo are not natural: you will not see those in the Greeks.' (*Autobiography*, December 1815). The Greek works he was referring to were of course the Elgin Marbles. Seven years before, Haydon had dragged Fuseli to see them on their arrival. On their way to Park Lane, they ran into a flock of sheep and Fuseli, like some diminutive Polyphemus, 'burst into the middle of them, and they got between his little legs and jostled him', but finally both got to their destination. At first Fuseli was enthusiastic according to Haydon, but later 'began to back out', for the good reason that he was expecting to see not an idealized naturalistic style, but a more abstracted one like Egyptian art.

It seems reasonable to surmise that his drawing of the Horsetamers may represent a double monument to Nelson and Wellington, for both were protectors of sea-girt Britain, as Castor and Pollux were of mariners in antiquity. And the naturalistic rendering of the left-hand figure, contrary to the original model, was his way of rendering tribute to Canova's reflection. Canova's tribute to Fuseli had gone further, and joined his name with Raphael's; to Haydon he had said, 'There are in art two things, fire and flame. Fuseli has the flame; Raphael the fire.' And Fuseli would have been pleased enough with that assessment.

163
164

56 *Fuseli. Woman with a stiletto. c.1816–17*

57 Fuseli. *The Oath on the Rütli*, 1778–81

58, 59 Two other 'patriotic' works, one influencing Fuseli, the other influenced by him: Polidoro da Caravaggio's *Camillus and Brennus* (left), and David's *The Oath of the Horatii* (below)

57

58

59

61

62

60

60–62 The pose of the head lying back and one limp arm touching the ground, which Fuseli used so dramatically in the various versions of *The Nightmare*, can be paralleled in antique and contemporary art. Above: antique group, *Menelaus and Patroclus*. Above right: James Barry, *Lear and Cordelia*. Right: Alexander Runciman, *Perseus killing Medusa* (detail)

63 Fuseli. *William Tell escaping from Gessler*. 1787

63

64

65

64, 65 Fuseli. Fear: *Three crouching Girls,*
c. 1780–82. A physiognomic exercise
perhaps inspired by Chodowiecki's engravings of Le Brun's *Passions,* used by
Lavater in the French edition of his *Physio-*
gnomy (right)

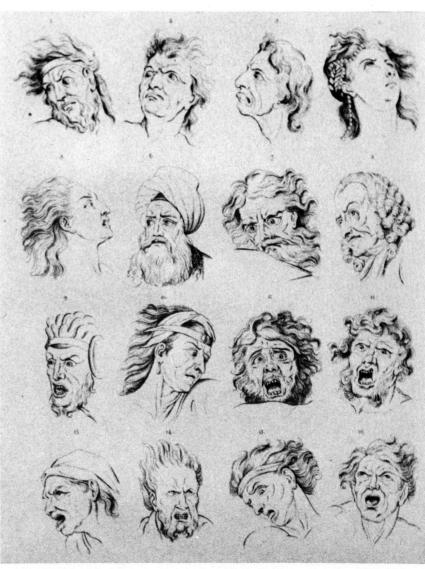

66 Fuseli. *An Executioner, c.* 1780

66

67 Andrea del Sarto. *Decapitation of St John the Baptist* (detail), the source of Fuseli's drawing

67

68

68 (left) Francesco Furini. *Hylas and the Nymphs*. The influence of Florentine early Baroque on Fuseli is chiefly a matter of tonality. But compare the head of Hylas with Fuseli's Brutus (pl. 46)

69

70

69, 70 In his illustrations to Shakespeare, Fuseli sought to give moral depth to the scenes chosen by relating them to accepted allegorical types. Lady Constance, from *King John* (1783), is identified with melancholy. Left: Cesare Ripa's *Malincolia*, from *Iconologia*, 1764–66

71

72

71, 72 The motif of the overlapping profile heads was borrowed by both David (*The Oath of the Horatii*, left) and Fuseli (*The Three Witches*, 1783, right) from Roman coins and bas-reliefs

73 Fuseli. *Oedipus announcing his Death*, 1784

73

74 Fuseli. *Subject from Milton's 'L'Allegro'*, c. 1785

75 Correggio. *Danae*. Probably the starting point for
Fuseli's *L'Allegro* composition

76 Fuseli. *The Awakening of Titania*, c. 1785–90

74

75

76

77

77 Fuseli. *The Shep-
herd's Dream*, 1785.
Beside the sleeping
shepherd is Pandora
with her open box.
The flying figures, in
particular, look back
to Rococo artists like
Fragonard, illustrated
below. For the finish-
ed painting, see pl. VII

78 Fragonard. *Coresus
sacrifices himself to save
Callirhoe*

78

79 Hogarth. *Strolling Actresses dressing in a Barn.*
There are several striking parallels between this
and Fuseli's two Titania paintings (pls. IV and 76)

80 The motif of the demon rider was common in
folklore. Left: an illustration by Chodowiecki to the
poem of *Lenore*

81 Fuseli. *Jack o' Lanthorn*, 1799, a union of Shakespeare and Milton in Fuseli's mind

80

81

83

82 Fuseli. *Henry V surprising Cambridge, Scrope and Grey with their death Sentence* – the original painting (top left) of *c.* 1786–89 and the engraved version, 1803, by Thew. The composition is inspired by David's *Oath of the Horatii* (pl. 59), reversed

83 Fuseli. *The Nightmare*, second version, 1790–91

84 Fuseli. *The Appearance of Christ at Emmaus*, 1792

85 John Brown. *Rest on the Flight* (detail). Fuseli may have owned this drawing, and borrowed from it the exhausted figure of Joseph

86 John Hamilton Mortimer. *Falstaff in the Buckbasket*. To be compared with Fuseli's treatment of the same subject, pl. VI

86

88

87

89

87–89 Vanity and her glass. The motif of the woman and her mirror, used by Fuseli in his Falstaff picture, pl. VI, has a long allegorical pedigree. Top: Ripa's *Lascivious Love*. Left: Charles Ansell's *The French Toilet*. Fuseli's own *Allegory of Vanity* (above) of 1811 retains the same formula

90

92

91

90 Fuseli. *The Fall of Satan*, 1802

91, 92 Fuseli. *Death and Sin bridging the 'Waste' of Chaos and met by
Satan on his return from Earth*. The
two figures on the bridge go back
to a detail (above) of Piranesi's
frontispiece to *Antichità di Roma*

94

93

94 Fuseli. *Sin intervening between Satan and Death*, c. 1793–96

93, 95 Two other versions of the same subject, by James Barry (above) and Hogarth (right). Hogarth is the model for both Barry and Fuseli

95

97

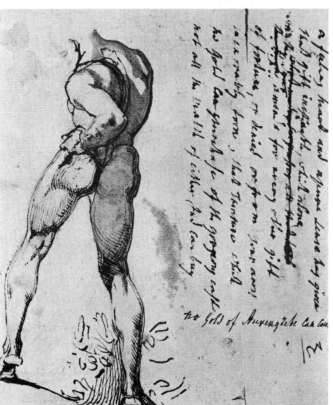

96 Two illustrations by
Francis Hayman to *Para-
dise Lost*: *Satan, Sin and
Death* and *Satan with Adam
and Eve*. Both are com-
parable to Fuseli's treatment of the same subjects
(pls. 94 and x)

97, 98 Fuseli. *Nude figure
of a man seen from the back*,
c. 1790–91. And its source,
Veneziano's engraving of
Michelangelo's *Battle of
Cascina*

98

99

100

99 Fuseli. *Titania, Bottom and the Fairies*, 1793–94

100 Detail from a Greek vase, the source of Fuseli's fairy, above right

101 Fuseli. *The Vision of the Lazar House*, 1791–93. This is another variant of *The Escapee* (pl. 43), both being based ultimately on the antique *Gladiator* (pl. 29)

101

102

102 Fuseli. *Britomart frees Amoret from Busirane*, 1793. The subject comes from Spenser's *Faerie Queene*

104

103 Andrea del Sarto. *The Naming of St John the Baptist* (detail)

104 Parmigianino's *Moses with the Tablets of the Law*, a likely source for the figure of Fuseli's Busirane

103

105

106

105 Fuseli. *Ixion and Nephele*, 1809

108

106 Fuseli. *Venus appearing to Ulysses*, 1803. From the *Odyssey*

107, 108 An antique gemstone, illustrated by Winckelmann (below), served as Fuseli's model for his *Celadon and Amelia* (right), 1801, an illustration to Thomson's *Seasons*

107

UNDE · UNDE · EXTRICAT

109 Fuseli. *Unde, Unde Extricat*, 1795. From Horace's *Satires*

110 Fuseli. Tailpiece from Lavater's *Physiognomy*, 1792. Both these figures derive from a wood-cut by Altdorfer

111 Fuseli. *Titania finds the Ring on the Shore*, 1804–05. From Wieland's *Oberon*

112 Fuseli. *A Woman in Tudor Costume, c.* 1803. The style is reminiscent of Holbein. All the works on this spread show Fuseli's recurring interest in German art and literature

113 Fuseli. *Hephaistos, Bia and Crato securing Prometheus, c.* 1810

114 Baldung Grün. *The Bewitched Groom.* Both this woodcut and an engraving by Altdorfer were in Fuseli's mind when he drew the Prometheus above

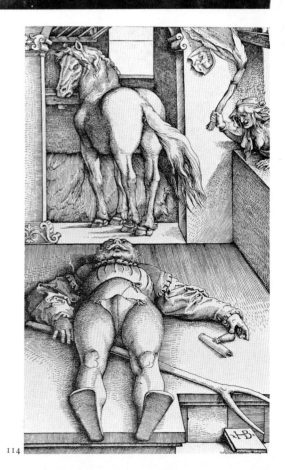

114

P. Croß. 23 May. 05.

Die schönen prunk losen ligen man dô lach
Kriemhilde jâmer ward ũ maßen groz
Daz bluot ir uz dem munde vor herzen jâmer bra.

117

118

115 Fuseli. *Chriemhild in a dream sees Siegfried dead*, 1805

116 Fuseli. *Chriemhild throwing herself on the dead Siegfried*, 1805. (See pl. XII.) Both illustrations to the *Nibelungenlied*

117 Fuseli. *Lear and Cordelia*, 1805. The artistic source is again the antique *Menelaus and Patroclus* (pl. 60)

118, 119 Fuseli. *Othello and Desdemona*, 1805. The composition looks back to another classical sculpture, *Satyr and Nymph*

119

120

121

122

120 Fuseli. *Diomedes and Cressida*, 1805

121 Fuseli. *The Daughter of Herodias with the Head of St John the Baptist, c.* 1779

122 A source for both the above engravings was the Hellenistic relief of a *Dancing Maenad*

123, 124 Fuseli. *Pericles*, 1805. And its source, Michelangelo's *Aminadab* from the Sistine ceiling

125 (right) Fuseli. *The Taming of the Shrew*, 1805

126 (far right) Raphael. *The Freeing of St Peter* (detail)

123

124

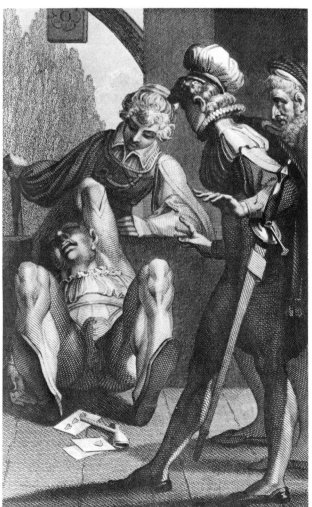

125

126

127

128

127 Fuseli. *Queen Katherine's Dream*, from Henry VIII, 1805. Griffith, with the book, is probably taken from Andrea del Sarto's *The Naming of St John the Baptist* (pl. 103)

128 Ludovico Carracci. *St Benedict exorcising the demon from the kitchen*. The demon's legs were borrowed by Fuseli for his picture of Queen Katherine

129

130

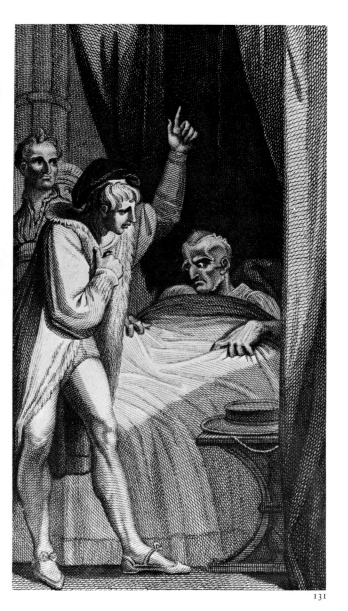

131

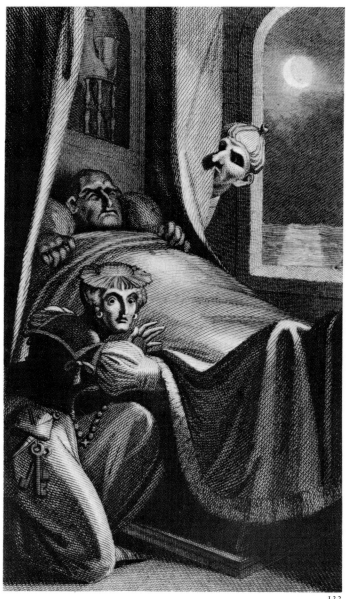

132

131 Fuseli. *Death of Cardinal Beaufort*, Henry VI, Pt 2.
Fuseli had done a more melodramatic version of this scene
thirty years earlier (pl. 25)

132 Fuseli. *Death of Falstaff*, 1805. The sketch (right, 133)
may be a rejected idea for this scene

133 Fuseli. *A man in bed*, c. 1805

133

129 (far left) Raphael. *The Freeing of St Peter* (detail)

130 (left) Fuseli. *Hamlet and the Ghost*, 1805

134 (left) Fuseli. *Roland at Roncesvalles (Fame)*, 1800–10

135 (below left) Fuseli. *Eros and Psyche*, 1808

136

138

136, 137 Blake's *Death of the Strong Wicked Man* (above) may be compared with the 1810 version of *The Nightmare* (below). In both, the forces of evil disappear through a rear window

138, 139 Veronese's *St John the Baptist Preaching* (above) is ingeniously adapted by Fuseli as an illustration to the graveyard scene in *Hamlet* (below), 1804

137

139

140

Sketched by Fuseli for Blake to engrave from

141

142

140, 141 Fuseli. *The Fertilization of Egypt*,
1791. Fuseli's sketch was used by Blake for his
finished engraving in Darwin's *Botanic Garden*
(below)

142 Fuseli. *Virtue reclaiming Youth*, 1806–07.
An illustration for Cowper's *The Progress of Error*

143 Fuseli. *The Ladies of Hastings*, after 1813

144 Fuseli. *The Lost Shepherd*, 1801. From Thomson's *Seasons*

145 Ludovico Carracci. *The Temptation of St Benedict*. The same reclining figure as in *The Ladies of Hastings*, the same sloping bank with women

146

147

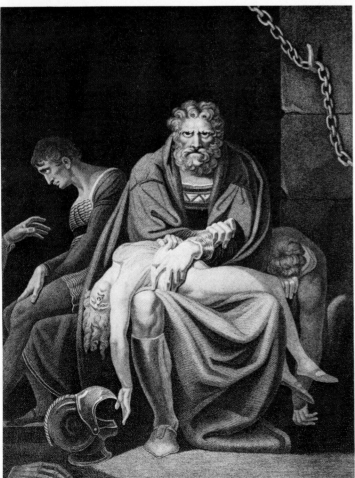

146 Fuseli. *Undine displeased leaves the Fisherman's Hut*, 1822

147 Fuseli. *Count Ugolino and his Sons*, 1806

148 Sir Joshua Reynolds's earlier version of the same scene, 1773. Reynolds has modelled his Ugolino on Michelangelo's *Aminadab* (pl. 124), Fuseli perhaps on the same artist's *Moses* and *Pietà*

148

IV Themes and Symbols

Genius either discovers new materials of nature, or combines the known with novelty.

Aphorism 5

INVENTION

There has been sufficient evidence advanced so far to indicate Fuseli's capacity to invent, but here (after considering first his own observations on this capacity) aspects and elements which lie embedded within his oeuvre require extraction and examination.

In his third Lecture (1801) he remarked 'The term invention never ought to be so misconstrued as to be confounded with that of creation . . . admissible only when we mention omnipotence: to invent is to find: . . . the visible universe . . . and its counterpart, the invisible one that agitates our mind with visions bred on sense by fancy, are the element and the realm of invention; it discovers, selects, combines the possible, the probable, the known, in a mode that strikes with an air of truth and novelty, at once.' Earlier in the same lecture, he had answered the question of whether the artist could invent 'without recourse to tradition or the stores of history and poetry? Why not, if the subject be within the limits of art and the combinations of nature, though it should have escaped observation?'

These quotations exactly define the artist's position as it appears from examining his work and surely require no further enlargement. To suggest that this position of Fuseli was consciously somewhere between Neo-classicism and Romanticism, as some have done, is an art-historical *bêtise* of this century, for neither term existed in his day, nor surely does any artist ever think of himself as a hyphenation between two abstractions! Most artists of that time exhibited in greater or lesser degree, a subjective tendency, but against the criticism that this tendency was 'entirely paramount' in Fuseli, one may quote Leslie's comment:* 'and yet his ghosts and demons are, to the imagination, more truly ghosts and demons than those of any other painter'; concluding that since the artist succeeded he then must be classed as objective. Since Leslie wrote this in 1855, it

*See C. R. Leslie, *Handbook for Young Painters*, London, 1855.

indicates how much Fuseli's inventions had become acceptable even to the conservative imagination.

That is looking a long way ahead, but how 'more truly' Fuseli maintained the continuity of his invention and its impact is discussed in the following sections.

As we know, Fuseli from the outset of his career was closely involved with Lavater's studies. Although he reserved his opinion on some of his friend's too enthusiastic analytic excursions and deplored its excesses it is clear that he had a serious interest in physiognomy. This extract comes from *The Advertisement* to the English edition which he supervised: 'By consulting Physiognomy only can History hope to discriminate the forms of various climates, and to stamp its figures with national character. We feel regret and shame . . . that the most celebrated names [of artists] have contented themselves hitherto with the grossest distinctions only; with white, tawny or black; with the thick lip or the slit; with the hooked or flattened nose ridge.' Implied here is a criticism of Winckelmann, for Lavater had taken objection to that authority's conjecture that the ancient Greeks had foreheads and noses forming a straight line; from such a trait 'wisdom and beauty will fly with equal rapid steps'. In the copies of ancient busts, 'I generally find the expression of meanness; and, if I dare so say, of vague insipidity'. To Winckelmann's 'Greatness will be expressed by the straight and full and tenderness by the gently curving', Lavater replied, 'All greatness has something of the straight and full; but all that is straight and full is not greatness.' The major objection, however, of the entomologist Fuseli to Winckelmann (as of the physicist Lichtenberg to Lavater) was their respective use of unscientific generalization. The taxonomic system referred to already lies behind Fuseli's linking of various climates and national character. Generally he distinguishes between the brachycephalic type of head of Brutus and the Ezzelin Bracciaferro, belonging to the central Mediterranean area, and the doceocephalic of the ancient Greek and (*pace* Winckelmann) of the Nordic races – for instance Satan, who is derived from the Apollo Belvedere, and any one of the Northern heroes. Into the former type Fuseli places correctly the gnomes, in the latter the fairies. But the scientist in the artist must have clearly recognized the fallacious nature of such broad classifications, particularly on the analogy of anthropology to entomology, for in reviewing Edward Smith's *Rarer Lepidopterous Insects of Georgia* (Analytical Review, Jan. 1798), he remarked, 'Every day discomposes the cobweb labours of precipitate classification, and the systems erected on the fragments of former observation totter already on the ruins. . . . The reason is obvious; nature dictated the classes, transient appearances, and frequently whim, the subordinate parts.' By 'whim' he means 'accident' and 'transient appearances' intrusions of one kind or another. Here lay a contentious issue with Lavater, who made no allowances whatsoever for regional

47
II

physiognomic traits. Indeed, in the German edition of his Essays he objected to Hogarth's 'caricatures', lumping together on a couple of pages vile engravings after various heads guillotined from the well-known series. On the other hand it was through the caricature process that Fuseli, first through Hogarth and secondly through Mortimer, approached the problem of national character.

By 'caricature process' is meant that selecting out and emphasizing of the dominant traits of individual or racial appearance, without necessarily arriving at the distortions of caricature proper. This is true of Mortimer's painting* in which Fuseli has already been identified, for there is an air of verisimilitude in each portrait, not only to individual characteristics, but those of race. These can be determined by comparing Mortimer's drawing *Choir and Orchestra* (1779, H.M. Queen) where he distinguishes English, Swiss, Italian, German and Prussian musicians. In the painting the two men at the end of the table could be, left and right, Moser and Cipriani respectively, while all the rest are clearly English, Welsh and Scots. There is no space to digress on their possible identities here, but as with all men of genius, they all share notable noses. Since most are artists, J. T. Smith's[†] report of Fuseli saying, on observing Rembrandt's large nose in one of his self portraits, 'What a nose! Why his nose is as big as his face! Well, he was a fine fellow; I like to see a great man with a great nose. Richard Wilson had a great nose', would indicate that Mortimer shared the same sentiment.

In Fuseli's drawing *Garrick as the Duke of Gloucester* (1766) *12* which is virtually contemporary with the Mortimer, he has gone to some pains to establish English physiognomies for the players. Going forward to the Rivington Shakespeare plates of Falstaff alive and dead, one may see Falstaff as a more aged *149, 132* version of Hogarth's old Earl in *The Marriage Contract* (National Gallery London), the English nose of Bardolph may be compared with the man on the extreme right in the *3* Mortimer, and the Hostess is as English as they come. The other *132* English plays of Shakespeare show the same emphasis, but for **3* the principals in all his subjects, Fuseli maintained an anonymous aristocratic mien.

149 *Fuseli. Illustration from the Rivington Shakespeare edition of 'The Merry Wives of Windsor'. 1805*

†J. T. Smith, *Nollekens and his Times*, vol. 2, London, 1828.

THE HEROIC TYPE

Since most of Fuseli's heroes were damned one way or another, there is no better example than Satan. The most specific relationship with the Apollo Belvedere is established by the plate of the *Head of Satan* in Lavater's Essays, despite the over- *168* heavy hand of the engraver. Winckelmann explained that 'The Vatican Apollo was intended to represent this duty (Jupiter's) in a state of anger over the serpent Python, . . . and at the same time with a feeling of contempt for his victory, which to a god was an easy achievement. . . . the skilful artist . . . to personify the most beautiful of the gods, expressed only the anger in the nose, – this organ, according to the old poet being its appro-private seat, – and the contempt on the lips.'[‡] In a note, Fuseli

‡J. J. Winckelmann, *Geschichte der Kunst des Altertums*, 1764.

explained that the original drawing showed the mouth expressing contempt not fear. Lavater found it hard to accept the head *in toto*, 'What a singular production!... a borrowed and affected manner: the original sin of all Painters who have genius, or who imagine they have it', was his acid comment in the text, peeved no doubt, that his friend could ennoble Satan but would not portray Christ. As one scans Fuseli's gallery of heroes, their faces are immobile, enmarbled while they are still alive, as men of destiny, blood brothers above race and creed and therefore unrewarding material for the physiognomist.

While the heroic type is stony in expression, the head is nearly always alert, raised or projected to make sure its magnetism is positive. In contradistinction the head of Sloth is always acutely tilted in a 'lost' threequarter view, negatively magnetic, in a state of total inertia. We may call this type Sloth and let it stand in for all related conditions.

THE HEAD OF SLOTH

166

The source is the prone figure in Michelangelo's *Brazen Serpent* spandrel in the Sistine Chapel. Initially, Fuseli introduced it in *Dante on the Ice of Cocytus*, in the head at the poet's foot, and it is clear that these two heads were the prototypes of two he drew for the French edition of Lavater's Essays, for the text comments as follows: 'the idea [of them]... has been taken from Dante's Hell. They express [there were four heads in all] the most horrible sufferings; but even in this state they announce characters actually energetic, though destitute of real greatness.' In general terms the state is induced paralysis, a form in its clinical types familiar to the artist through his two close medical friends, Drs Armstrong and Carrick-Moore. Thus Bottom in *The Awakening of Titania* is in drugged sleep, while the afflicted in *The Vision of the Lazar House* demonstrate the effects of mental instability on muscle control; epileptics at this time were also classed as insane.* Supernatural fear is another inducing agent as one sees in the horseman in *Puck* from *A Midsummer Night's Dream*. Alcohol is another paralyser, accounting for Sly's condition in *The Taming of the Shrew* plate from the Rivington series. The Lord aptly remarking:

167
29

76
101

169
125

*See Gregory Zilboorg, *A History of Medical Psychology*, New York, 1967, for a useful survey of medical opinion and treatment of the insane.

> O monstrous beast! how like a swine he lies!
> Grim death, how foul and loathesome is thine image!
> (I.i)

In this context the Gravedigger in the *Hamlet* drawing is an interesting variant, for although very much alive he is in the grave too! But death paralyses the dead Siegfried, as Chriemhild throws herself upon him. To complete the catalogue, it will be noticed that Death himself affects this condition in *Sin intervening between Satan and Death*. Other variants of the type may be observed in the illustrations here, evidence not only of a consistent imagery, but one which is applied with an almost clinical accuracy, bespeaking a solid background of observation. Something of this potent observation must have abetted the impact of *The Vision of the Lazar House*. In 1816 writing to his sister, Leslie recalled 'The Lazar House, I believe from Milton.

137

116

94

101

The figures glare across the picture like a horrible dream. He (Fuseli) has certainly never been equalled in the visionary.'* Five years later Leslie would have changed the term 'visionary' when he saw Géricault's *Raft of the Medusa* (Louvre) when it was exhibited in London.

*C. R. Leslie, *Autobiographical Recollections of the Life . . .*, ed. Taylor, London, 1860.

SYMBOLIC ANATOMY

No one, to this writer's knowledge, has traced the origin of that image of the resolute manly man, so popular in this century, fitted like a mask to fighter pilots, football players and east of the Elbe to tractor drivers and other worker heroes, of which the twentieth century prototype is the World War I recruiting poster of Kitchener – *Your Country Needs You.* It does not in fact seem at all impossible that an earnest iconographer would find his way back to Fuseli's *King Lear* as he renounces Cordelia! *240*

But Fuseli also used means other than this implacable mask to designate the condition of his heroes. One must look a little further than gesture or posture and see that the artist emphasizes the principal joints, since these are the main springs of articulation. He often employs, for instance, the clenched hand, the knuckles whitened with the intensity of the emotion, whether it is in his *Self-Portrait* or in *The Death of Cardinal Beaufort.* *Frontispiece, 25* Inevitably he pays close attention to the positions of fingers in a hand gesture, the best example being of *Balaam* from Lavater's *170* Essays (French ed. *c.*1778), for as the text explains 'this figure represents the Magician Balaam on the summit of the mountain blessing the Children of Israel, whom he intends to curse'. Few of his later heroes were given to blessing, so that Balaam's right hand is not repeated, but the *monstrari digito* and its no less articulated companions appear in extraordinary variety through *King Lear* and others to Gray's *Bard,* the Welsh *240* descendant of Balaam. Even when the hero is at rest – the artist himself in the self-portrait with Bodmer, Hotspur listening to *7* Glendower and the Rivington plate of *Timon of Athens* – the *172, 171* V formed by the index and middle finger is not a prop but a signal of mental energy. The fact that Kemble sat for both Hotspur and Glendower reveals that the source was once again the stage. That Fuseli had no time for the cliché gesture is discovered in his criticism of Northcote's Solomon, whose fingers he thought resembled a pair of scissors – 'Cut him' he had Solomon say.

It would be difficult to establish the time when Fuseli began to think seriously of the symbolic possibilities of dismembered anatomy, but the forearms and hands, borrowed from the Veneziano engraving appear in *The Descent of Odin c.*1775–78 *174* (Art Institute, Chicago). Whereas Veneziano's arms, and equally so Michelangelo's in the *Battle of Cascina* (copy by Aristotile di Sangallo, Holkham Hall) from which the engraving is derived, belong to a bather eager to get on shore, Fuseli's are a symbol of a powerful, primitive earth or water force. Since he drew attention in one of his lectures to the copy of the Michelangelo at Holkham, it is possible that it re-awakened his interest prior to his work on Darwin's *Botanic*

Garden 1791. In the frontispiece plate *Flora attired by the Elements*, *173*
a gnome thrusts up his arms to hold out jewels from the earth,
for as Darwin explained with Augustan aplomb, 'the Rosicrucian doctrine of Gnomes, Sylphs, Nymphs and Salamanders
was thought to afford a proper machinery for a Botanic Poem'.
He cites Francis Bacon as his authority, but since his own
couplets echo those of Pope, he might have referred to the
Preface of *The Rape of the Lock*, where the poet wrote, 'The
best account I know of them [the Rosicrucians] is in a French
book called "Le Comte de Gabalis" . . . According to these
Gentlemen, the Four Elements are inhabited by Spirits, which
they call Sylphs, Gnomes, Nymphs, and Salamanders'. But
times had changed and Darwin, who was acquainted with
Jacob Bryant the mythologist, took a serious view, observing
in a note 'it is probable that they [Nymphs, Gnomes, Sylphs]
were originally the names of hieroglyphic figures of the
elements, or of Genii presiding over their operations'. Whereas
these gnomish arms are a fresh invention in the Fuseli plate,
Flora and her attendants are taken almost directly from Albani
(e.g. *Earth*, Pinacoteca, Turin), except that this Darwinian Flora
is also Venus, as she was with Spenser, a goddess of vegetation
and generation. At first, one might share Goethe's opinion on
receiving a copy of the *Botanic Garden*, (it) 'is embellished with
crazily allegorical engravings' (to Schiller, 26 January 1798),
but it must be reiterated that Fuseli was also a scientist, and that
an allegory of this kind does not represent the bizarre end of a
tired iconographic tradition, but is absolutely true to the contemporary scientific decision to use Latin or Greek for the
nomenclature of classes. Just as any living vernacular language
was held to be open to change so Fuseli would shun contemporary imagery, for it, too, was subject to the whim of fashion.

It is with scientific consistency that this motif of uplifted
arms is employed in *The Great Father and Ancient Night c.*1810, *156*
a consistency which has a literary justification, for Armstrong's
poem *On Preserving the Health* (1744) formed with William
Mason's *The English Garden* (1772–81) the lineage of Darwin's
poem.

There is, however, a difference between what can be called
amputated and what can be called dismembered. The hand and
wrist in Fuseli's work is a pathetic symbol, the last signal of a
drowning person. It appears in *Percival frees Belisane from the
Spell of Urma*, 1783, and in the *Count Ugolino and his Sons*, 1806. *III,147*
Finally the dismembered lower half of a figure in the Rivington
Queen Katherine's Dream has to be recalled to indicate how fre- *127*
quently Fuseli turns to late Italian Mannerism or to its Emilian
hybrid in such an artist as Ludovico Carracci, for a suitable
motif to apply to his own vocabulary of symbolic abstractions.

The most powerful and frequently employed motifs in this
vocabulary were the knees and the forelegs. At their most
energetic, already in evidence in the Roman period and
derived, of course, from Michelangelo, they are seen in a rising
position as in the Boydell *King Lear*. When their latent energy *240*
is at rest, they are frequently crossed as in the three Rivington

plates of *Brutus*, *Timon* and *Richard II*. When, however, this 220, 171, 175
energy is in check, whatever the reason, then knees and forelegs
are either locked by the hands as in *Titania, Bottom and the* 99
Fairies or, rather subtly, made unstable by placing the feet close
together as in the Rivington *Pericles*. Then in two major in- 123
stances these two members are rendered impotent by women,
namely in *Oedipus announcing his death* and in the Rivington 73
plate of *Falstaff* with the combined weight of Mrs Page and Mrs 149
Ford. Lastly in the most enervated condition they are to be seen
splayed apart as Bottom sleeps in *The Awakening of Titania*. 76
These variations stem from the same figure in Michelangelo's
Brazen Serpent fresco that provided the head of Sloth. This 167
demonstrates more than anything the nature of Fuseli's critical
acumen, for he realized that Michelangelo himself saw more in
legs than merely articulated variety.

It is proper to anatomy to consider now the sum of all these
parts in the figure of Fuseli's *Executioner* type derived from 66
Andrea del Sarto. Paradoxically it is a male figure seen from
the back, therefore faceless, but nonetheless all-powerful.
Starting from his own source figure of an executioner *c.* 1780–
85, it reappears in the same role, as Hephaestus securing 113
Prometheus to the rock in *c.*1810, but in between those dates
it stands in for the god Anubis in *The Fertilization of Egypt*, 140
engraved by Blake for Darwin's *Botanic Garden* 1791 and in
minuscule, for Mustardseed in *Titania and Bottom c.*1786–89, IV
standing on Bottom's hand.

Darwin explained in a note, his authority being the Abbé la
Pluche, that the rising of Sirius, the dog star, and the flood
waters of the Nile coincided, so that the Egyptian priests hung
the figure of the dog-headed Anubis on their temples at this
time. Fuseli, however, has turned Anubis into the Nile itself,
basing the conception of the figure straddling the river from old
engravings of the Colossus of Rhodes, as Pliny described it,
'the colossal statue of the Sun . . . seventy cubits in height.
. . . Few men can clasp the thumb in their arms and its fingers
are larger than most statues',* an ancient Brobdingnagian ex- *Pliny, *Natural History*.
perience, indeed. It is also relevant that in the Odyssey,
Αἴγυπτος in the masculine is the Nile and in the feminine,
Egypt. In 1790, Fuseli had reviewed James Bruce's *Travels to
discover the source of the Nile*, in which he recounted his discovery of the source of the Blue Nile, but the White Nile
he knew to be the larger river. Hence Fuseli's Nile figure
has his face turned away, replacing the seventeenth-century
mode of covering the head of the river god, as in Bernini's
Four Rivers Fountain (Piazza Navona, Rome). Nile/Anubis,
his star overhead, calls in Jupiter Pluvius, to be seen clearly in the
Blake engraving and sketched lightly in the drawing. This 141
figure is taken from the Marcus Aurelius Column in Rome,
where, as a *deus ex machina*, he helped, through his rain storms,
the Roman army to annihilate the enemy. While the Nile
flood waters were beneficial once they had run their course,
they were immensely destructive. For this reason, then, does
Fuseli employ his executioner type here.

From the Nile one only has to move northwards across the Mediterranean to the wood near Athens, where Bottom, like some Middle Eastern potentate, is giving orders to the fairies – Cobweb to kill a bee for its honey bag – Peaseblossom to scratch his head – Mustardseed first to desist from his excessive courtesy and then to join in scratching his master's head. The gesture of the hands above the head is typical of Eastern obsequiousness, but the motif of a tiny figure on the hand is probably derived from the engraved reconstruction of Phidias' colossal Jupiter Olympus at Elis and is also connected with Gulliver's experience. For an explanation of the use of the executioner type, one may turn to Act III Scene I of the same play, where Bottom speaks to Mustardseed:

IV

Good Master Mustardseed, I know your patience well: that same cowardly giant-like oxbeef hath devoured many a gentleman of your house: I promise you, your kindred hath made my eyes water ere now.

Thus Mustard, hot and sharp, is a kind of gourmet's executioner! If this peck of wit is too hot to swallow, then Addison in Zurich may provide a salivant: 'I have indeed observed in several Inscriptions of this Country, that your men of Learning here are extremely delighted in playing little Tricks with Words and Figures; for your Swiss Wits are not yet got out of the Anagram and Acrostic.'

There was no time in the artist's life when women were absent, either personally or in his work, but it is not until after his friendship with Mary Wollstonecraft, about 1790, that one senses that they become a dominant and consistent theme as subject matter. What has not been generally realized is that it is more than a theme, it is a cycle – a cycle in the sense that the artist explores in a variety of contexts the whole gamut of the evolution of woman from hoyden to heroine, from maiden to mother. These parallel developments will be examined in that order along with their diverse effects on man, that subject, equal and object of their affection, which is nowhere more clearly stated than in Aphorism 227: 'Woman fondles, pities, despises and forgets what is below her; she values, bears and wrangles with her equal; she adores what is above her.'

Rome was a proving ground in many fields and Fuseli had had eight years to find his proofs, to establish for himself his own definitions of the roles that women could play and perhaps rid himself of that antipathy towards the emancipated woman which most of the *Stürmer und Dranger* had. In Rome it was possible for both sexes from the North to relax the conventions of their respective homelands, both among themselves and with the Romans.

In the Palazzo Bolognetti alone, Fuseli may have felt that he had fallen amongst the Three Graces themselves, for of the three daughters of a superannuated servant of the family, Angela had 'wit in conversation', Leonora 'sang and played the pianoforte with vast expression' and Nannina (Fuseli's favourite) had a 'surprising capacity of mind'. These descriptions are owed to

150 Title page of 'Parthenia'. 1611

168

Northcote, who may not have been so privy to Fuseli's liaisons with nymphs whose accomplishments lay in other directions. Carnival time in Rome allowed for more licence than at others and girls could escape their chaperones. The two drawings by John Brown aptly illustrate this situation, one, *Three Women with Baskets* fitting the account given by Northcote in one of his *176* letters of carnival activities, while the other demonstrates normality, the rear vision of the delectable but unattainable flower with its attendant thorn, *A Roman Lady with her Duenna. 177*

Drawings of this type by Fuseli do not come earlier than 1779, when he was at Ostend about to embark for England and one suspects that he had a selection of Brown's drawings with him, an influence already observed. However he was perfectly well aware of the tightrope that a young girl walked on her way to mature virtue; he had written about it in his *Remarks on the Writings of J.-J. Rousseau* (1767) apropos of *La Nouvelle Héloïse*,

what consequencies will it have for wenches to know that there are kisses, out of family. . . . To know that stays paint to the eagle eye of love there their luxuriance of bosom and milky orbs of rapture, and there the slender waist and rising hips; that with the perfumes of their toilet contagion spreads, that aprons will invite Hamlet to build tabernacles between Beauty's legs. . . . What will be the consequencies of all this? They will open them – yea, and dream at the same time that virginity may drop a maidenhead, and matrimony pick it up: . . . your daughter may prove a harlot – very like – and may have read Héloise.

It was in 1785–6 in four *tondi* of Perdita's upbringing (*The 179 Winter's Tale*, III 3 and IV 3), which are extra-textual, that Fuseli employed the motif of a girl at a spinet, a seventeenth-century invention to represent the transition between virginity and the breaking of the hymeneal chord. Robert Burton (*Anatomy of Love* XI) explained that, 'To hear a fair young gentlewoman play upon the virginals, lute, viol and sing to it . . . must needs be a great enticement', and for a pictorial example one cannot do better than refer to the title page of *Parthenia 150* (1611), which requires no explanation. It may indeed be possible that Fuseli knew this work, for he was friendly with Dr Burney, the musician and historian; besides, almost every woman of his acquaintance seems to have been an adept at these dangerous keys – Angelica Kauffmann, Maria Cosway, Anna Landolt – affecting their audience as Lotte did Werther, when at the piano: 'Never have I seen her lips so charming; it was as if they opened up in a famishing desire to sip in those sweet sounds . . . I resisted no longer, . . . and vowed: "never will I dare . . . And yet – I will – Ha! do you see . . . – this bliss – and then lost forever to expiate that Sin – Sin!" ' (Letter 24 November).

While the fatal kiss between Lotte and Werther was to come over the reading of *Ossian*, Fuseli might almost be illustrating this *amore pianoforte* in his *Young man kissing a girl at a Spinet 181* (1819). Earlier in 1800, he had made a drawing to illustrate *Folly and Innocence* for Cowper's *Progress of Error*, in which he *180* makes clear that Vanity, or looking in the mirror, reveals to the innocent her charms, so that any consequent playing at the keyboard will lead to folly. To emphasize the richness of innocence Fuseli inscribed on this drawing the 'paradox' of Hesiod 'the half is fuller than the whole', better to sing of innocence than from experience is the moral drawn, but the same paradox would fit Burton's anonymous couplet:

> She seems not won, but won she is at length
> In such wars women use but half their strength.
> (*Anatomy of Love* XI)

For it is the Ripa interpretation of a woman before her mirror as *Lascivious Love*, whether it be the type with the armoured headgear in his *Allegory of Vanity* (1811) or the more domestic type of *A woman gazing in a mirror* (*c.* 1814). In the former there is the moral addition of Time speeding away to ring the changes, an invention of the artist derived in part from Milton's Limbo of Vanity (*Paradise Lost*, III, 440 ff) and Shakespeare's *Time*, as Chorus (*A Winter's Tale*, IV prologue), who announced among other things: 88 89 54

> so shall I do
> To the freshest things now reigning, and make stale
> The glistening of this present . . .

Lascivious love is very obviously at the back of this allegory for on the verso side there is *Three female nudes and an amorino surround a prostrate male figure*, the debilitated finale to the activity in another drawing of a similar group (Victoria and Albert Museum). Since one of the women holds an apple, the scene could be described as a 'Parisian' aftermath to that famous contest and judgment of Antiquity. London could provide similar entertainment, the harlot or courtesan being, par excellence, the emblem of sexual pleasure without love. 182

If Fuseli assumed a moral antipathy to loveless sex, he was also persuaded by a care for his health. Armstrong had so warned in his *The Art of Preserving the Health*:

> nor in the wanton arms
> of twining Lais melt your manhood down.
> For from the colliquation of soft joys
> How chang'd you rise! the ghost of what you was!
> Languid, and melancholy, and gaunt, and wan;
> Your veins exhausted, and your nerves unstrung.
> Spoil'd of its balm and sprightly zest, the blood
> Grows vapid phlegm. (IV)

Worse followed if there was over-indulgence, epitomized by what Fuseli called 'a prettier simile' (of the effects of the arts and sciences on society) in his work on Rousseau, namely 'rosy harlots, who by coaxing and magic embraces give momentary springs and elasticity to those limbs which their abyss of pleasures sucked into languishment and impotence'. In any case, Fuseli as a choleric would avoid anything which might render him phlegmatic!

The many drawings of courtesans, singly but more often in twos and threes, like *Two Courtesans with fantastic hairstyles* (*c.*1796–1800), therefore, represents such an 'abyss of pleasures', with an appropriate hardness of line and strong colour tones. The relationship of this drawing to the one by John Brown, *Three Women with baskets*, in the way the heads are turned, is a 178 176 reminder of the likely source in Michelangelo's *Judith and Holofernes*, in which the heroine and her companion are similarly shown. *36*

It might be going too far to suggest that Fuseli would have considered Judith, as he did Salome, as a Bacchic maenad, but a male head was *her* trophy, and it was well known that Cristofano Allori's painting of this subject represented *his* head carried by his mistress. Thus one can follow through Fuseli's oeuvre the conjunction of the Bacchic type of femme fatale, tragic, comic and domestic and a male head, rendered more degrading by being still attached to the body. As examples, the *Siegfried and Chriemhild, Falstaff in the Buck Basket* and *Falstaff* *52, VI* *with Doll Tearsheet* can be cited. This motif is a combination of *183* 'twining Lais' and Fuseli's brand of agoraphobia, induced possibly by his small stature. A specific occasion of his violent reaction was when he and Opie were beset by a crowd of beastly Eton boys and had to fight their way out, when they were visiting Windsor to see the Royal collection. A prime example of this same motif is to be seen in the Pasinelli *Salome with the Head of St John the Baptist*, engraved in the same Boydell series *184* (1769–1772) cited earlier, for this treatment of the head on a charger as though it was some choice viand is not so different from Fuseli's own version for Lavater's Essays. *121*

The commencement of the true femme fatale as a maenad is well shown in the *Lady Macbeth Sleepwalking* 1775–77, and as an *30* incipient maenad/harlot in the Rivington plate of *Cressida,* who *120* exclaims to Diomedes:

> O pretty, pretty pledge!
> Nay, do not snatch it from me;
> He that takes that doth take my heart withal.

The fallen woman may lead, by change of tense only, to the falling woman motif, but this is also induced by a kind of Bacchic frenzy, in the case of the heroine in James Thomson's *Tancred and Sigismunda* (1792, but here in a hand-coloured reprint of *185* 1827), who, throwing herself down in grief beside the mortally wounded Osmund, her husband, is killed by him for her supposed infidelity with Tancred. The motif has a possible stage source in the action of Mrs Beverley playing *The Gamester,* who won approbation in a similar scene, when she 'flung herself as if for union of death on the prostrate form before her':* in *See Downer, *op.cit.,* p.14. essence, Chriemhild re-enacts this mortal fall in the death scene from the *Nibelungenlied*. In another context, the converted *116* Moslem girl Amanda/Rezia locked in embrace with Huon, *186* falls into the sea, a true lover's leap. The source for this group is the famous *Eros and Psyche*, but true to form Fuseli has Amanda/ *187* Rezia clutching Huon's head and not vice versa as in the Roman work.

Very rarely indeed does Fuseli carry this theme into real life, for even the courtesan drawings have no great air of reality about them. One instance, *Woman seated on a Sofa* (c. 1795–1802) *188* does give a slice of life, a fashionable demi-mondaine in an erotic but inelegant pose, but possibly not so, once one remembers that the prototype was a Fragonard Sultana in pantaloons!

171

The Turkish cult was so worked in, that postures like this among the avant-garde were commonplace. That this woman is the Western houri is supported by the earlier work of the Rev. Matthew William Peters, *Love in her Eye sits playing* (1778), which was the typical English smoking room version of the Rococo oriental type. But one has to remember that Mary Wollstonecraft *smiled* when she read in a 'book of education', 'It would be needless to caution you against putting your hand . . . under your neck-handkerchief, for a modest woman never did so!' (1792). The sofa probably gained respectability when Cowper wrote *The Task* (1785), of which Book I was titled *The sofa*, and Fuseli's illustration to the later edition had the poet seated in one, listening to his Genius. *189*

The most extreme type of the Bacchic maenad occurs when frenzy turns to madness. As one knows, Fuseli had been told that Bedlam was dominated by women in love, but the times also provided a great variety of other women possessed, like Joanna Southcott with religion and the less notorious case of Marianne Davies* who was driven out of her mind by playing the harmonica (wineglasses set ringing by the wetted finger). This instrument was warranted so dangerous that several states banned its use! Madness was also possible in advanced pregnancy. Indeed the bars over windows in the maternity wards of the older London hospitals were only removed this century. There was then no lack of contemporary evidence of the fragile balance of the female mind.

*See Stephen Gwynn, op.cit., p.30.

The Vision of the Lazar House has already been referred to, but further attention might be drawn to the lovelorn girls in the right background. But the most lonely and extraordinary case that Fuseli treated was *Mad Kate* (1806–07, Cowper *The Task* I 534–556). The poet recounts how Kate, a serving maid, fell in love with a sailor lost at sea. Crazed with grief she took to wandering, deluded into expecting his return. Fuseli illustrates all this dramatically, turning Kate into some deranged Sibyl, a modern Penelope perhaps, with no Athena to save her roving sailor. Neither he nor Cowper were exactly inventing a new character, for Laurence Sterne had much earlier (*A Sentimental Journey*, 1768) produced the very popular image of Maria and her dog, and artists as diverse as Wright of Derby and Angelica Kauffmann had painted that subject. Maria of course was French, so if one excepts The Lady in Milton's *Comus*, as an English equivalent, there was a truly British frenzied prototype in Mortimer's *Britannia* (1777), the frontispiece to Thomson's poems in Bell's *The Poets of Great Britain*. The lines illustrated from the poem of that title read: *192*

101

190

> Bare was her throbing bosom to the Gale
> Loose flowed her tresses, rent her azure robe.

Britannia was distraught, because as Samuel Johnson said these verses were 'a kind of poetical invective against the Ministry (Walpole's), whom the nation thought not forward enough in resenting the depredations of the Spaniards'.† However, this seashore maenad does owe something to Angelica Kauffmann's

†Samuel Johnson, Lives of the Poets, London, 1779–81.

172

Ariadne or the engraving made from it. Finally, Reinagle's *The Fair Maria*, engraved by Caldwell in 1797, substitutes the *193* seashore for the previous rural setting. Fuseli's *Mad Kate*, therefore, combines and continues this new myth, but characteristically endows Cowper's deranged housemaid with the gesture and expression of a much higher caste, for instance Dante's Hecuba, after she had seen both Polyxena slain and

> Polydorus dead by the seashore, fell insane
> And howled like a dog, so fearfully distraught
> Was she, so wrenched out of her mind with pain.
>   (Inferno xxx 10–21)*

Inferno. The Divine Comedy, trans. Dorothy Sayers, London, 1949.

There might be some injustice, perhaps, in suggesting that *Mad Kate* is a more mythical rendition of Mary Wollstonecraft,† but both have certain things in common. Not only does Fuseli's epithet 'termagant' fit them both, but Miss Wollstonecraft at the time of their closest association irritated the fastidious artist by affecting a 'revolutionary' appearance, her hair unbound topped by a working class cap, a nondescript dress and black worsted stockings, an appearance which also matches David's *La Maraichère* (*c.*1793–95 Musée Lyons), an educated revolutionary. Mary in France had had an affair and a child with Imlay, before returning to England to find some stability in her marriage with Godwin. His memoirs of her, however, provoked a violent anti-Jacobin attack on her memory, the worst describing her as little more than a prostitute. 'Poor Mary' was all Fuseli had to say when she died, but in the discussion of the other part of his 'cycle', it may be that there lies his serious valediction of that impulsive prophetess without honour in her own country – at least until almost the end of the nineteenth century.

†See Ralph M. Wardle, *Mary Wollstonecraft*, University of Kansas Press, 1951.

What is quite clear is that Fuseli despite the obvious drift of Cowper's poem, had no intention of indulging in rural genre as Thomas Barker of Bath does in his *Crazy Kate* (*c.*1794–1803). *191* While this work represents a much more true to life observation, the girl epitomizing the nadir of despair, it cannot be claimed as an example of social realism, but rather of 'proto-realism', if the term can be forgiven, since it indicates the absorption of the figurative into the corpus of the rural picturesque.

It is apposite to begin the 'better half' of the cycle with some reference to that force which directs the young girl on her progress to virtue or vice – Love. An etching by the artist of *194* about 1805, with its inscription describing the origin of the two loves from a common source, illustrates both the notion held within the circle of Erasmus Darwin and also Fuseli's own view. The crawling Cupid is the elder Eros, as Darwin explained in a footnote to the *Botanic Garden*, 'the first that came out of the great egg of night, which floated in Chaos, and was broken by the horns of the celestial bull; that is, was hatched by the warmth of spring'. His source was Bacon's *Cupid or an Atom. Explained of the Corpuscular Philosophy* (xvii *Wisdom of the Ancients*), described there as the most ancient of all the Gods, but also interpreted as 'a particle' and linked to the atom or corpuscle theory of Democritus. At the end of the eighteenth century this theory was being applied albeit in a very vague formulation to molecular structure – microcosm to macrocosm – and inevitably to the union of spermatozoa and ova (of 'the formation of the fetus in the womb we are very ignorant: but it appears . . . probable, that an accidental physical cause may account for . . . it' – Mary Wollstonecraft, 1792). The armed Cupid is the younger, the son of Jupiter and Venus, the archer and harbinger of Love. Fuseli, very effectively, illustrates an endless cycle of Love and Life in contra-distinction to the Renaissance and Neo-Platonist theory of Sacred and Profane Love.

But he went further than this by establishing Northern equivalents for these two Cupids – Puck and Jack O'Lanthorn. *169, 81* The latter, alias Will-o'-the-Wisp, was also *ignis fatuus* (foolish fire), the phenomenon caused by the spontaneous ignition of the gas (methane) which escapes from the decayed vegetable matter in marshes. The resulting action may be described, therefore, as a metamorphosis of chemical matter to animate form. To substantiate this conception there are the following analogies: in 1772 Priestley (*On Different Kinds of Air*) had demonstrated how plants were capable of restoring exhausted air: in 1774, by passing electric sparks through 'alkaline air' (ammonia) he had separated it into nitrogen and hydrogen and followed this by isolating 'dephlogisticated air', which his French colleague, Lavoisier, named oxygen. At this point, one may interpolate that Venus as Goddess of Vegetation was also the mother of Cupid, who, according to Bacon, was Atom. Before 1800, both Richter and Cavendish had explored the principles of equivalency and reciprocal proportions (in 1784 the latter had discovered that two parts of hydrogen and one part of oxygen composed water). However, it was not until 1811 that John Dalton formulated the atomic theory. Thus, Fuseli, following Darwin, was substituting 'stricter' analogies drawn from Natural Philosophy for those 'looser' ones 'which dress out the imagery of poetry'.

Turning to the polyautograph or lithograph, one of the first to be made in England, *A Woman looking out of a Window* (1803), *195* one finds a young girl, expectant of love, for it is inscribed in Greek, 'Evening thou bringest all'. This is the crepuscular threshold to love itself, for Ripa through Albani's agency in the Palazzo Verospi ceiling, illustrates this time of day by a *37* Cupid raining down arrows on the earth, while next to him is Night, the mother of Love. This young girl of Fuseli's is also stylistically related to Ludovico Carracci's nymph in *The Temptation of St Benedict,* as mentioned. *145*

Certainly up to his meeting with Mary Wollstonecraft, Fuseli would have held the views of his generation on the up-bringing of the young girl, and very probably those outlined by Rousseau* in his novel *Émile* for his young man's mistress and wife, Sophie. Its purpose was 'To please, to be useful to us (men), to make us love and esteem them, to educate us when young, and take care of us when grown up, to advise, to console us, to render our lives easy and agreeable', upon which purpose and its methods of attainment Miss Wollstonecraft

*All the extracts from Rousseau were quoted by Mary Wollstonecraft in her *A Vindication . . . .*

heaped her scorn in *A Vindication of the Rights of Women* (1792). It is clear from some turns of phrase, the language of the invective and rather more direct references, that this tract grew out of discussions with Fuseli and others of the Johnson circle. One reference is surely directed towards Fuseli, when she opines that a careful education will produce either fine ladies, or 'mere notable women', 'friendly, honest creatures' but the intellectual world is shut to them. 'A man of sense', she continues, 'can only love such a woman on account of her sex, and respect her because she is a trusty servant. . . . Besides, how many women of this description pass their days, or at least their evenings, discontentedly. Their husbands acknowledge that they are good managers and chaste wives, but leave home to seek for more agreeable – may I be allowed to use a significant word – *piquant* society'. Later she returned to the same theme (repetition was her strong suit), 'if women be not, in general, brought more on a level with men, some superior women, like the Greek courtesans, will assemble the men of abilities around them, and draw from their families many citizens, who would have stayed home had their wives had more sense, or the graces which result from the exercise of the understanding and fancy'. All this was true of the Fuselis, and Mary Wollstonecraft's suggestion of a *ménage à trois* was to supply the missing link of intellectual friendship, since, she observed, 'In a great degree, love and friendship cannot subsist in the same bosom': and contrasted 'The vain fears and fond jealousies' of love with 'the tender confidence and sincere respect' of friendship.

She was also familiar with the discussion of electrical fluids as in a footnote: 'when inclined to laugh at materialists' she would ask whether 'the passions might not be fine volatile fluids that embraced humanity', then in another passage, inveighing against allowing the imagination to revel in the reading of novels, she ends in a typical Fuselian way, 'every trifle produces those phosphoric bursts which only mimic in the dark the flame of passion'. About Fuseli as an artist the following shaft goes home, 'the lively heated imagination . . . directed by a mind, condemned in a world like this, to prove its noble origin by panting after unattainable perfection. . . . An imagination of this vigorous cast can give existence to insubstantial forms, and stability to the shadowy reveries which the mind naturally falls into when realities are found vapid.'

Almost as a riposte to those remarks, a trifle feline for a reformer who decried 'cattish affection', Fuseli endowed his wife with a catalogue of Rousseauesque identities. In the *Portrait of Mrs Fuseli with her Workbasket* (c. 1790–2) he shows her as a   *202* glamorous companion, her workbasket shut, yet in another he shows her sewing. In *The Fireplace* (1791) she is the dominat-   *201* ing mistress of the hearth, the reddish purple of her gown lending an extra imperiousness. Although childless, they may not in early years have expected to be so, and she is shown as the educator, switch in hand, as Miss Wollstonecraft declaimed,   *198* 'The wife . . . who is faithful to her husband, and neither

175

suckles nor educates her children, scarcely deserves the name of a wife.' A better known drawing of Mrs Fuseli with a switch (Kunsthaus Zurich) has in the past been hinted at as an example of Fuseli's sadistic eroticism, so it may prove disappointing to some to note Ripa's engraving of *Educazione*, and of *Correzione*, both showing women with switches. So far as she could, therefore, his Sophia, like her namesake in *Émile*, was both mistress and wife.

The naturalistic coloured drawings of her are firmly ensconced in the English portrait tradition, either of the formal, *Mrs Fuseli seated with her Workbasket* and the portrait from Belfast, or the informal and more French Rococo *Bust Portrait of Mrs Fuseli* and *Mrs Fuseli Sleeping*.

The first drawing, with the artist's notes of his articles for the *Analytical Review* providing a *terminus post* date of 1790, is too late to be a wedding portrait, but it might be an anniversary one, for Mrs Fuseli's couture contains all 'the fleeting whimsies of depraved elegance', which Mrs Nollekens, according to J. T. Smith, supposed herself to be above. Fuseli in no way exaggerated the 'way out' fashions of his day. There was in fact no need to, as a brief extract from Smith may show. Mrs Nollekens' hair was 'arranged over a cushion made to fit the head to a considerable height . . . the whole being surmounted by a small cap of point lace'. By wearing, in addition, shoes with three inch heels, Smith thought, maliciously as ever, that 'she meant to exult in out-topping her little husband'. Mrs Fuseli's statistics have not been preserved, but judging from the drawing of her, *The Fireplace*, she out-topped her husband without these artificial extensions. Even in his own home Fuseli must have been constantly aware of the dominating role of woman in his time.

While he looked to Gainsborough on occasion, Reynolds was his most favoured source for portraiture, as may be gathered by comparing Fuseli's portrait of his wife with Reynolds's *Mrs Robinson (Perdita)* (1782), Fuseli employing most of the stylistic characteristics displayed in it. The two informal studies cited above are immediately reminiscent of Greuze and Baudouin, the former's influence being particularly evident in *Mrs Fuseli Sleeping*; Greuze's *La Philosophie endormie* was exhibited at the Salon of 1765 in which Fragonard's Coresus had also appeared. In that same Salon *Young Girl weeping over a dead Bird*, by Greuze, had been pronounced as 'delicious' by Diderot. That epithet gives one a precise clue to explain the survival of the Rococo style well into the nineteenth century, for almost without break its courtly association elided into one with fashionable high life and its *debutantes* nymphs. Fuseli had broken too many pitchers with that age group, perhaps, before his marriage to permit him to express true innocence, and Mrs Fuseli in the bust portrait, with that formidable arrow thrust through her coiffure, gives the promise of experience, rather than a virginal invitation.

There is one aspect of technique in this latter drawing which indicates the degree to which engravings contributed to the

196

202, 203
199
200

201

203
204
199, 200

199

176

other media, for the 'pointillist' method of rendering the tight little curls of the hair seems derived from engravings of Roman heads; the one here reproduced by Winckelmann may serve *197* as an example, although better existed. From his earliest days the graphic media had been a 'natural' source for the artist.

It was the fortunate discovery of an inscribed drawing in the Liverpool Public Library that permitted Dr Schiff to identify Mrs Fuseli in so many drawings. Still untraced is the portrait of her by John Opie which formed a pair with the portrait of Fuseli now in the National Portrait Gallery, but establishing her identity has provided a key to the artist's range of interpretation in this genre. For these studies from life help to determine that other, seemingly domestic, scenes, are not so.

Apart from his vindication of Mrs Fuseli's role, the artist was in agreement with most of what Miss Wollstonecraft proposed. His drawing of *A Woman on a Sofa,* for instance, *188* could easily be that 'weak woman of fashion' of Miss Wollstonecraft's acquaintance, who 'thought a distinguishing taste and puny appetite the height of all human perfection. . . . I have seen this weak sophisticated being neglect all the duties in life, yet recline with self-complacency on her sofa, and boast of her want of appetite as a proof of delicacy that extended to, or, perhaps, arose from, her exquisite sensibility'. The crescendo of her indignation rising, Miss Wollstonecraft bursts out, 'Such a woman is not a more irrational monster than some of the Roman emperors, who were depraved by lawless power.' Since then kings have been more restrained and honour however weak had prevented too many instances of 'folly and cruelty', 'nor does the despotism that kills virtue and genius in the bud, hover over Europe with that destructive blast which desolates Turkey, and renders the men, as well as the soil, unfruitful'. Certainly here, Miss Wollstonecraft points to a different reason for emasculation, but her main argument is that if women are to be kept enslaved and ill-educated, they will continue to act as capricious tyrants, rendering effeminate true manly dignity. Nothing drew more scorn from her than the marriage market and the training of the debutante to that end and Rousseau must have made her spit when he opined that a young Englishwoman should cultivate her talents as 'a Circassian cultivates hers, to fit her for the harem of an Eastern bashaw'.

In this light two drawings by Fuseli can be examined, *The Debutante* (1807) and the earlier *Woman seen from the back,* *208* *drawing a curtain* (1798–1800). In the first one sees the victim *209* sewing (one form of slavery to Miss Wollstonecraft) and also leashed up to the wall like a 'lap dog'. In the background, however, there is her jailer and governess, the old order of calling and not the new, exemplified by Miss Wollstonecraft's own career and expounded in her *Thoughts on the Education of Daughters* (1787). This old order represents the ignorant duenna, a procuress, the female eunuch and major-domo of the modern seraglio. Salvator Rosa's *Soldier seen from the back* (Mortimer *210* made a copy of this etching) is not only a possible source but expresses the androgyne nature of the female guardian of the second drawing, and for this reason cannot, surely, be identified as Mrs Fuseli, whose own form was not as expansive as those here.

One cannot do better in summing up this part of the 'cycle' than referring to the watercolour, *An Elegant Establishment for Young Ladies* (*c.*1810) by Edward Francis Burney, a relative of *211* Dr Burney and his daughter Fanny, whose novel *Evelina* had given such a vivid, contemporary account of the rural teenager in London. Burney was a close follower of Fuseli, and he provides in this drawing a succinct catalogue of his master's images – the girls at the pianoforte, right; the female major-domo at her desk, left background; the poor wretch attached by a neck iron to a chair (a reference to *The Debutante*) in the *208* foreground; and rather more dramatically the girl being hoisted up by her jaws in the centre. Other dangers are demonstrated – being fondled by a French dancing master, handled by a Nubian, squeezed by the soldiery and measured up by a lascivious tailor. Across the street there is a seminary for young boys. Both institutions and their lamentable influence provoked Miss Wollstonecraft into advocating co-education up to the teenage level, stating as one reason, 'marriage will never be held sacred till women, by being brought up with men, are prepared to be their companions rather than their mistresses'.

Fuseli appears to imply a happy equality of the sexes in his *The Newspaper in the country* (1806–07 Cowper's *The Task* IV *212* 36–56), for he changes the sex of the reader in illustrating the lines:

> This folio of four pages . . .
> . . . that holds
> Inquisitive attention, while I read,
> Fast bound in chains of silence, which the fair,
> Though eloquent themselves, yet fear to break –

As with *Mad Kate*, he monumentalizes the everyday genre *190* scene – not however to everyone's satisfaction. Leigh Hunt (*Lord Byron and some of his contemporaries*, 1828) accused Fuseli of turning 'the quiet tea table scene in Cowper . . . into a preposterous conspiracy of huge men and women, all bent on shewing their thews and postures, with dresses as fantastical as their minds. One gentleman, of the existence of whose trousers you are not aware till you see the terminating line at the ankle, is sitting and looking grim on the sofa, with his hat on, and no waistcoat.' Which is a reminder that Fuseli experienced that kind of social criticism long before Manet.

As to marriage itself, Milton and Homer offered the two types of spouse. *The Return of Milton's Wife* (*c.*1799) shows us *214* one who deserted her husband only to come back and plead and implore his pardon, while *Ulysses and Penelope* (1806 *213* Duroveray edition) contains the classic example of the faithful wife. In both there is that rare posture for a woman in Fuseli's work, that of kneeling before a man. (The most notorious example of the reverse is *Adam and Eve* from the Milton

178

Gallery, where he is agreeing to share her Sin.) In the more conventional union of marriage, Fuseli maintained the man as *magister*, expecting loyalty but charitable enough to forgive on occasion. Perhaps his own lack of experience led him to picture, nearly always, mothers alone with their children and a rare example of a *toute ensemble* is the engraving of the Milton Gallery painting *Silence (Il Penseroso* 78–82):   *215*

> Some still removed place will fit,
> Where glowing embers through the room
> Teach light to counterfeit a gloom,
> Far from all resort of mirth,
> Save the cricket on the hearth,

Mary Wollstonecraft's heart 'throbbed with sympathetic emotion' at the sight of a husband, . . . 'who, returning weary home in the evening, found smiling babes and a clean hearth', although Fuseli in *Silence* was thinking of one of Hayley's anecdotes of Milton as a youth in Italy being taken in to rest by an Italian woman with a small child. Guercino's *Night* again   *158* plays a part in providing a melancholic brooding over a sleeping child and a similar sad lassitude afflicted John Brown's Holy Family in his *Rest on the Flight*.   *85*

   Silence is yet another example of Fuseli's choice of a melancholic light counterfeited here by the embers or truly dyed by evening, timeless in effect, but indicative that night will replace day. And time itself was running out for Fuseli as it was for *Richard II* in the Rivington plate: *175*

> I wasted time and now doth Time waste me

with the added reference to death; the motif of the skeleton moving on the hands of the clock comes from the *Nun* plate of Holbein's *Dance of Death*,* of which a set was in Ottley's collection.

*Illustrated and discussed in W. Y. Ottley, *An Inquiry into the Origins and Early History of Engraving . . .*, 2 vols, London, 1816.

   To complete this 'cycle', Fuseli's *Parental Care* (*c.*1805) does   *216* duty as a reflection both on old age and on the concern of children for their parents. For a sentimental and conventional view there is William Hamilton's engraved work, *Charity*   *217* (Royal Academy 1799), which would appear to stem from Fuseli. It is utterly redolent of every cliché connected with the subject but, as one knows, would have been accepted as being absolutely true to life. On the other hand, Fuseli's couple do not belong to the 'old folks' home' tradition at all, but represent two elderly heroic characters. Their nature may be guessed at by quoting from Mary Wollstonecraft's chapter, *Duty to Parents*: 'If parents discharge their duty they have a strong hold and sacred claim on the gratitude of their children, but few parents are willing to receive . . . respectful affection . . . on such terms. They demand blind obedience, . . . and to render these demands of weakness and ignorance more binding, a mysterious sanctity is spread around the most arbitrary principle.' Later she adds, 'the indolent parent of high rank, may, it is true, extort a show of respect from his child, and females on the Continent are particularly subject to the views of their families.' One wonders whether Fuseli is defending here that feudal relationship that is attacked in the second quotation, or demonstrating the tyranny exposed in the first.

There was one class of women which was nonpareil to Fuseli – the Greek goddess and the Northern fairy queen. For them he reserves a Rococo svelte figure and in all such cases man is in a subservient position, seated or kneeling. His penchant for the Sibyl type, the eternal woman, positive and energetic, is shown in two examples based on the theme of *The Tiburtine Sibyl and Augustus,* either from Antonio de Trenta's print after Parmigianino or from Pietro da Cortona's painting in the Royal Collection at Windsor: *Virtue reclaiming Youth* (1806–07, Cowper *The Progress of Error* V 71–2) and the frontispiece to John Bonnycastle's *Astronomy* (1786 and 1811), the goddess here being Urania. Even in their more terrestrial or oceanic exploits, these goddesses are calm and serene, like *Nephele and Ixion* (1809) – though that union was to spawn the centaur – and *Venus appearing to Ulysses* (1803), where the hero is a sprawling survivor behind her. In general Fuseli's treatment of this class is consistent with the eighteenth century's belief that men would be brutes without women.

There is one last class of the female species to be dealt with – the woman artist; of which there were a phenomenally large number in the last half of the eighteenth century, a high proportion of them also blessed with good looks. It is highly improbable that Fuseli had any regard for them as a class. One of them he definitely disliked. Northcote recorded that if anyone suggested that Maria Cosway was an imitator of his, 'Fuseli was put in a passion'.

Some evidence suggests that the drawing *Woman before the Laocoon** (c. 1802–03) represents Maria Cosway before that great sculpture. The watermark date on the paper is 1802, the year that Fuseli visited Paris. Maria Cosway was already there, having been in France for some time in circumstances which Horace Walpole in a letter to Miss Berry (1791) puts as well as anyone: 'I am glad Mrs Cosway is with you – she is pleasing, but surely it is odd to drop a child and her husband and country all in a breath' – particularly as she had earned the title of '*The all accomplished Maria*' before her departure. As far as her style was concerned she followed in the footsteps of Miss Kauffmann, and as far as her subjects were concerned she followed everyone, turning vapid everything she borrowed. She was, however, very pretty and it was perhaps in Italy that Fuseli had been put out by her.

His moment came, one may surmise, when he saw her standing looking at the Laocoön group which was one of the great works brought by Napoleon from Italy to be exhibited in the Louvre. He shows her clenching her fists in frustration, artistic presumably, but with the possible *double entendre* that this was one heroic male that this lively harpy could not claw.

The conception was not exactly new. Mrs Cosway had painted her fair share of Sibyls (*The Persian Sibyl*, Sir John Soane's Museum, London). A start may be made with Salvator Rosa's well known *Apollo and the Cumaean Sibyl*, here illustrated

142

105

106

151 Salvator Rosa. The Cumaean Sybil and Apollo

*218

by the etching, but a painting of the same group in a landscape is in the Wallace Collection. The tragedy of the story lies in the fact that the Sibyl had had her wish for long life granted by the god, but she had forgotten to ask for lasting beauty and youth as well. The connection of the theme with art was initiated by Mortimer's *Origin of Painting* (1770–71), in which the Corinthian maid outlines the silhouette of her lover on the wall. No woman artist would have missed that evidence of female primacy in the art of painting, so a logical sequel is to be found in Angelica Kauffmann's painting of *Design* (c.1779), with three others set in the ceiling of the Royal Academy council room in Somerset House and later transferred to Burlington House. Here the artist studies the Farnese Torso. Even the satirical side of such a juxtaposition prompted artists of this period, like St Aubin in his drawing, *Rendezvous in the Tuileries* (c.1764–65, National Gallery, Washington), showing an elderly woman sitting at the foot of a statue of a Greek youth.

219

But one may be sure that Fuseli's primary target was Maria Cosway's uncritical confidence in her own powers; Cunningham records that she considered her masterpiece to be her picture containing all the paintings in the gallery of the Louvre! If this was not enough, she issued in 1800 her series *The Progress of Virtue*, and that may have been the last straw.

Since much has been said already about these themes in Fuseli's art the discussion now will centre on the psychological elements which underlay his invention.

APPARITIONS, DREAMS AND NIGHTMARES

It is worth repeating that the evolution of Fuseli's apparitions runs from the shadowy, ectoplasmic type seen in the *Witch of Endor* and *Ulysses and Tiresias* to the solid embodiment of the spectre in *Hamlet and the Ghost* (c.1788). The repetition of this last subject in the Rivington Shakespeare introduces an important change, for in this *Hamlet and the Ghost*, the dead king is given the prominent front plane position and Hamlet, staring under his hand, rather as Reynolds had painted himself in an early self-portrait (1753–54, National Portrait Gallery), is relegated to a minor position. Similarly in the scene from *Julius Caesar* in the same series, the ghost is given full physical shape and the front position. That this promotion of the ghost may have been due to compositional demands is possibly true, but it also fits the artist's view that man remains dominated by extra-terrestrial forces. Since these forces, whatever their vehicle, may be considered as super-realities, there is good reason to give them solid form.

42, 41
221

130

220

This leads naturally to Fuseli's much quoted aphorism (231), 'One of the most unexplored regions of art are dreams, and what may be called the personification of sentiment'; the rider is important, for feelings so acutely personified in so many dream sequences can be carried in consequence into the realm of painted reality. Thus the dissonances of scale, irrational space and other phenomena of dreams are the instruments which Fuseli employs to purvey an overall expression of feeling.

In his own time the works involving fairies from Spenser's *157*
Faerie Queene and Shakespeare's *A Midsummer Night's Dream* *IV*
were instantly acceptable because everyone knew that fairies
and elves were very small, but in the case, for instance, of
Undine appearing to the Fisherman and his Wife, the rational *XIII*
spectator around 1820 would likely jib at such arbitrary space
and scale, even though he might be familiar with the work of
Rembrandt.

The only work connected specifically with the aphorism is
the plate engraved by Dadley for the 1807 edition of Erasmus *152*
Darwin's *Works, The power of Fancy in dreams* to illustrate the
lines starting with 'So holy transports' . . . to:

> Charm'd o'er thy bed celestial voices sing,
> And Seraphs hover on enamour'd wing.

Here are contrasted the sleeper and the dreamer, a young woman
being awakened to the power of celestial love via the imagery
of Saint Cecilia and her harpsichord as a symbol of virginity.
In the later *Queen Katherine's Dream* the moment of awakening *127*
from the dream is chosen, and in *Chriemhild in a dream sees* *115*
Siegfried dead (1805), the super-reality of the future is seen
simultaneously with the present reality of Siegfried looking
on. Opinion may differ on the success of these examples, but
in the context of the contemporary knowledge of such
phenomena, they are not 'crazy' to use Goethe's word.

Fortunately, Darwin inserted *Interludes* between the bookseller (Johnson) and the poet, amongst his verses, in which he
expanded on his subject matter. Thus he explained, 'you will
allow that we are perfectly deceived in our dreams: and that
even in our waking reveries, we are often so much absorbed
in the contemplation of what passes in our imaginations, that
for a while we do not attend to the lapse of time or to our own
locality; and thus suffer a similar kind of deception, as in our
dreams'. In an earlier note he had explained that 'we experience
variety of passions and even hunger and thirst in our dreams.
Hence I conclude, that our nerves of sense are not torpid or
inert during sleep.' Returning to the *Interlude*, Darwin continues, 'When by the art of the Painter or Poet, a train of ideas
is suggested to our imaginations, which interests us so much
by the pain or pleasure it affords, that we cease to attend to the
imitations of common external objects, and cease also to use
any voluntary efforts to compare these interesting trains of
ideas with our previous knowledge of things, a complete
reverie is produced', but one suspects only a few people at that
time were able to slip over into that irrational world, which
Darwin describes with such mundane assurance. It is proper to
interpolate here, that when Fuseli refers to 'poetic painting',
he means this type of art. Lessing (*Laocoön*, 14, note b.) says the
ancients called 'poetic pictures' *phantasiae* and the illusion they
create, *enargia*, and quoting Plutarch (*Amatorius* II) he declares
that because of this combination they were in fact 'waking
dreams'.

As with dreams Fuseli was concerned with different types of

152 *Fuseli. The Power of Fancy in Dreams,
from Erasmus Darwin's 'Botanic Garden'. 1807*

nightmare, or to be more clinically exact according to a recent article, sleep paralysis. The principal symptom is 'someone or something sitting on the chest', which in fact is the description given for the nightmare in eighteenth century dictionaries. The main difference between the two best known *Nightmares** of 1781 and 1792, is that the former is highly subjective, possibly to be described as the dream of a nightmare, since the artist by some process of sympathetic magic wishes to punish the indifferent Anna Landolt, and the latter is objective – indeed clinically so. Darwin's verses describe other symptoms named by Dr Schenk in the article cited above:

> O'er her fair limbs convulsive tremors fleet
> Start in her hands, and struggle in her feet;
> In vain to scream with quivering lips she tries,
> And strains in palsy'd lids her tremulous eyes;
> In vain she *wills* to run, fly, swim, walk, creep;
> The WILL presides not in the realm of SLEEP
> On her fair bosom sits the Demon-Ape
> Erect, and balances his bloated shape.

153 *Fuseli. Hercules destroying the horses of Diomedes. 1800–05*

One can assume that with the specialized knowledge of Dr Armstrong and Erasmus Darwin combined, Fuseli would have been familiar with all these characteristics; the one non-clinical element being the horse head of Swiss folklore. He seems indeed to have had no affection for the horse, for it is so often included in scenes of terror like *Hercules destroying the horses of Diomedes* (c.1805: engraved 1806) and *The Devil taking the Sompnour to hell* apart from the Nightmare variants. On the other hand he may be following Edmund Burke, who pointed out how some animals will react instinctively *before* the event. For example, Fuseli uses the motif of a dog with its tail between its legs in the Boydell work of *King Lear* and in the scene from Thomson's *Seasons* of the shepherd cowering in a storm, which accords with Burke's observation that 'dogs, under an apprehension of punishment. . .have writhed their bodies, and yelped, and howled as if they had actually felt the blows'.

161

240
144

If there was a poetic trigger for the first *Nightmare* then it must be in Bürger's *Lenore* (1774), for there in the opening verses a girl is oppressed in sleep and hears the clattering hooves of her dead lover's horse; Chodowiecki's engraving for the poem, *inter alia*, would have provoked Fuseli's competitive instinct to do better. A poetic change of another kind is worth noting. In Thomson's *Seasons* there are the lines:

80

> Still interrupted by distracted dreams,
> That o'er the sick imagination rise,
> And in black colours paint the mimic scene
> (*Spring* 1051–1053)

and in Armstrong's *The Art of Preserving the Health* (III),

> whose delirious brain,
> Stung by the Furies, works with poison'd thought:
> While pale and monstrous painting shocks the soul;
> And mangled consciousness bemoans itself
> For ever torn; and chaos floating round.

Both are describing a nightmare; Thomson's older type is black *I,83

183

and Armstrong's new type is white or pale. While this change is perhaps not so evident in the first *Nightmare* it certainly is in the second. *I 83*

Mention of Dr Armstrong introduces the second type of Nightmare (1810). The Greek inscription makes quite clear *139* that overeating will bring bad dreams during the night or in the poet's words:

> Not all a monarch's luxury the woes
> Can counterpoise of that most wretched man,
> Whose nights are shaken with the frantic fits
> Of wild Orestes;

and the lines already given for the nightmare follow. In a preceding canto Armstrong had given this advice:

> But would you sweetly waste the blank of night
> In sweet oblivion;
> Oppress not Nature sinking down to rest
> With feasts too late, too solid, or too full;
> But be the first concoction half-matur'd
> Ere you to nightly indolence resign
> Your passive faculties.

And as related, Fuseli followed his old friend's advice and never partook of a late supper. This practice in itself should be sufficient to dispel the belief put about in the *Public Advertiser* (1790) that the artist's creative fancy sprang from 'an animal process, and is brought about after regular intervals by Mr Fuseli's eating raw pork for supper'. It may be remarked that about the same time, Thomas Beddoes M.D., a friend of Darwin's, an enthusiastic admirer of the French Revolution and a kind of batty ecologist dreaming (Virgil *Eclogue IV*) of a change in the natural order that could make hedgerows produce butter, wrote a tract proposing that sailors should eat their food (salt pork) raw to prevent obesity, the first symptom of scurvy. It was a good thing for the future of the Royal Navy that Cook introduced more effective anti-scorbutics!

Fuseli was very well aware of this supposed gastronomic stimulant to the imagination. It must have been about the same year that he called on Blake and, as related by Cunningham, feigned astonishment at finding the other artist supping off a dish of cold mutton. 'Is that what you do it on?', Fuseli is supposed to have remarked. This legend did not die out for Thomas De Quincey repeated it, 'we hear it reported of Dryden and of Fuseli in modern times, that they thought proper to eat raw meat for the sake of obtaining splendid dreams: how much better for such a purpose to have eaten opium.'* But there is no evidence of Fuseli even doing that.

**Op.cit.*, p. 118.

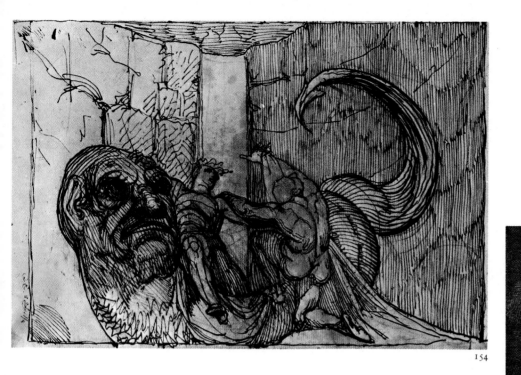

154 Fuseli. *Virgil, Dante and Geryon*, 1811

155 Fuseli. *Michelangelo in the Colosseum*, 1801. The walls of the Colosseum enclose him as the cliffs enclose Dante

156 Fuseli. *The Great Father and Ancient Night*, c. 1810. From Armstrong's *Art of Preserving Health*

157 Fuseli. *The Dream of Prince Arthur*, 1788. From Spenser's *Faerie Queene*

158, 159
Guercino's *Night*
(above) was used
(in reverse) by
Fuseli as the basis
for his etching
*The Witch and
the Mandrake*
c. 1812–13

160 Fuseli.
Garrick and Mrs Pritchard as Macbeth and Lady Macbeth, c. 1766.
For a later version, see pl. XI

161 Fuseli.
The Devil taking the Sompnour to hell, 1821. From Chaucer's *Canterbury Tales*

162 John Hamilton Mortimer.
The Devil, the Sompnour and the Widow

160

161

162

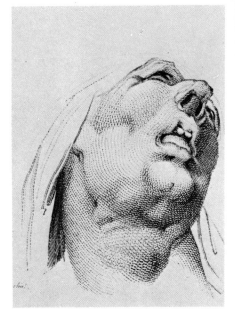

163

165

164

OPVS PRAXITELIS   OPVS FIDIAE

163, 164 Fuseli. *A Capriccio of The Horsetamers*, c. 1810–11. The original classical group is shown (left) in an eighteenth-century engraving. Fuseli's 'Caprice' may actually have been planned as a double monument to Nelson and Wellington

165 Fuseli. *Undine and Huldbrand*, c. 1819–22

166, 167 Fuseli. *Two Heads from Dante, c.* 1779. Made to illustrate Lavater's *Physiognomy*. The left-hand head represents Sloth, and its source is a head (right) from Michelangelo's *The Brazen Serpent*

SATAN.

168 Fuseli. *Head of Satan, c.* 1779. Another 'type' for Lavater – heroic pride

169 Fuseli. Puck, from *A Midsummer Night's Dream*, 1802

171

170 Fuseli. *The Prophet Balaam*, c. 1779. An example, also for Lavater, of the 'physiognomy of gesture' – the right hand conveying a blessing, the left a curse

171 Fuseli. *Timon of Athens*, 1805

172 Fuseli. *Kemble as Hotspur with Glendower*, 1784. Note, in this and the Timon pictures the V formed by the two fingers – a sign of mental energy. Compare also pl. 7

172

173

173 Fuseli. *Flora attired by the Elements*, 1791.
The frontispiece to Darwin's *Botanic Garden*

174 The curious motif of the dismembered
arms reaching upwards, which appears at the
bottom of the Flora picture and also in pl. 156,
is no doubt derived from Veneziano's copy of
Michelangelo

174

176 John Brown. *Three Women with Baskets*

177 John Brown. *A Roman Lady with her Duenna*

178 (below) Fuseli. *Two Courtesans with fantastic hairstyles and hats, c.* 1796–1800. The poses may be influenced by Michelangelo's *Judith* (pl. 36)

179 (below right) Fuseli. *Girl at a Spinet with an Elf, c.* 1785–86. One of four illustrations – but not of particular scenes – to *The Winter's Tale*

180 Fuseli. *Folly and Innocence*, 1800

181 Fuseli. *A Young Man kissing a Girl at a Spinet*, 1819

182 Fuseli. *Three women, an amorino and a prostrate man*, 1811

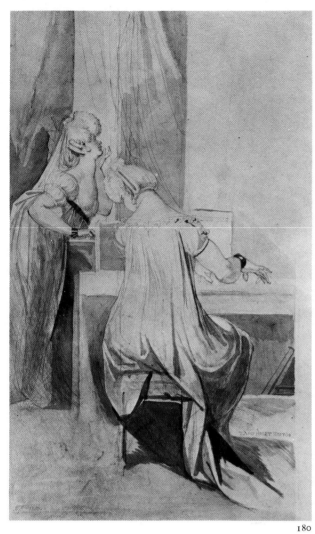

180

181

182

183

183 Fuseli. *Falstaff with Doll Tearsheet*,
1789. The femme fatale holds and kisses a
male head as if it were a sort of trophy:
another example is pl. 52

184 Pasinelli. *Salome with the Head of St
John the Baptist*. Compare Fuseli's version,
pl. 121

184

185

186

187

185 Fuseli. *Tancred and Sigismunda*, 1792.
An illustration to Thomson's play.
Sigismunda throws herself beside her
mortally wounded husband, who kills her
for supposed infidelity

186, 187 Fuseli. *Amanda/Rezia falls with
Huon into the sea*, 1804–05. Fuseli's source
was again classical – *Eros and Psyche* (left)

188 Fuseli. *Woman seated on a Sofa*, 1802–08

189 Matthew William Peters. *Love in her Eye sits Playing*

190 Fuseli. *Mad Kate*, 1806–07. The story comes from Cowper's *The Task*: a serving maid loses her lover at sea and crazed with grief wanders by the shore expecting his return

191 Thomas Barker of Bath. *Crazy Kate*. The same subject as Fuseli's, but treated in a more genre style

192, 193 Two more mad maidens. Below left: Mortimer's *Britannia*, an illustration to Thomson's poem of that name. Below right: Richard Reinagle's *The Fair Maria*, a character in Sterne's *Sentimental Journey*

194

197

195

196

198

194 Fuseli. *Venus/Night and the Two Cupids*, *c.* 1805. The crawling Cupid is the elder Eros, the armed Cupid the younger, also identified by Fuseli with Puck (pl. 169) and Jack o'Lanthorn (pl. 81) respectively

195 Fuseli. *Girl on a sofa looking out of a window*, 1803. The (reversed) Greek inscription means 'Evening, thou bringest all'

197 A Greek coin illustrated by Winckelmann, showing a method of rendering the curls of the hair copied by Fuseli in the portraits reproduced opposite

196, 198 An erotic meaning has been read into Fuseli's drawing of *Mrs Fuseli seated, with a switch*, *c.* 1790–92 (below), but comparison with the figure of *Educazione* by Ripa (below left) shows that the intention is more allegorical than sexual

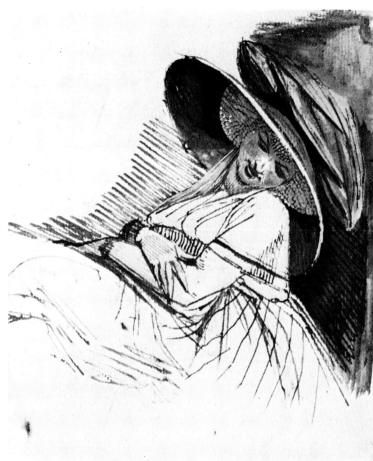

199 Fuseli. *Bust portrait of Mrs Fuseli, c.* 1790–95

200 Fuseli. *Mrs Fuseli Sleeping, c.* 1795

201 Fuseli. *The Fireplace,* 1791

202 Fuseli. *Mrs Fuseli seated with her work basket, c.* 1790–92

203

204

203 Fuseli. *Portrait of Mrs Fuseli*, 1794

204 Sir Joshua Reynolds. *Portrait of Mrs Robinson
(Perdita)*. Reynolds was the main influence on Fuseli
as a portraitist

V Fuseli's Influence

... perhaps even this barren age has produced a genius, ... who may live to astonish, to terrify, and delight all Europe.
(Armstrong: *The Influence of Climate upon Genius*, 1770)

Dr Armstrong's prophecy may have been overstated as a generalization, but in one particular he was absolutely right – *The Nightmare*.

It is now well-known that the influence of Reynolds's *Ugolino in his Cell** was effected entirely through the mezzotint by John Dean (1774). Therefore in this period of European art the historian, if he is to consider the influence of one artist on another, must concern himself more with the existence of a print than with the availability of the original painting. And, of course, because of the proliferation of reproductive engravings of all periods, a source could stimulate a similar image from two artists who were unknown to each other.

The following selected catalogue shows that prints of *The Nightmare* and its variants were published throughout the artist's life. The 1781 version was engraved by T. Burke (1783) and the 1791 version by T. Holloway (1791): a very coarse coloured engraving appeared in 1802 by Raddon, who also made the engraving of the one illustrated here in 1827, both of these from variants by the artist. The influence of the 1781 version was almost immediate after its exhibition in 1782. Rowlandson, for instance, used it in his *Covent Garden Nightmare* (1784) depicting Charles Fox, the Opposition leader. Here a point may be raised which also applies to Gillray; some commentators see such cartoons as 'mocking' the artist who painted the model. This is no more true of the eighteenth century than it is today, for surely the cartoonist is using the original work as a vehicle, not to ridicule the artist, but to ridicule the subject of his wit. To use a phrase of Gillray's, 'Mock Sublime' is the classification into which such a work falls, pointed as it was towards an informed audience. A different audience is the goal of Newton's *A Nightmare* (1794). This exemplifies an interesting process – the commonplacing of a

NIGHTMARES

I, 83

148

*See Frances Yates, 'Transformations of Dante's Ugolino', *Journal of the Warburg and Courtauld Institutes*, 14, 1951.

222

223

224

201

myth – an action which was taking place in many fields during the last two decades of the century, due to the growth of awareness produced by the expanding urban populations. By 'awareness' is meant that sharpening of the intellect towards political and social conditions which urban living creates. As the vernacular and the broadsheet idiom was chosen for its relevant stratum of audience, the cartoon was constructed likewise. To put it in a slightly more grandiose manner, Newton's print represents the metamorphosis of an 'aristocratic' myth into folklore, and it is no small claim for an artist, to have originated so popular an image. For a much more sophisticated audience, Gillray employed *The Nightmare* for his cartoon of 1798, *Nightly Visitors at St Ann's Hill*.

Next in chronology, and demonstrating its influence on the Continent, there is Chodowiecki's obvious use of the nightmare maiden in his etching *The Sleeping Courtesan* (*Das Mädchen aus* 225 *der Waldhütte*) of 1799. Implicit here is the transition between the 'and then' anticipatory moment of the Gothic novel and the early romantic erotic motif of the fully clothed man and the half-draped woman. Chodowiecki's back view of the man is almost coincidental to Fuseli's use of the same motif in the Rivington Hamlet, or in the earlier *Rosicrucian Cavern* (1803). 130, 233

The trail becomes a little unclear in the following years, but it is safe to assume that Raddon's print of 1827 was most responsible for *The Nightmare* appearing again in France in the 222 full Romantic period. Fuseli's variant and the original were in the Countess of Guildford's collection in 1831 and therefore quite out of sight to any visiting artist. The three vignettes illustrated here, by Gavarni, Ramelet and Callot, from the 226, 227, 228 journal *Macedoines* (1830) are literally thumbnail sketches in size. The titles are *Scène diabolique* (Gavarni), and *Reverie diabolique* (Ramelet); Callot's work is untitled, understandably in its particular circumstances! All three demonstrate the sturdy survival of the Rococo. Chodowiecki himself can hardly count as survival, since he had belonged to the original German Rococo movement. But Gavarni's minute lithograph, excluding the little devil, is a reincarnation of Greuze's *La Philosophe endormie*. The book in the picture would not be philosophic but a novel, which both Fuseli and Miss Wollstonecraft had warned against. The other principal aspect is the vignette form itself. In Raddon's engraving of *The Nightmare* 222 two small female figures adorn themselves on the dressing table, a fairy interpolation. Mention was made in respect of vignette motifs to the Woodmason Shakespeare *Titania, Bottom and the Fairies* (1793–94) and here that discussion can continue, for it will 99 be noticed that the three French vignettes are unframed, even faded out into the sheet, contrary to the Rococo vignette which was always framed. The underlying concept of the Romantic vignette is, to borrow from Ramelet's title, the reverie, the 227 realized image of the 'picture' in the mind derived from the printed page. It was common practice on both sides of the Channel to 'decorate' the margins in this manner during the Romantic era.

The principal source of this idea must lie in Fuseli's paintings of dreams. Since space does not allow a full treatment, one may turn quickly to two stages of this evolution. First to Gillray's *Shakespeare-sacrificed : – or – The Offering to Avarice* (1789), an attack on Boydell for his supposed commercial motives. No less than four 'vignettes' are drawn from Fuseli's paintings, and the manner in which all are shown is identical to that adopted by Fuseli. What is more, these images appear in the smoke caused by the burning of Shakespeare's plays. Since Gillray himself and his medium were less constricted by traditional conventions, his compositions, quite apart from their artistic quality, had artistic influence. The next stage of this evolution still requires closer investigation, but a *Sheet of Studies* (c.1820) by W. Y. Ottley and another *Sheet of Studies* (c.1827–30) by Theodore von Holst* can be considered as typical sheets of the Romantic artists, where vignette-like studies are scattered over the page, as though they were random jottings, but usually, (well-known sheets of Delacroix will come to mind), there is an overall connection despite differences in scale and handling. Von Holst carried this idea into a painting, *Dream after Reading Goethe's Walpurgisnacht* (1827, Private Collection, England), in which motifs from the text appear in a cloud around the reader's head. Both Ottley and von Holst were followers of Fuseli, and the latter was closely connected with Romantic circles in France and Germany. This is not to suggest von Holst as an influence but he was certainly an agent of Fuseli's influence. Until book illustration methods in the late 1780s and 1790s have been carefully studied, Fuseli cannot be awarded the whole crown, but as he might have averred 'the half is as full as the whole'.

229

230
231

*See Gert Schiff, 'Theodore von Holst', *The Burlington Magazine*, January 1963.

It is somewhat astonishing to note that Leslie in a letter to his sister in 1813 could say, 'I find that pictures from modern poets do not take. Even Shakespeare, Dante and Milton are scarcely sufficiently canonised to be firm ground.'[†] It would seem that twelve years after the Milton Gallery shut its doors, there was hardly a ripple left on the surface. Such were the rapid shifts in fashion at that period, not unlike our own, that yesterday's gasp was today's yawn in other fields besides painting. But Fuseli's Milton did surface as one knows from an engraving of *Silence* of 1844, which puts it close to the Pre-Raphaelites.

While Fuseli was not alone in his devotion to Milton, he certainly was the most prolific and various artist in this field. There seems no doubt at all that it was *his* Satan, that slim Apollo-like hermaphrodite, the conjunction of Sin and Death, that captured the imagination of most men, including that of Hazlitt, who in his essay, *Why are the Heroes of Modern Novels so insipid?* was thinking of more than the text, when he said that Satan was an acceptable hero, since he possessed both good and bad qualities, was proud and prepared to fight back. The sublime conception of Satan was not Fuseli's in the first place, and the initial source has been continuously overlooked, most

MILTON

†*Op.cit.*, p. 165.

215

being satisfied in finding the reference in Burke. But long before Burke, Jonathan Richardson had included in his essay on the Sublime (1719, 1773), the whole extract of Milton's description of Satan, in particular the lines:

> but his face
> Deep scars of thunder had intrenched, and care
> Sat on his faded cheek, but under brows
> Of dauntless courage, and considerate pride
> Waiting revenge: cruel his eye, but cast
> Signs of remorse and passion, to behold
> The fellows of his crime,

Not only is this a physiognomic portrait of most of Fuseli's heroes, but there is a coincidence in the fact that the 1773 edition of Richardson's essays had been dedicated to Sir Joshua Reynolds by the author's son (who had died the previous year, but obviously before his death had approached Reynolds about the new edition); and it was in the same year that the President had painted his *Ugolino*, inspired by Richardson's inclusion of Dante's verses on the episode and also by the author's wish that some artist might paint the subject. There is some reason to believe that Fuseli was likewise inspired, even perhaps before he came to England since there was the French edition of 1728, and certainly Bodmer was familiar with Richardson. Then when he read Winckelmann's description of the Apollo Belvedere, quoted earlier, the coincidence in the expressions must have struck him.

This is perhaps taking a long way round to discuss the influence of Fuseli's Milton series, but it does make the point that it was neither Barry's Satan nor Blake's which successfully mirrored Milton's. Fuseli, indeed, did rather more than that, for his is the only pictorial exemplar which parallels the literary metamorphosis of Satan as hero.* He recognized that satanic sublimity present in the psychological make-up of the tragic hero from Oedipus to Macbeth. It is not incurious, then, that Hazlitt, in order to preface his approbation of Satan, said that Werther and other heroes 'of the philosophical School of Romance' were not 'insipid' but 'one violent and startling paradox'.

*See Mario Praz, *The Romantic Agony*, 2nd ed., Oxford, 1951.

There is of course in Fuseli's interpretation the presence of an equation between Satan and the Promethean myth. It is then not irrelevant to mention here the question of Mary Shelley's *Frankenstein or The Modern Prometheus* (1818) and the distinct possibility of the Fuselian nature of her invention. It is hardly necessary to explain that they knew each other, she being the daughter of Mary Wollstonecraft and William Godwin, at whose house Fuseli was still wont to dine as late as 1813. In 1816, Byron, Shelley and young Mary were in Switzerland, 'when they talked of the experiments of Dr Darwin', some of which Mary Shelley granted were fictitious, but 'Perhaps a corpse would be reanimated: galvanism had given token of such things: perhaps the component parts of a creature might be manufactured, brought together, and endued with vital warmth.' Her own imagination warmed by this notion, she continued, 'I saw the hideous phantasm of a man stretched out, and then on the working of some powerful engine, show signs of life, and stir with an uneasy, half vital motion.'* It is interesting to find in Addison and Steele's *Spectator* (v, No. 379) the story of Rosicrucius' Sepulchre: 'A certain person having occasion to dig . . . in the ground where this Philosopher [the founder of the sect] lay interred met with a Small Door.' Curiosity led him inside to 'a very fair Vault' and there seated at a table was the statue of 'a Man in Armour', a truncheon in his hand and a lamp burning before him. Thus disturbed, the statue rose and moving jerkily, 'broke the lamp into a thousand pieces'. It was later found to be made of brass and 'nothing more than a piece of clockwork'. This was the text of Fuseli's *The Rosicrucian Cavern*, exhibited at the Academy in 1804, and engraved here *233* by Sharp for the 1805 edition of the *Spectator*. Later in her novel, Mary Shelley describes her 'phantasm': 'his yellow skin scarcely covered the work of muscles and arteries underneath': the coloration and appearance of many a male figure by Fuseli. To the modern mind, the analogy may seem distant from Milton, but the rapid pulse beat of the Romantic imagination could lend enchantment to a view of an analogy whatever the distance.

*Mary Shelley in her Preface to the 1831 edition.

Thus spake Fuseli in Aphorism 215: 'Things came to Raphael and Shakespeare; Michelangelo and Milton came to things', and Horace, too, would join the former company with his *et mihi res, non me rebus* (*Epist.* i. i. 19). This division between the 'secular' and 'divine' nature of artistic creativity also sheds some light on the divided loyalties of Fuseli's own period. Fuseli went to Shakespeare, therefore, much as Italian artists of the seventeenth century had gone to the *novelle* of Bandello,[†] for examples of social morality. It would take too long here to examine all the details of that transformation, so it must remain sufficient to emphasize that one of the principal motives of Fuseli's choice of episode is its inherent moral persuasiveness. The other principal is, naturally, its dramatic strength, 'big with the past and pregnant with the future'. These two conditions, always present in the Boydell series, are instrumental in separating Fuseli's from all other contributions to the Shakespeare Gallery. In the next century the brothers Redgrave were in no doubt when they said that Fuseli's works were clearly the most outstanding. The Boydell prints were re-issued constantly in one form or another throughout the nineteenth century, and as lately as 1923 an edition of Shakespeare, *The Complete Works* appeared, illustrated by thirty-two of the Boydell prints, of which five, the greatest number, were Fuseli's. It would seem that in our time opinion remains the same. Even if it is over-working the message, it should be stressed that here is another example of that subterranean influence on popular myth, discussed before. Is it Fuseli's *Hamlet and the Ghost* or Olivier's that, even for this generation, materializes like a vignette from one's reveries?

SHAKESPEARE

†For some discussion see P. A. Tomory, 'Profane Love in Italian . . . Baroque Painting', *Essays in Honor of Rudolf Wittkower*, London, 1967.

As related, Fuseli was deep in Shakespeare long before the Boydell scheme, so before contrasting his works with others which belong to it, his *A Scene from Timon of Athens* (1783) can 232 serve as an introduction, particularly, since this version is oiled or 'fixed', it is probably the one used by Blake for his engraving, almost identical in size, which he published from Poland Street in 1790.

First of all there is a striking contrast between Fuseli's and Nathaniel Dance's *Timon of Athens* of 1767, the latter a Poussin- 234 esque but somewhat supine rendering of the same episode. The conception remains static in the *ut pictura poesis* tradition and bears no sign of the influence of the contemporary stage, except that Alcibiades, by his bored presence, might represent a pre-Garrick 'walk-on' interpretation. In the work by Fuseli there is a true confrontation between the misanthropic eternity of Timon and the humane ephemerality of Alcibiades, with the 'timing', distance and grouping sure evidence of dramatic observation.

But Fuseli shows Alcibiades almost as weak and futile as his two companions, although in the play he emerges as a well-balanced man, able to compromise but possessing integrity.

What might have influenced Fuseli's reading was Salvator Rosa's Fourth Satire *La Guerra* in which the poet converses with Timon of Athens. Significantly an annotated edition of the satires by Salvini had nine printings in Amsterdam and London between 1719 and 1791 (the relevant London dates are 1780, 1787), with an Italian text for a publisher in Livorno. Of particular relevance are Rosa's criticisms that men are no longer men for they are dressed like women, that painters who paint only dwarfs, deformed and lascivious characters debase taste in art and society, and worse that the sexual deviations of certain gentlemen pervert and warp the mind. Timon replies that it is a waste of time trying to change the world, for it always has been wicked and will continue to be so. He also advises the poet to keep silent to avoid being harmed. One does not have to go to Japan to find martyrs (a reference to the Jesuit missionaries there). Rome itself, he observes, does not open its mouth.

The reason for so many printings might well be found in the same satire for Rosa expands on the need for patriotism; by making Italians one makes Italy. Only the leaders can set the example, but they pander to foreigners in order to preserve their own power. The ordinary people are too ill-educated to know what to do. In general, these thoughts were shared by Pietro Verri, who founded *Il Caffè*, a journal concerned with taste, morality and liberty, in Milan in 1764, and by Beccaria, the virtual founder of the Italian Enlightenment, who also lived there. Knowing Fuseli's interests, it is inconceivable that he was unaware of the analogies to be found in Rosa's satire.

Nor is there much need to labour the point that the artist more or less identifies himself with Timon. Evidence has already been given for that, and a glance at the Rivington plate of *Timon of Athens* (1805) will reveal the close similarity in pose 171 with that of Fuseli himself in *The Artist in Conversation with* 7 *Bodmer* (1781).

Conveniently, Fuseli confirms this interpretation in two ways. First by adding to his drawing Pindar's line '. . . man is the dream of a shadow', (Pyth. 8.) which Jonathan Richardson also quoted, in his essay on *The Sublime*, linking it to Shakespeare's '. . . we are such stuff as dreams are made on' (*The Tempest* IV I). Second, the whole manner of the drawing of Alcibiades and his companions is a pastiche of Bartolozzi's style, a witty reminder of Fuseli's lines in his incomplete *Dunciad of Painting*:

> There as the wedded elm and tendril'd vine
> Angelica and Bartolozzi twine

which not only establishes the artist's identity with Timon, but *inter alia* that the date of the poem must be close to that of the drawing, 1783.

The theme of Timon continued to be significant for the Romantic generation. Witness Byron's *Addition to the Preface* (1813) of *Childe Harold's Pilgrimage*, 'Had I proceeded with this poem this character would have deepened . . . ; for the outline which I once meant to fill up for him was, with some exceptions, the sketch of a modern Timon'. And, as we know, Fuseli admired Byron.

Plutarch's *Life*, of course, was everyone's fundamental source, but it might not be irrelevant to quote Robert Burton on Alcibiades, since his description is echoed by Fuseli's pictorial treatment, for example, 'dallying with wanton young women, . . . effeminate in his apparel, ever in love, but Why? He was over-delicate in his diet, too frequent and excessive in banquets' (*Anatomy of Melancholy*).

However, it may have been the same edition of the Satires that, apart from stylistic reasons, turned Fuseli away for ever from Rosa. In the Third Satire the poet castigates Michelangelo for showing such shameful things (buttocks, backsides and scrotums) in the *Last Judgment*. Fuseli's riposte occurs first, c.1780–89 in his *Dunciad of Painting*, where he calls Rosa a 'Critic self-damn'd . . . for he . . . bade a monarch fall' and second in his Lecture II (1801), 'the rod which he had the insolence to lift against the nudities of Michael Angelo, . . . would have been better employed in chastising his own misconceptions.'

Rosa's influence, supporting Walpole's comment quoted earlier, is marked in many paintings of the Boydell Gallery. His ragged contours fitted Burke's maxim that irregularities in forms were both natural and picturesque. Thus it is that Hoppner's figure of Pisano in his scene from *Cymbeline*, comes *235* directly from Rosa (*Diverses figures*), and likewise the landscape with its broken stumps.

It is, however, Reynolds in his two major works, *Macbeth and the Witches* and *The Death of Cardinal Beaufort*, who pre- *237, 236* serves Rosa's imagery to a much greater extent than any other artist. The *Macbeth and the Witches* contains all the Rosaesque bric-a-brac of the occult, which Fuseli would have none of. Otherwise Reynolds borrows from Michelangelo's *Last*

Judgment for one of the witches, and Macbeth is a more activated version of Raphael's guard captain in *St Peter in Prison*. Posterity in the shape of Hazlitt (*Essays on Art*) approved of the work, 'the apparatus of the witches contains a very elaborate and well arranged inventory of dreadful objects.' Fuseli, on the other hand, is absolutely silent on all Reynolds' history pictures except *The Infant Hercules*, considering in his lectures the late president as only an excellent portrait painter. Neither was Fuseli inclined to accept that imitation is a form of flattery at this stage, for it is clear that the *Death of Cardinal Beaufort* repeats in the main figure his own of 1772, grinning more wolfishly, it is true, and with the addition, to the distress of most critics, of a demon hovering over the head of the cardinal. That item of demonology came directly from Rosa's *Job*. This *14* was unnoticed by Hazlitt, who felt that the cardinal was 'too much of a physical horror, a canine gnashing of teeth, like the picture of a man strangled'.

The fact that Fuseli appears to repeat the Reynolds format in his Rivington plate of this scene, was not out of respect, but *131* rather that Reynolds himself had initially borrowed from one of Fuseli's sketched variants.

To recognize Fuseli's superiority in dramatic selection and execution, one need look only at the Hoppner (*Cymbeline*) and *235* the two Reynoldses (*Macbeth* and *Henry VI, pt. II*). All three are *237, 236* examples of arrested action, divorced from the continuity of the drama, similar to the 'stills' that illustrate theatre books today, giving as much information on a play as a programme note does on a symphony.

Two comparisons may help to elucidate this comment. First, Gavin Hamilton's *Coriolanus* and Fuseli's *King Lear*. The *239, 240* situations are very similar, the hero in conflict with his family. Coriolanus is denying his family and Rome, because he is too proud of his own name, even though he is a traitor leading the Volsces against his native city. He accedes in the end to his mother's entreaties, and agrees to arrange a peace, knowing the outcome will be his own death. Nothing of this appears in the painting because Hamilton chooses the flattest moment in Scene 3:

> Down ladies; let us shame him with our knees

presenting not a tragic turning point, but a scene of a mother and her girls moistly reproving her soldier son for being out all night. Fuseli chooses *the moment* in the first act of *King Lear*, which sets up the whole tragic course of the play, when Lear drives out Cordelia because she refuses to indulge in the hypocritical exaggeration that he demands, and receives, from her sisters. Thus Lear's authority, his ensuing madness, the devotion of Cordelia, the unnatural ambitions of her sisters Goneril and Regan and the continuously strained loyalty of Kent are all projected in an ensemble in which every character reacts according to his or her role.

Second, Northcote's Hubert and Arthur from *King John* can *238* be compared with Fuseli's Roman period drawing of the same *22* scene. Fuseli himself was to criticize Northcote for choosing

208

the wrong moment, when all the passion is spent, with Hubert saying to the attendants:

Go stand within; let me alone with him

instead of Fuseli's moment, when it is still not clear that Hubert will be won by the boy's entreaties and the irons are still red hot.

These examples should suffice, although there is more evidence, to show not only that Fuseli knew his Shakespeare but had the critical acumen to seize the dramatic apogee of the chosen episode. With the Rivington series he was to do something different, as described, but he could not have done that without laying the groundwork up to and including the Boydell Shakespeare Gallery.

Some interactions between Fuseli, David and Girodet have already been noted; what remains to be said is tentative until more evidence appears.

At least there is no doubt about Fuseli's liaison with David in Rome, even if one bit of evidence, Fuseli's name (corrupted) appearing in Jules David's enormous list of David's pupils, is ambiguous, since the truth might be the reverse. There is a set of coincidences, however, which might support the first assumption. There is the similarity in pose of Fuseli's Caius Marius and the plague-stricken man in David's *St Roche* 241 *interceding with the Virgin for the Plague stricken* (1780), though 242 admittedly both artists may have turned independently to Poussin's *Philistines struck by the Plague*. This might be so, but 21 the younger Drouais, David's great friend and pupil, began working on *his* Caius Marius (Louvre) shortly after David's work was finished, although it does not follow Fuseli's composition.

Then there was Fuseli's *Oath on the Rütli*, whose importance 58 lay in the fact that it proclaimed patriotic unity, the substance of the theme of David's Horatii, four years later, and the fact 59, 71 that Fuseli was working on the illustrations for the French edition of Lavater's Essays before he left Italy, thus forearming David, who was to apply the four temperaments of Chodowiecki's engraving in that edition to characters in his *Death of Socrates* (1786). From the same edition, even, may have come the stimulus for his painting of *Brutus and the Lictors* (1788), a different Brutus to be sure, but Bodmer and his circle had many years before established the name of Brutus as synonymous with patriotism. It seems preferable to suggest a close liaison of interests, of exchanged sources, between David and Fuseli rather than press for that twentieth-century characteristic of art history – one-upmanship – which often does more for the reputations of art historians than for those of the artists they are studying!

The relationship is no more exact with the next generation of French artists, except that by, say 1802, the year of the brief armistice, prints after many of Fuseli's paintings were available on the Continent. Known, for instance, is Ingres's ownership of Flaxman's outline engravings, and Géricault's dependence on

English sporting prints and engravings after Stubbs and James Ward. It would be a little ridiculous to maintain that these were the only prints from England in their folios. Look, for instance at the eroticism of Ingres's *Thetis and Jupiter* (1811). Its source is established in Flaxman's engraving of the same episode, but Thetis there does not press her breast against Jupiter's knee. But in Fuseli's painting of Oedipus, engraved by William Ward in 1785, one daughter certainly does, and Titania presses hers against Bottom's arm in *Titania, Bottom and the fairies* engraved by Rhodes in 1794.

Finally amongst the Frenchmen the case of Delacroix* should be referred to, simply because of his series of prints after Shakespeare (1826–30). The group of Hamlet and Marcellus in *Hamlet and the Ghost*, although pivoted follows Fuseli's Boydell composition. There may be more to note in this artist, for Delacroix, on his visit to England in 1824 with Bonington, spent a little time with Edward Calvert, who had worked with Fuseli. Calvert's own minute engravings like *The Bridal Bower* reflect his master's voice in small.

There is no evidence of Fuseli being considered 'a foreigner' by his English contemporaries, or his art being outside the English context: on the contrary it was considered an integral part of the variegated pattern of English painting, for the idiom that he employed was much in tune with the local vernacular.

73

99

*See E. G. Dotson, 'English Shakespeare illustration and Eugène Delacroix', *Marsyas*, New York University, Suppl: II, 1965.

221

Each of these artists had a kind of tangential connection with Fuseli: Romney and Barry because they had already mature styles before their contact, Flaxman because he was a sculptor, and also because his removal to Italy enabled him to find his own style before he became dominated by either Blake or Fuseli. Romney's *Dream of Atossa* (1777–80), for instance, incorporates ideas from Fuseli's *Death of Cardinal Beaufort* (1772) and *Samuel appearing to Saul, before the Witch of Endor* (1777). Barry's *Satan, Sin and Death* (c.1790–93) has Fuseli's precision in the delineation of individual forms, which could hardly grow independently out of his own earlier, impacted 'symplegma' forms of *Lear and Cordelia* (1774). Flaxman in his drawing for the Collins monument, made in 1787, the year he arrived in Italy, demonstrates on the left-hand side clear hints of Fuseli's influence. He was never to use such strained postures again.

The mention of symplegma above, the Hellenistic practice of intertwined or touching figure groups, is maintained by Fuseli in its purest form. While his figures are often close together, they remain separate, merging only at pivotal points like knees. But in the early works by Romney and Barry cited above, the symplegma becomes more a coagulation of bodies. This is also true of Flaxman in his later work. Thus Fuseli emerges as the purest classicist of the four in that respect. In terms of outline and proportion, Flaxman is the purest, with Barry and Fuseli somewhere in between. Romney however stands apart, since he uses wash to determine the form and line

ROMNEY, BARRY AND FLAXMAN

243
25
42
93

61
244

205 *George Romney. Anger, Envy and Fear*

210

only to keep it in check. In other ways, Romney remains a traditionalist. In his drawings of *Anger, Envy and Fear* (*c*.1791), a *205* preliminary sketch for *The Infant Shakespeare attended by Nature and the Passions* of the Boydell Gallery, the last-named are clearly drawn from Le Brun, despite the subjective nature of *65* his drawing. It is the subjective element in each of these four artists which now seems to separate them; to a contemporary viewer it was that characteristic which linked them together.

In such a brief space, less than justice can be done to the most subjective of all Fuseli's contemporaries. Blake* and Fuseli were intimates in many projects, and each had in the other the most disinterested admirer of his work. Fuseli, alone, was to come through unscathed from Blake's doggerel invective against his brother artists, and the last of Fuseli's comments on Blake was on the latter's visit (1815) to an Academy life class, 'Mister Blake, *you* should be teaching us.'

BLAKE

*On his relationship with Fuseli and others, see Anthony Blunt, *The Art of William Blake*, New York, 1960.

As suggested, the two must have met soon after Fuseli's return to England, if for no other reason, because Fuseli was too good a judge to pass up an artist of imagination, whatever his age.

There is no doubt that Blake borrowed a great deal from Fuseli, certainly in the first decade of their acquaintance. The opportunities were considerable. Until about 1792 they worked together on the Lavater English edition, supervised by Fuseli, and on Darwin's *Botanic Garden*, though Blake published his *140, 141* *Timon of Athens* plate independently in 1790. One of the most *232* striking of Blake's borrowings, if only for the span of time involved, is the figure 'Laughter' in his stipple engraving of *Mirth and her Companions, c*.1815–20, which is taken from 'Laughter holding both his sides' from the Fuseli *Subject from Milton's L'Allegro* (*c*.1785). Since Fuseli's work was never en- *74* graved and no artist could hold in his memory an image for that number of years, it must be assumed that Blake still owned a variant at the time he made his print, for he even shows Care being thrust down by Sport.

From the Lavater edition he was clearly impressed by Fuseli's group of four damned heads, particularly the one labelled in this text as the head of Sloth (for he made a large independent *166* engraving of it). The derivative appears in his watercolour of *The Stoning of Achan* (*c*.1800–05), but it is characteristic of *245* Blake that his figures are always more contorted than Fuseli's and his vision of apocalyptic punishment is double imaged.

As to visions themselves, his own *Queen Katherine's Dream* *246* (1808) may be compared to his engraving of Fuseli's version in *127* the Rivington Shakespeare (1805) for he seems to have joined the fairies of Fuseli's *Shepherd's Dream* (1793) to the earthbound *VII* figures of 1805. Blake, to whom visions were as real as everyday life, would hardly recognize the distinctions in dreams that Fuseli made.

Blake's plate from Blair's *The Grave* (1808), *Death of the Strong Wicked Man*, whose effect on Fuseli has been noticed, is *138* derived in part from Blake's own *The House of Death* (1795) but this in its turn is derived from Fuseli's *Vision of the Lazar House*.* Nothing demonstrates more clearly the artistic relationship between the two artists and is also proof that there is no case of one dominating the other. It is clear, for instance, that Fuseli never thought of Blake as just another engraver, for although Blake was away in Felpham from 1800 to 1803 Fuseli must have sought him out to make the Michelangelo engraving[†] for his published lectures in 1801.

There is a well-known anecdote of Blake showing Fuseli a drawing, saying that the Virgin Mary had thought it very good and what did his friend think of that. Fuseli replied, 'Nothing, only that her ladyship's taste is not immaculate!' Implicit here is not only Fuseli's wit but his obvious familiarity with Blake's easy intimacy with the spiritual world. One only has to recall Crabb Robinson's rather embarrassed account of his first meeting with the poet to see that this is so. However, it must have been Fuseli's imaginative powers that saved him from consignment to the deep waters of materialism by his friend. In one instance they were irrevocably divided over the identity and meaning of Satan, illustrated by Blake's annotation to Bacon's *Essays* (1798): 'Did not Jesus descend and become a servant? The Prince of Darkness is a Gentleman and not a man; he is a Lord Chancellor.' Satan was only a hero to Blake when he was 'in all his original Glory'.

Necessarily, therefore, in all matters spiritual Fuseli and Blake differed strongly. Paradoxically it was the spiritualist Blake who found it so easy to materialize the soul, whereas Fuseli the materialist never did so. A work by each artist, close in date, exemplifies their respective conceptions. Blake's *The Soul hovering over the Body reluctantly parting with Life* (Blair's *The Grave* 1808) and Fuseli's *Achilles grasps at the Shade of Patroclus* (1803), while similar in the conjunction of the living and the departed, represent in Blake's case his conception of the soul as an *alter ego*, embodied as the twin of its possessor, while in that of Fuseli, the departing spirit is merely the insubstantial shadow of its physical housing. Fuseli, therefore, so distinguishes the 'shade', in contrast to his embodiment of the apparition and the dream.

Finally, there is an interesting feature relating the artists in Fuseli's practice of 'drawing through' the image on one side of the paper to the other. Generally this was done to obtain a reverse image for engraving, but Fuseli worked endless variations, for instance his erotic scene *Three women, an amorino and a prostrate man* is drawn on the reverse of his *Allegory of Vanity*, so that Vanity herself 'doubles' in two roles. More significant is the drawn-through *écorché* treatment of his drawing of *A Woman seen from the back, drawing a Curtain* (c.1798–1800), which in its symmetrical treatment resembles anatomical drawings of insects – an easy analogy for an entomologist. The connection proposed with Blake is his drawing of *The Ghost of a Flea* (c.1819–20 Tate Gallery), which despite Varley's account of its creation, is an *écorché* study of an entomological specimen.

247
248

182
89

209

*101   †155

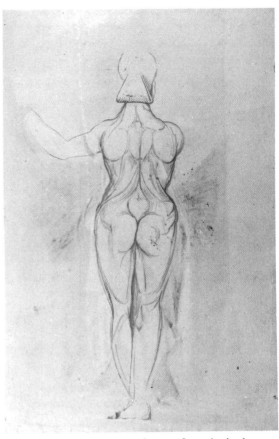

206 *Fuseli. A woman nude seen from the back*

There is a decision in the Scottish courts, 'not proven', which may be applied by some to the evidence given here, but whatever the final judgment, Fuseli can no longer be considered as the nightmare *alter ego* of the visionary Blake.

This artist follows naturally, for he and Blake were fellow students in the Royal Academy schools in 1779 and they were colleagues, under the aegis of Fuseli, in making designs for Lavater's *Essays on Physiognomy*. Gillray's* contribution was *The executioner with the head of St John* after a drawing by Fuseli.

*See Draper Hill, *Mr Gillray, The Caricaturist*, London, 1965.

In the first instance, the impression which has been drawn from Gillray's remarks to Sneyd of Fuseli's 'Mock Sublime', 'mad Taste' and 'the use to be made of him', should be corrected, for in the cartoon *Shakespeare-sacrificed:* . . . Gillray acknowledges Fuseli's contribution to the Boydell Gallery and also in *Titianus Redivivus:* . . . (1797) his refusal to take part in the ridiculous episode of Miss Provis's recipe, the 'Venetian Secret'. The real truth of their relationship comes out in a quotation from Thomas Paine in his *Age of Reason* (Pt II. 1794): 'One step above the sublime makes the ridiculous, and one step above the ridiculous makes the sublime again.' Gillray's art epitomizes this delicate balance and shows his acuteness in using Fuseli's works as vehicles for his satire. Indeed the whole quality of Gillray's imagination rests on that distinction and not on the metamorphosis described by the late Mr George Robey as 'From the sublime to the gorblimey'!

[marginal note: 229]

Gillray's quickness in uptake is demonstrated by his *Sin, Death and the Devil* which appeared on 9 June 1792, Fuseli having completed his painting on 28 May, a celerity to be explained only by a close acquaintanceship. Not all his borrowings were that spontaneous, for Gillray's *Weird Sisters* (1791) follows a long way behind Fuseli's painting of 1783, but the dedication at the top to Fuseli is a proper acknowledgment and not a mocking bow in his direction. Comparison of the two works not only reveals the stylistic kinship of the artists, but the one step of exaggeration required to produce what Gillray calls the *Caricatura-Sublime*. This accuracy of his should be remembered in analyzing *The Nuptial Bower* (1797). His model for it was *Satan's first address to Eve* of Fuseli's Milton Gallery which opened in 1799. This is confirmed by Gillray's sub-title, *–with the Evil-one, peeping at the charms of Eve,* and he must have seen it before it was publicly exhibited. The original, now lost, would have been a horizontal rectangle, with the tree of knowledge occupying a large proportion of the canvas, confirming that the 1802 painting, which is all that survives, is not a variant but a much reduced vertical replica.

[marginal notes: 249 / 72 ; 250 ; X]

Finally, Gillray's *The King of Brobdingnag and Gulliver* (1803) representing George III with Napoleon standing on the palm of his hand, is clearly derived from Fuseli's *Titania and Bottom* (1786–90). The mutual connection with Swift points to their own connection a step apart, in the art of the satirical sublime.

[marginal note: IV]

Fuseli was of the opinion that Genius had no following, so perhaps when he looked at the work of these three artists he might have exclaimed like Picasso, 'Michelangelo was not responsible for the cupboards of the Renaissance'. For neither Tresham nor Ottley were to live up to their early promise; neither moved out of a kind of amateur status explained by the pressure of their other interests in dealing and collecting. Fuseli had known Tresham since the Roman days, so it is curious to note in Tresham's drawing of *Psyche and Charon** (Apuleius *Metam*: 6) dated 1796, and intriguingly inscribed on the transom of the boat, *Johann Kasp. Lavat . .* , the survival of Runciman's style cross-bred with that of Fuseli. Charon's head, moreover, belongs to the generic type of Mortimer's and Barry's *Lears*.

Ottley kept up a close friendship with Fuseli till the latter's death – in fact was to have dined with him the night he fell ill. These friends were two of England's first art historians before the profession was invented, in the way they linked searching stylistic analysis to the broader appraisal of periods. Ottley's drawing style fluctuates between the 'heavy' treatment of *A Nude from the back* and the 'light' of *Various Sketches*[†] (*c*.1819–20). The former, undated, depends on Luca Cambiaso, but a comparison with *The Rosicrucian Cavern*[‡] (1803) makes it possible to classify it as a caricatura-sublime study after Fuseli. The various sketches are almost an album of Fuseli themes and motifs – Cupid and Psyche – Paolo and Francesca – a female nude from the back, top right – but there is more than a hint of Flaxman in the figures bottom right.

Von Holst was more consistent and, as mentioned, constituted the artistic and generation link between Fuseli and the Romantics. His style is closer to French artists like Gavarni than it is to anyone's in England, except perhaps Etty in an uncharacteristic moment of frivolity. To both von Holst and Wainewright, whose artistic career was arrested when he was (for poisoning) can be ascribed many of those pornographic drawings once given over-generously to Fuseli. In Von Holst's *Sheet of Studies*, already discussed, there is the motif of Chriemhild and Siegfried from Fuseli's painting of 1817 and, bottom right, a Fuseli-derived female nude but now lifted out of context and placed, expectantly, in the plush ambience of the *maison clos*.

Fuseli thought a great deal of Lawrence for his qualities as a man and companion, rather than for his painting, where 'flesh was glass'. Lawrence, too, never deviated from his high opinion of Fuseli. But as an artistic disciple, he left off almost as soon as he started or at least as soon as he completed his *Satan summoning his Legions* (1797 Royal Academy London) – their ensuing conversation on that matter has been related. However in his portrait 'in character' of *John Philip Kemble as Hamlet* (1801), Lawrence indirectly follows his own Satan and that of Fuseli in defining the demoniac nature of Hamlet's temperament. The portrait reflects both the stage machinery of

207 *William Y. Ottley. A nude from the back*

231
XII

LAWRENCE, TURNER, HAYDON, WILKIE AND ETTY

252

*251, †230, ‡233

the period, the grave being a 'trap' upstage, so that the actor would look as if he was standing at the edge of the abyss, and Fuseli's setting of the grave in his *Hamlet, Horatio and the Grave-digger* (1804). The source of Lawrence's low viewpoint for his portrait is confirmed by a letter of his of 1828, where referring to Tintoretto, he writes of his 'delighting in novel, foreshortened views of the figure, in which . . . he and Fuseli are the highest authorities'. There is little wonder then that on Fuseli's death Lawrence purchased 804 of the artist's drawings, paying for them with an interest-bearing bond of £200 per annum; the principal still being outstanding at his death, the drawings returned to Fuseli's executor, who sold them to the Countess of Guildford. In addition, Lawrence bought 16 of the 97 lots put up at the Christie's sale of Fuseli's studio on 28 May 1827. As a connoisseur, Lawrence made very few mistakes about artistic quality. *137*

Fuseli may not have had a very high opinion of landscape painting as a genre, indulging in it himself mostly when his godfather's son J. C. Gessner, the landscapist and lithograph pioneer, was in England 1799–1803, but this did not apply to individual painters. He had great admiration for Constable, and Cunningham's absurd interpretation of Fuseli calling for his umbrella as he went to view six Constables as a statement of censure, when it was really the reverse, only confirms the suspicion that Cunningham was sorely deficient in humour. Fuseli's championship of Turner is perhaps better known, supporting him for Academician when Northcote and Opie voted against him. Later to Farington in 1802, Fuseli praised Turner's *Calais Pier* and expressed his admiration for that artist's colour. Later still, when Turner painted his *Woman reading a letter* (Tate Gallery) and the *Music Party at Petworth* (Tate Gallery), he was making a gesture in Fuseli's direction, despite the fact that with his reputation established he had no need to depend on anyone.

Three of Fuseli's major pupils remain to be considered and the last shall come first. No illustration of an Etty is included, since right through his work Fuseli's art is present. But as with von Holst, Etty, a much more gifted painter, turned Fuseli's pantheon images into replicas fit for the parlour. Thus Fuseli's *Theseus and Ariadne* (1788) became *The Parting of Hero and Leander* (1827 Tate Gallery).

Wilkie, whose gifts Fuseli recognized quickly, was too much the genre painter to be much influenced by his master, except in borrowing a type. Since this is the same as one borrowed by Haydon, the two may be considered together. The thematic character starts with Fuseli's *Timon of Athens* of 1805, which *171* Leslie, another pupil, selected as his subject for a painting of 1812 (Private Collection, Philadelphia). Then in 1814, Wilkie exhibited his *Duncan Gray*, the text being the poem by Robert *253* Burns, but Duncan Gray himself shows all that implacability and determination to go it alone if necessary, characteristic of the Fuselian 'outsider' hero. This same *Indifferent* is present in Haydon's *Mock Election* of 1828, the only man to take no notice *254* whatsoever of the proceedings, and indeed bears all the traits of a Byronic 'modern Timon'.

In Haydon one might like to see the anything but mute, yet inglorious end of Fuseli's lineage, but the truth is not so strange as the fiction that history painting died with Haydon. In his lifelong defence of it, Haydon never, at any stage, was aware that terms can change. He really was championing 'serious' painting, the work of an artist with integrity, or as Fuseli put it in Aphorism 167: *Dignity is the salt of art*, and if an artist lose his savour how can he be then exalted? What Haydon really lacked was Fuseli's historical perspective. Fuseli knew the reasons for and the causes of his own neglect, but he never yielded, preserving his integrity intact and encouraging his students to do likewise, whatever their bent.

'Fuseli was indeed', as William Roscoe wrote to Knowles in 1831, 'a most extraordinary and accomplished person.'

208 Fuseli. *The Debutante*, 1807. Woman, the victim of male social conventions, is tied to the wall, made to sew and guarded by governesses. The picture reflects Mary Wollstonecraft's views in *The Rights of Women*

209 Fuseli. *Woman seen from the back drawing a curtain*, c. 1798–1800. Another duenna figure, almost masculine in its aggressive pose

210 Salvator Rosa. *Soldier seen from the back*. A possible source for the drawing above

211

212

213

214

215

211 (opposite, above) Edward F. Burney. *An Establishment for Young Ladies*. Ordeals and risks of the pursuit of elegance

212 Fuseli. *The Newspaper in the Country*, 1806–07

213 Fuseli. *Ulysses and Penelope*, 1806

214 Fuseli. *The Return of Milton's Wife*, 1796–99

215 Fuseli. *Silence*, 1799. The subject is a passage for Milton's *Il Penseroso*, but it is revealing for Fuseli's attitude to women. Despising the fashionable marriage market, he revered them as companions (pl. 212), wives (pl. 213) and mothers

216

216, 217 Fuseli. *Parental Care*, *c.* 1805. Fuseli's 'parents' are two aged tyrants, still exerting authority on the edge of the grave, worlds away from the normal sentimental view of old age exemplified in William Hamilton's *Charity* (left)

218 Fuseli. *A Woman before the Laocoon*, *c.* 1802. Possibly a malicious sketch of Maria Cosway

217

218

219 (below) Angelica Kauffmann. *Design*. Fuseli's drawing
(below left, pl. 218) is a satirical comment on such
allegories

220, 221 Two Fuseli illustrations of Shakespearean ghosts.
Right: *Julius Caesar*, 1805. Below: *Hamlet and the Ghost*,
1789. The later picture promotes the Ghost to a more
dominant position. Compare also his 1805 Hamlet
illustration, pl. 130

219

220

221

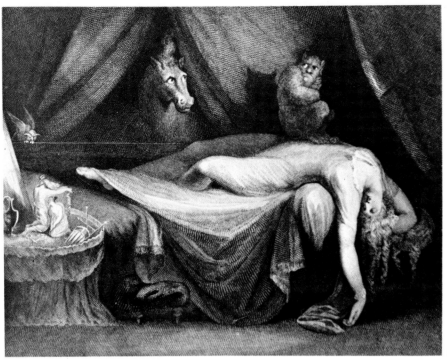

222 Fuseli. *The Nightmare*. An engraving by W. Raddon, 1827, close to Fuseli's first version (pl. 1), but note the interpolated fairies on the dressing-table. It was through engravings that this subject became so widely known and copied. A selection of such imitations and caricatures is shown on these two pages.

222

THE COVENT GARDEN NIGHT MARE.

223

224

DRAWN and ETCH:d by R:NEWTON

A NIGHT MARE

223 Thomas Rowlandson. *The Covent Garden Nightmare*, 1784. The girl has become Charles James Fox. The composition is the 1781 version (pl. 1) reversed

224 Richard Newton. *A Nightmare*, 1794. The sublime well and truly vulgarized

225

226

227

228

225 D. Chodowiecki. *The Sleeping Courtesan*, 1799. The erotic element emphasized, the terror diminished

226–228 Three illustrations from the journal *Macedoines*, of 1830, by Gavarni (top), Ramelet (above) and Callot (right)

229 James Gillray's *Shakespeare – sacrificed* is an attack on Boydell's Shakespeare Gallery. Of the vignettes that appear in the smoke rising from Shakespeare's burning works, four are taken from Fuseli (see pls IV, 221, 240) and one from Barry (pl 61)

229

231

230

230, 231 Two pages from sketchbooks by typical Romantic artists, William Y. Ottley (left) and Theodore von Holst (above). Both are full of reminiscences of Fuseli (see, for instance, pls 116, 135, 178, 182)

232

233

232, 234 Fuseli and Nathaniel Dance as interpreters of Shakespeare. The scene is the visit of Alcibiades and his two courtesans to Timon in his cave. Fuseli (above, 1783) gives it a tension that is both theatrical and powerfully symbolic. Dance (below) is Poussinesque but lifeless

233 Fuseli. *The Rosicrucian Cavern*, 1803. A man opens the tomb of Rosicrucius. Inside is a statue made of brass which rises up and breaks the lamp

234

235 John Hoppner. Illustration to *Cymbeline*

236 Sir Joshua Reynolds. *The Death of Cardinal Beaufort*, from *Henry VI*, Pt 2. Compare Fuseli's two versions of the same scene (pls 25, 131)

237 Sir Joshua Reynolds. *Macbeth and the Witches*. All the pictures on this spread belong to Boydell's Shakespeare Gallery

238 James Northcote. Hubert and Arthur, from *King John*. Compared with Fuseli's version of the same scene (pl. 22), this fails because Northcote selects a moment when the action is over, not the real moment of tension

239, 240 The dramatic moment. Gavin Hamilton, illustrating the climax of *Coriolanus* (above), shows not Coriolanus's actual decision but a point some time before this is made. Fuseli's *King Lear* (below) chooses the precise moment of Lear's rejection of Cordelia

241

241 Fuseli. *Caius Marius and the Cimbrian Soldier, c.* 1764

242 David. *St Roche interceding with the Virgin for the Plague-stricken*, 1780. Note the similarity of pose between Caius Marius and the plague-stricken man

243 George Romney. *The Dream of Atossa*, 1777–80. To be compared with Fuseli's 1772 version of *The Death of Cardinal Beaufort* (pl. 25)

244 John Flaxman. *Designs for a Monument to William Collins*, 1787. Flaxman's cool classicism is given an unusual tension by the influence of Fuseli

242

Nº 1

Nº 2

& Hope enchanted smil'd & wav'd her golden hair

Revenge, Anger, Fear. Despair &c retiring on one side, on
the other Joy & Mirth led on by Love, heads of Exercise
Sport &c amongst the trees

Nº 2 would be the design for the Monument in which the
basreleif Nº 1 or Nº might be introduced

Nº 2 with the basreleif Nº 1 might be executed with the figures about 2 feet
high, low relief, the length of the whole about 5 feet &, the whole heigth about
4 feet 6 Inches for about 70 £ — but the basreleif being the principal object
of the Monument would not be sufficiently large & distinct to produce
a good effect, on the contrary the figures in Nº 6 forming only a
kind of framework to the inscription could not fail I think of producing
exciting the spectators attention to observe & decypher the former whilst
he read the latter

247

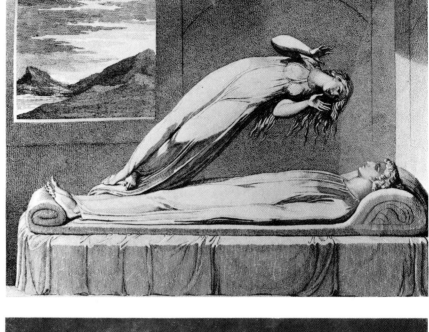

246

245 William Blake. *The Stoning of Achan*. Blake borrows the head of Sloth from Fuseli's illustrations to Lavater (pl. 166)

246 William Blake. *Queen Katherine's Dream*. Compare with Fuseli's version of the same scene (pl. 127) and also with the fairies of *The Shepherd's Dream* (pls VII and 77)

247 William Blake. *The Soul hovering over the Body*, 1808

248 Fuseli. *Achilles grasps at the Shade of Patroclus*, 1803. Blake's 'soul' is as substantial as his 'body'. Fuseli makes the distinction visual.

248

249 James Gillray. *The Weird Sisters*. A 'Caricatura – Sublime' version of pl. 72

250 James Gillray. *The Nuptial Bower – with the Evil One* This is a caricature of Fuseli's early version of *Satan's first address to Eve*, which has since disappeared. The painting which survives (pl. x) is a reduced vertical replica

251 Henry Tresham. *Psyche and Charon*, 1796. A stylistic combination of Fuseli and Runciman

252 Sir Thomas Lawrence. *John Philip Kemble as Hamlet*, 1801. A portrait much in Fuseli's theatrical vein

253 Sir David Wilkie. *The Refusal (Duncan Gray)*, 1814. Fuseli's demonic 'outsider' in a domestic setting

254 B. R. Haydon. *The Mock Election*, 1828. The same Fuseli character on the right – indifferent, uninvolved, Byronic

Appendix: Fuseli's Library

Bibliography

List of Illustrations

Index

Appendix: Fuseli's Library

The following titles of books, given in order of lot number, have been extracted from the Sotheby Sale catalogue of Fuseli's 'small and very select Classical Library', his collection of prints and drawings, on Friday July 22 and the three following days, 1825. Of the comprehensive selection of classical writers and poets in his possession, I have included only those that have a particular relevance to the present work.

62	Priestley's (J.) Essay on Government	1768
64	Roger's (S.) Italy, a Poem	1823
69	Mirabeau Mémoires Secrets sur la Russie, 2 tom.	1800
75	Raynal Histoire Philosophique des deux Indes, 10 tom.	*Geneve*, 1781
89	Johnson's (S.) Lives of the English Poets, 4 vol.	1781
101	Ramond sur les Pyrénées, 2 tom.	*Paris*, 1789
109	Perouse's Voyage round the World, 3 vol, *plates*	1798
111	Leonardo da Vinci on Painting, *plates*	1796
112	Johnson's Journey to the Western Islands of Scotland	1775
119	Byron's (Lord) Don Juan, 6 vol.; Sardanapalus; Werner and Manfred; *together* 9 vol.	1822
127	La Fontaine Contes et Nouvelles, 2 tom.	1780
128	Life of Colley Cibber, by Bellchambers	1822
131	Priestley's History of the Christian Church, vol. 3 to 6	1802
132	Rousseau (J. J.) La Nouvelle Heloise, 3 tom.	*Paris*, 1819
134	Wollstonecraft's History of the Revolution	1794
135	Burke on the Sublime 1798 – Price on the Picturesque,	1801
146	Wieland Oberon 3 tom. *in a case*	
152	Burger's (G. A.) Gedichte, 2 tom.	1796
153	Herder's Philosophie, 4 vol. 1785 – (Motte-Fouqué) Undine	
171	Bewick's British Birds, *first edition*, LARGE PAPER	1797
173	Boccaccio Il Decamerone	*Venet.* 1538
176	Motte Fouqué, Tigurd der Schlangentodter	*Berlin*, 1808
177	Camper sur la Physionomie des Hommes, *avec planches Par.*	1791
186	Moore's (J.) Narrative of the Campaign in Spain	1809
188	Chevy Chase, a Poem	1813
197	Bellori (G. P.) Vite de' Pittori, Scultori, et Architetti moderni, *con fig.*	*Roma*, 1672
215	Myller der Nibelungen Lied	*Berlin*, 1782
218	Mengs (Raffaello) Opere, 2 tom. in 1	*Bodoni.* 1780
222	Winkellmanns Geschichte der Kunst des Alterthums	*Wien*, 1776
227	Lanzi (Luigi) Storia Pittorica della Italia, 3 tom.	*Bassano*, 1795–6
231	Zuccaro (F.) l'Idea de Pittore et Scultori	*Roma*, 1768
247	Vasari (G.) Vite de Pittori, Scultori et Architetti, 7 tom. *con fig.*	*Livorno*, 1767
255	Bentleii (R.) Epistolae, *Presentation Copy from Dr. C. Burney*	*Lond.* 1807

Bibliography

This is not an exhaustive list, but includes only those sources consulted in writing and revising the text. More bibliographical sources appear in the text, including articles which have appeared since the text was completed, but are of direct interest.

Antal, Frederick *Fuseli Studies* London 1956

Beutler, E. *J. H. Füssli* Goethe, Viermonatschrift des Goethe-Gesellschaft IV, 1939

Boase, T. S. R. *English Art 1800–1870* Oxford 1959

Cunningham, Allan C. *The Lives of the Most Eminent British Painters* Vol. 2 (ed. Heaton) London 1879

Federmann, Arnold *Johann Heinrich Füssli, Dichter und Maler* Zurich/Leipzig 1927

Fischer, Marcel *Das Römische Skizzenbuch von Johann Heinrich Füssli* Zurich 1942

Ganz, Paul *The Drawings of Henry Fuseli* New York 1949

Irwin, David *English Neo-Classic Art* London 1966

Jaloux, Edmond *Johann Heinrich Füssli* Geneva 1942

Janson, H. W. *Fuseli's Nightmare, Arts & Sciences* Spring New York 1963

Kalman, Harold D. 'Füssli, Pope and the Nightmare', *Pantheon*, III, 1971

Knowles, John *The Life and Writings of Henry Fuseli, Esq., MARA* 3 vols. London 1831

London *Fuseli* Exhibition Catalogue Arts Council of Great Britain 1950

MacAndrew, Hugh *Henry Fuseli and William Roscoe* The Liverpool Bulletin Walker Art Gallery Liverpool 1959–60

MacAndrew, Hugh *Selected Letters from the Correspondence of Henry Fuseli and William Roscoe of Liverpool* Gazette des Beaux-Arts 62 July-August 1963

Mason, Eudo C. *The Mind of Henry Fuseli* London 1951

Mason, Eudo C. *Unveröffentliche Gedichte von Johann Heinrich Füssli* Neujahrsblatt der Zürcher Kunstgesellschaft Zurich 1951

Mason, Eudo C. *Remarks on The Writings and Conduct of J. J. Rousseau* (Johann Heinrich Füssli) with a German translation Zürcher Kunstgesellschaft Zurich 1962

Muschg, Walter *Heinrich Füssli Briefe* Basel 1942

Powell, Nicholas *The Drawings of Henry Fuseli* London 1951

Schneck, Jerome M. *Henry Fuseli, Nightmare and Sleep Paralysis* Journal of the American Medical Association, Vol 207 4 January 1969

Schiff, Gert *Zeichnungen J. H. Füsslis aus seiner Römischen Zeit* Oldenburg 1957

Schiff, Gert *Zeichnungen von Johann Heinrich Füssli* Zurich 1959

Schiff, Gert *Johann Heinrich Füssli in Zürich* Librarium 7, III, Zurich 1964

Schiff, Gert *Johann Heinrich Füsslis Milton-Galerie* Zurich/ Stuttgart 1963

Schiff, Gert *J. H. Füssli und Michelangelo* Schweizerisches Institut für Kunstweissenschaft, Jahresbericht 1964

Schiff, Gert *Echtheits- und Zuschreibungsprobleme bei J. H. Füssli*, Schweizerisches Institut für Kunstwissenschaft Jahresbericht 1965

Schiff, Gert *Johann Heinrich Füssli: Oeuvrekatalog* Zurich (in preparation). (S. numbers in the illustrations list refer to the *Oeuvrekatalog* numbers. Only the catalogue entries relevant to the Fuseli drawings at Auckland have been consulted.)

Todd, Ruthven *Tracks in the Snow* London 1946

Tomory, P. A. *Drawings by Henry Fuseli* (in the City Art Gallery Auckland) Auckland 1967

Zurich *Johann Heinrich Füssli* Exhibition Catalogue Kunsthaus Zurich 1926

Zurich *Johann Heinrich Füssli* Exhibition Catalogue Kunsthaus Zurich 1941

Zurich *Johann Heinrich Füssli* Exhibition Catalogue Kunsthaus Zurich 1969

List of Illustrations

Measurements of works by Fuseli are given in centimetres
S. = Schiff Catalogue (see Bibliography)
Except where otherwise stated, photographs have been supplied
by the owners of the pictures

Pencil and white chalk
40.1 × 53.7
Kunsthaus, Zurich
S.839

65 D. Chodowiecki
The Passions after Le Brun
Lavater, *Essays on Physiognomy*
1792
Columbia University
(Author)

66 Fuseli
An Executioner
*c.*1780
Ink
227 × 18.5
Staatliche Kunstsammlungen,
Weimar
S.693

67 Andrea del Sarto
Decapitation of St John the
Baptist
Chiostro dello Scalzo, Florence
(Alinari)

68 Francesco Furini
Hylas and the Nymphs
Palazzo Pitti, Florence
(Alinari)

69 Fuseli
Lady Constance, Arthur and
Salisbury
1783
Oil on canvas 63·5 × 53·3
Smith College Museum of Art
Northampton, Mass.
S.722

70 Cesare Ripa
Iconologia
1764–66
Malincolia
Columbia University
(Author)

71 J. L. David
The Oath of the Horatii (Detail)
Louvre, Paris
(Documentation
Photographique)

72 Fuseli
The Three Witches
1783
Oil on canvas 65 × 92
Kunsthaus, Zurich
S.733

73 Fuseli
Oedipus announcing his Death
1784
Oil on canvas
150 × 166
Walker Art Gallery, Liverpool
S.712

74 Fuseli
Subject from Milton's *L'Allegro*

*c.*1785
Pencil heightened with white
33 × 41.1
Art Gallery, Auckland
S.1757

75 Correggio
Danae
Villa Borghese, Rome
(Alinari)

76 Fuseli
The Awakening of Titania
*c.*1785–90
Oil on canvas 44 × 57
Kunstmuseum, Wintherthur
S.754
(Speich)

77 Fuseli
The Shepherd's Dream
1785
Pencil, red chalk and grey wash
40 × 55.2
Albertina, Vienna
S.829

78 Fragonard
Coresus sacrifices himself to
save Callirhoe
Louvre, Paris
(Documentation
Photographique)

79 William Hogarth
Strolling Actresses dressing in
a Barn
Engraving
British Museum, London

80 D. Chodowiecki
Lenore (G. A. Burger)
Engraving
Kupferstichkabinett,
Staatliche Museen, Berlin
(Steinkopf)

81 Fuseli
Jack o' Lanthorn
1799
Milton *L'Allegro*
Engraved M. Haughton 1806
Victoria and Albert Museum,
London
S.913
(Author)

82 Fuseli
Henry V surprising Cambridge,
Scrope and Grey with their
death Sentence
*c.*1786–89
Oil on canvas
48 × 61
The Shakespeare Memorial
Theatre Picture Gallery and
Museum, Stratford
S.725

82 Fuseli
Henry V surprising Cambridge,

Scrope and Grey with their
death sentence
1789
Boydell Shakespeare Gallery
Engraved R. Thew 1803
Royal Academy, London
S.725
(Author)

83 Fuseli
The Nightmare
1790–91
Oil on canvas
76 × 63
Goethe Museum,
Frankfort-am-Main
S.928

84 Fuseli
The Appearance of Christ
at Emmaus
1792
Oil on canvas
144 × 69
From the collection of Mr and
Mrs Paul Mellon
S.1759

85 John Brown
Rest on the Flight
Ink and grey wash
Royal Academy, London
(Author)

86 John Hamilton Mortimer
Falstaff in the Buckbasket
Engraved J. Collyer
Royal Academy, London
(Author)

87 Charles Ansell
The French Toilet
Engraved P. Tomkins
*c.*1784
Royal Academy, London
(Author)

88 Cesare Ripa
Iconologia
1764–66
Lascivious Love
Columbia University
(Author)

89 Fuseli
Allegory of Vanity
1811
Pencil, ink, watercolour
20 × 27.1
Art Gallery, Auckland
S.1809

90 Fuseli
The Fall of Satan
1802
Milton *Paradise Lost*
Engraved C. Warren
Victoria and Albert Museum,
London
S.1302
(Author)

Rivington *Shakespeare*
Engraved R. Cromek
S.1294

118 Fuseli
Othello and Desdemona
1805
Rivington *Shakespeare*
Engraved R. Rhodes
S.1297

119 Satyr and Nymph
Hellenistic
Museo dei Conservatori, Rome
(Alinari)

120 Fuseli
Diomedes and Cressida
1805
Rivington *Shakespeare*
Engraved J. Neagle
S.1286

121 Fuseli
The Daughter of Herodias with
the Head of St John the Baptist
c.1779
Lavater, *Essays on Physiognomy*
1792
Engraving
Columbia University
S.961

122 Dancing Maenad
Hellenistic relief
Museo dei Conservatori, Rome
(Alinari)

123 Fuseli
Pericles
1805
Rivington *Shakespeare*
Engraved R. Rhodes
S.1293

124 Michelangelo
Aminadab
Ceiling, Sistine Chapel, Rome
(Alinari)

125 Fuseli
The Taming of the Shrew
1805
Rivington *Shakespeare*
Engraved R. Rhodes
S.1272

126 Raphael
The Freeing of St Peter
Vatican

127 Fuseli
Queen Katherine's Dream
1805
Rivington *Shakespeare*
Engraved W. Blake
S.1285
(Author)

128 Ludovico Carracci
St Benedict exorcising the
demon from the kitchen
Engraved G. Fabbri
(Biblioteca dell'Archiginnasio,
Bologna)

129 *See* 126

130 Fuseli
Hamlet and the Ghost
1805
Rivington *Shakespeare*
Engraved J. C. Smith
S.1296

131 Fuseli
Death of Cardinal Beaufort
1805
Rivington *Shakespeare*
Engraved R. Cromek
S.1282
(Author)

132 Fuseli
Death of Falstaff
1805
Rivington *Shakespeare*
Engraved J. Lee
S.1280
(Author)

133 Fuseli
A man in bed
c.1805
Pencil, 18.1 × 22.6
Royal Academy, London
(Author)

134 Fuseli
Roland at Roncesvalles (Fame)
1800–10
Ink, brown and grey wash
57.5 × 68.6
From the collection of The
Detroit Institute of Arts,
Gift of John S. Newberry
S.1403

135 Fuseli
Eros and Psyche
1808
Pencil, ink, watercolour
23.3 × 35.8
Art Gallery, Auckland
S.1812

136 William Blake
Death of the Strong Wicked Man
Engraving
Blair *The Grave*
Victoria and Albert Museum,
London
(Author)

137 Fuseli
The Nightmare
1810
Pencil, watercolour 32 × 40
Kunsthaus, Zurich
S.1446

138 Veronese
St John the Baptist Preaching
Villa Borghese, Rome
(Alinari)

139 Fuseli
Hamlet, Horatio and the
Gravedigger
1804
Ink, grey, blue and pink wash
37.2 × 29.5
Art Gallery, Auckland
S.1802

140 Fuseli
The Fertilization of Egypt
1791
Pencil
24.1 × 19.4
British Museum, London
S.1038

141 William Blake
The Fertilization of Egypt
Darwin *Botanic Garden*
Engraving
British Museum, London

142 Fuseli
Virtue reclaiming Youth
1806–07
Cowper *The Progress of Error*
Engraved W. Bromley
Victoria and Albert Museum,
London
S.1330
(Author)

143 Fuseli
The Ladies of Hastings
after 1813 ?
Oil on canvas
111 × 86
Dr Martin Hürlimann, Zurich
S.927
(Schweizerisches Institut)

144 Fuseli
The Lost Shepherd
1801
Thomson's *Seasons*
Engraved W. Bromley 1802
Victoria and Albert Museum,
London
S.1315
(Author)

145 Ludovico Carracci
The Temptation of St Benedict
Engraved G. Fabbri
(Biblioteca dell'Archiginnasio,
Bologna)

146 Fuseli
Undine displeased leaves the
Fisherman's Hut
1822
Pencil, blue and grey wash
32 × 37.6
Kunsthaus, Zurich
S.1563

173 Fuseli
Flora attired by the Elements
1791
Darwin *Botanic Garden*
Engraved Anker Smith
Royal Academy, London
S.973
(Author)

174 Agostino Veneziano
Les Grimpeurs (after
Michelangelo)
Engraving
The Metropolitan Museum,
New York
(Author)

175 Fuseli
Richard II
1805
Rivington *Shakespeare*
Engraved R. Cromek
S.1277
(Author)

176 John Brown
Three Women with Baskets
Pencil, ink and brown wash
Museum and Art Gallery,
Nottingham

177 John Brown
A Roman Lady with her Duenna
Ink and grey wash
Courtauld Institute,
University of London

178 Fuseli
Two Courtesans with fantastic
hairstyles and hats
*c.*1796–1800
Ink, brown, pink and grey wash
17.9 × 16.2
Art Galley, Auckland
S.1774

179 Fuseli
Girl at a Spinet with an Elf
*c.*1785–86
Oil on canvas
diameter 47
Dr C. Ulrich, Zurich
S.746
(Schweizerisches Institut)

180 Fuseli
Folly and Innocence
1800
Pencil and brown wash
42.4 × 25.6
Museum and Art Gallery,
Nottingham
S.1074

181 Fuseli
A Young Man kissing a Girl
at a Spinet
1819
Black crayon. 24.7 × 20
Kunsthaus, Zurich
S.1584

182 Fuseli
Three women, an amorino and
a prostrate man
1811
Pencil
20   27.1
(verso of No. 90)
Art Gallery, Auckland
S.1810

183 Fuseli
Falstaff with Doll Tearsheet
1789
Boydell Shakespeare Gallery
Engraved W. Leney 1803
Royal Academy, London
S.724
(Author)

184 Pasinelli
Salome with the Head of
St John the Baptist
Engraved G. Vitalba 1767
Royal Academy, London
(Author)

185 Fuseli
Tancred and Sigismunda
1792
Thomson,
Tancred and Sigismonda
Engraved F. Legat 1792, 1827
Author
S.943
(Author)

186 Fuseli
Amanda/Rezia falls with Huon
into the sea: Fatma is held
1804–05
Oil on canvas
61 × 45
Frau H. R. Blattman-Roth,
Wädenswil
S.1224
(Schweizerisches Institut)

187 Eros and Psyche
Hellenistic
Museo Capitolino, Rome
(Alinari)

188 Fuseli
Woman seated on a Sofa
*c.*1802–08
Ink
18.5 × 20
Kunsthaus, Zurich
S.1057

189 Matthew William Peters
Love in her Eye sits Playing
Engraved J. R. Smith
The Metropolitan Museum of
Art, New York,
Whittelsey Collection, 1953
(Author)

190 Fuseli
Mad Kate
1806-07

Oil on canvas
91 × 71
Goethe Museum,
Frankfurt-am-Main
S.1234

191 Thomas Barker of Bath
Crazy Kate
Art Gallery, York

192 John Hamilton Mortimer
Britannia
Thomson *Britannia*
Engraved C. Grignion
Author

193 Richard Reinagle
The Fair Maria
Engraved J. Caldwell
Royal Academy, London
(Author)

194 Fuseli
Venus/Night and the Two Cupids
*c.*1805
Etching
19.9 × 27.7
The Metropolitan Museum of
Art, New York,
Whittelsey Fund, 1963
S.1508
(Author)

195 Fuseli
Girl on a sofa looking out of a
window
1803
Polyautograph
21.6 × 31.7
Victoria and Albert Museum,
London
S.1434
(Author)

196 Cesare Ripa
Iconologia
1764–66
Educazione
Columbia University
(Author)

197 Greek Coin
Detail from plate No. 17
Winckelmann *Geschichte der
Kunst . . .*
(Columbia University)

198 Fuseli
Mrs Fuseli seated, with a switch
*c.*1790–92
Ink, grey, brown and pink wash
Verso of 202
22.7 × 15.7
Art Gallery, Auckland
S.1775

199 Fuseli
Bust portrait of Mrs Fuseli
*c.*1790–95
Ink, black and blue wash,
heightened with white

17.4 × 14.4
Art Gallery, Auckland
S.1779

200 Fuseli
Mrs Fuseli Sleeping
c.1795
Ink with grey, blue and pink
wash
22.7 × 18.6
Art Gallery, Auckland
S.1778

201 Fuseli
The Fireplace
1791
Watercolour
28 × 16.5
Victoria and Albert Museum,
London
S.1091

202 Fuseli
Mrs Fuseli seated with her work
basket
c.1790–92
Ink, grey, brown and pink wash
22.7 × 15.7
Art Gallery, Auckland
S.1775

203 Fuseli
Portrait of Mrs Fuseli
1794
Pencil, watercolour heightened
with white
34.6 × 21.6
Ulster Museum, Belfast
S.1099

204 Sir Joshua Reynolds
Portrait of Mrs Robinson
(Perdita)
The Wallace Collection, London

205 George Romney
Anger, Envy and Fear
Pencil
Yale University Art Gallery

206 Fuseli
A Woman, nude, seen from
the back
(verso of 209)
Pencil 30.7 × 17.3
Art Gallery, Auckland
S.1782

207 William Y. Ottley
A Nude from the back
Pencil and ink
Victoria and Albert Museum,
London

208 Fuseli
The Debutante
1807
Ink, red wash
37 × 24
Tate Gallery, London
S.1444

209 Fuseli
Woman seen from the back
drawing a curtain
c.1798–1800
Pencil, ink, grey, brown and
pink wash
30.7 × 17.3
Art Gallery, Auckland
S.1782

210 Salvator Rosa
Soldier seen from the back
Etching
B.41 *Diverses Figures*
John and Mable Ringling
Museum of Art,
Sarasota, Florida
(Author)

211 Edward F. Burney
An Establishment for
Young Ladies
Watercolour
Victoria and Albert Museum,
London

212 Fuseli
The Newspaper in the Country
1806–07
Cowper *The Task*
Engraved J. Neagle
Victoria and Albert Museum,
London
S.1335
(Author)

213 Fuseli
Ulysses and Penelope
1806
Homer *Odyssey*
Engraved I. Taylor
British Museum, London
S.1257

214 Fuseli
The Return of Milton's Wife
1796–99
Oil on canvas
88 × 111
Walker Art Gallery, Liverpool
S.919

215 Fuseli
Silence
1799
Milton *Il Penseroso*
Engraved M. Haughton 1808
The Metropolitan Museum of
Art, New York,
Whittelsey Fund, 1962
S.915
(Author)

216 Fuseli
Parental Care
c.1805
Ink, grey and blue wash
19.2 × 28.8
Art Gallery, Auckland
S.1786

217 William Hamilton
Charity
Engraved P. W. Tomkins
Royal Academy, London
(Author)

218 Fuseli
A Woman before the Laocoon
c.1802
Ink
32 × 41
Kunsthaus, Zurich
S.1072

219 Angelica Kauffmann
Design
Royal Academy, London

220 Fuseli
Julius Caesar
1805
Rivington *Shakespeare*
Engraved C. Warren
S.1289
(Author)

221 Fuseli
Hamlet and the Ghost
1789
Boydell Shakespeare Gallery
Engraved R. Thew 1803
Royal Academy, London
S.731
(Author)

222 Fuseli
The Nightmare
after 1792 ?
Engraved W. Raddon 1827
Victoria and Albert Museum,
London
S.757a
(Author)

223 Thomas Rowlandson
The Covent Garden Nightmare
Etching
British Museum, London

224 Richard Newton
A Nightmare
Etching and aquatint
British Museum, London

225 D. Chodowiecki
The Sleeping Courtesan
Das Madchen aus der Waldhütte
Engraving
Kupferstichkabinett,
Staatliche Museen, Berlin
(Steinkopf)

226 Gavarni
Diabolic Scene
Les Macedoines
Lithograph
Private collection

227 Ramelet
Diabolic Dream
Les Macedoines

248

Lithograph
Private collection

228 Callot
Les Macedoines Untitled
Lithograph
Private collection

229 James Gillray
Shakespeare – sacrificed . . .
Colour engraving
The Metropolitan Museum of
Art, New York
Gift of Mrs Marshall P. Slade

230 William Y. Ottley
Various Sketches
Pencil, ink
British Museum, London

231 Theodore von Holst
Sheet of Studies
Ink and wash
Victoria and Albert Museum,
London

232 Fuseli
A Scene from Timon of Athens
1783
Ink, brown, yellow and pink
wash on oiled paper
20.5 × 29.9
Art Gallery, Auckland
S.1755

233 Fuseli
The Rosicrucian Cavern
1803
The Spectator V 379
Engraved W. Sharp 1805
Royal Academy, London
S.1310
(Author)

234 Nathaniel Dance
Timon of Athens
H.M. The Queen
(Cooper)

235 John Hoppner
Cymbeline
Boydell Shakespeare Gallery
Engraved R. Thew
Royal Academy, London
(Author)

236 Sir Joshua Reynolds
The Death of Cardinal Beaufort
Boydell Shakespeare Gallery
Engraved C. Watson
Royal Academy, London
(Author)

237 Sir Joshua Reynolds
Macbeth and the Witches
Boydell Shakespeare Gallery
Engraved R. Thew
Author
(Author)

238 James Northcote
King John
Boydell Shakespeare Gallery
Engraved R. Thew
Royal Academy, London
(Author)

239 Gavin Hamilton
Coriolanus
Boydell Shakespeare Gallery
Engraved J. Caldwell
Royal Academy, London
(Author)

240 Fuseli
Lear, Cornwall, Albany,
Goneril, Regan, Cordelia,
King of France, Duke of
Burgundy, Kent and
Attendants
1789
Boydell Shakespeare Gallery
Engraved R. Earlom 1803
Royal Academy, London
S.739
(Author)

241 Fuseli
Caius Marius and the Cimbrian
Soldier
c.1764
Ink and grey wash
30.6 × 48.6
Art Gallery, Auckland
S.1731

242 David
St Roche interceding with the
Virgin for the Plague stricken
Ministère de la Santé Publique,
Marseilles
(Giraudon)

243 George Romney
The Dream of Atossa
Black chalk heightened with
white
Walker Art Gallery, Liverpool

244 John Flaxman
Designs for a Monument to
William Collins
Ink
British Museum, London

245 William Blake
The Stoning of Achan
Watercolour
Tate Gallery, London

246 William Blake
Queen Katherine's Dream
Watercolour
Fitzwilliam Museum,
Cambridge

247 William Blake
The Soul hovering over the
Body and reluctantly parting
with Life
Engraving
Blair *The Grave*
Victoria and Albert Museum,
London
(Author)

248 Fuseli
Achilles grasps at the Shade of
Patroclus
1803
Oil on canvas 91 × 71
Kunsthaus, Zurich
S.1192

249 James Gillray
The Weird Sisters
Colour engraving
British Museum, London

250 James Gillray
The Nuptial Bower – with the
Evil One
Colour engraving
British Museum, London

251 Henry Tresham
Psyche and Charon
Apuleius *Metam* VI
1796
Brown ink and brown wash
23.7 × 27
Professor Julius Held

252 Sir Thomas Lawrence
John Philip Kemble as Hamlet
Tate Gallery, London

253 Sir David Wilkie
The Refusal
(Duncan Gray)
Victoria and Albert Museum,
London

254 Benjamin Robert Haydon
The Mock Election
H.M. The Queen
(Cooper)

Index

Numerals in italic refer to
illustrations